THE TWO-TERM JINX!: WHY MOST PRESIDENTS STUMBLE IN THEIR SECOND TERMS, AND HOW SOME SUCCEED

THE TWO-TERM JINX!: WHY MOST PRESIDENTS STUMBLE IN THEIR SECOND TERMS, AND HOW SOME SUCCEED

Volume 1, George Washington-Theodore Roosevelt

EDWARD P. MOSER

ISBN 10: 1530790514
ISBN 13: 9781530790517

*To historians of scope and sweep: Arnold Toynbee, Francis Parkman,
Paul Johnson, and Edward Gibbon*

INTRODUCTION

An examination of over 225 years of presidential history reveals a second-term 'jinx'. A large majority of two-term Presidents have experienced significant setbacks and misfortunes in their second four years in office. The jinx ranges from tragic deaths—the assassination of Abraham Lincoln and William McKinley early in their second terms—to unpopular wars, financial and real estate panics, and even severe physical ailments that have plagued assorted Chief Executives.

Luck and skill, or their lack, have much to do with dodging or succumbing to the jinx. Through little or no fault of their own, Presidents Grant and Cleveland had severe recessions erupt during their second terms. So did President Monroe, although he escaped blame, partly because the politics of the time gave a small economic role to the federal government.

President Andrew Johnson had the misfortune of having to replace Lincoln in serving out the latter's second term. He fumbled away any good will that might have accrued to him by sticking to outdated beliefs, regarding the post-Civil War treatment of the freed slaves and the defeated South, thus mangling relations with a hostile Congress. President Theodore Roosevelt, on the other hand, lessened the effect of the Wall Street Panic of 1907 by exhibiting flexibility during that crisis. The corporate trustbuster permitted corporate titans, usually his political enemies, to band together to stop a further run on the stock market.

President Jefferson, after an extremely successful first term, stumbled toward the end of his second. Slow to recognize the treason of his former Vice-President, Aaron Burr, he ignored his Cabinet's advice in imposing a harsh trade embargo. During his own second term President Madison found himself pushed into a role, Commander-in-Chief, for which he had no experience. However, he was able to make changes in personnel to help him regain some of the popularity which the initial phases of the War of 1812 had stripped away.

Presidents Cleveland, Washington, and Jackson all suffered from severe health problems, including cancer, pneumonia, and possible blood poisoning, respectively, in their second terms.

For many Presidents elected twice, time seems their enemy, not their ally. After about six years in office, the issues that elect someone in the first place often begin to fade. They are replaced by another set of issues, matters often associated with an opposition faction or party. Among more recent Presidents, this phenomenon may have occurred for Presidents Dwight Eisenhower and George W. Bush, who both lost momentum about six years after key episodes which helped define their presidencies. Namely, ending the Korean War in 1953, and starting to wage the War on Terror in 2001.

A frequently cited constitutional reason for the presidential hex, at least in recent times, is the 22nd Amendment. The Amendment—ratified in 1951 in the wake of President Franklin Roosevelt's four terms—limits the Chief Executive to two terms. It has undercut the clout of second termers by underscoring the lame-duck status of their final years. Modern Presidents can no longer threaten their foes, nor inspire their allies, with the prospect of a third term. It seems no coincidence that, since the passage of the 22nd Amendment, the second-term jinx has become considerably more frequent.

Another oft-cited reason for the curse is that, at some point after a re-election triumph, many of a President's key staff and advisors leave the White House for other jobs. This strips the Chief Executive of critical experience and expertise. The 22nd Amendment has intensified this trend, as it ends any hope of employment for such aides in a third term of an Administration.

Aimed at history and politics lovers from middle school on up, this work is written in an accessible, journalistic style. Its aim is to entertain as well as to inform and enlighten. Enjoy!

Edward P. Moser
Alexandria, Virginia

QUOTATION

"No man leaves this position with the reputation he had on assuming it."

OVERVIEW

This book outlines all of the two-term presidencies, and sketches their successes and failures, and the reasons why they succumbed to, or avoided, a common second-term falloff, or 'jinx'. Such a misfortune, the book shows, has afflicted most second-term Presidents.

To provide context, many of the one-term Presidents are also discussed in brief. Some of the 'two-term presidencies' considered actually consist of two successive Chief Executives, where one man succeeded another man who died or was killed in office.

Two-term Presidents are evaluated by various means. These include their popularity while in office, their historical reputation, and their ability to handle the major political issues of their time. The most objective way to assess presidential success or failure seems to be election results. This is true of White House elections, but also of congressional elections—both midterm elections and congressional elections during a presidential election year. Congressional elections are an excellent, if indirect, means of judging a President's popularity and success, especially for those Chief Executives who held office before the emergence of public opinion polls. The book therefore sketches the results of congressional elections since 1790, in addition to presidential elections since 1788.

This book is the first of two volumes. It covers President George Washington to President Theodore Roosevelt.

The second volume, due out by autumn 2016, covers President Woodrow Wilson through President Obama and the campaign of 2016.

TABLE OF CONTENTS

THE SECOND-TERM FALLOFF, A
COMMON PRESIDENTIAL MALAISE

In presidential politics, the second-term "jinx" seems an established fact. It is remarkable, looking back to the founding of the American republic, to see how many second-term presidencies have gone through rough water, or have foundered outright.

Of the 20 'two-term' presidencies that this book considers, only four have been outright successes that dodged the two-term hex. Fully 10 of the two-termers have been unsuccessful. Furthermore, five have been judged as "close calls" that might be called modestly successful or modestly unsuccessful. Even George Washington had a difficult, if arguably successful, second term. (The second term of the current President, Obama, is discussed, but not categorized, as he has yet to complete his time in office.)

LIST AND RANKING OF TWO-TERM PRESIDENTS

SUCCESSFUL SECOND TERMERS

James Monroe
Andrew Jackson
Theodore Roosevelt
(Warren Harding)/Calvin Coolidge

UNSUCCESSFUL SECOND TERMERS

Thomas Jefferson
(Abraham Lincoln)/Andrew Johnson
Ulysses S. Grant
Grover Cleveland
Woodrow Wilson
Franklin Roosevelt, second term
Franklin Roosevelt, fourth, or 'second second' term

(John Kennedy)/Lyndon Johnson
(Richard Nixon)/Gerald Ford
George W. Bush

N.B.: The book considers the terms of Andrew Johnson, Calvin Coolidge, Lyndon Johnson, and Gerald Ford as the completion of the 'second terms', respectively, of Abraham Lincoln, Warren Harding, John Kennedy, and Richard Nixon.

CLOSE CALLS

George Washington
James Madison
Dwight Eisenhower
Ronald Reagan
Bill Clinton

IN PROGRESS

Barack Obama

THE TWO-TERM PRESIDENCIES

A description and evaluation of the two-term presidencies follows.

SECOND-TERM WOES FOR
THE FIRST FOUNDER
GEORGE WASHINGTON, 1793-1797

The second term of President George Washington was a somewhat troubled, if still accomplished, follow-up to his landmark first. In his initial term, Washington merely invented the presidency, in setting up the executive branch of the new federal government, thus establishing many norms and precedents that endure to this day.

In the election of 1788-1789, President Washington, at age 57, had been chosen almost unanimously under the limited suffrage of the time. Although technically running as an independent, Washington was the standard bearer for the Federalist movement which had sought to put the new Constitution into practice under a strong federal government.

In the first federal presidential election, Washington basically ran without opposition. He took a remarkable 90.5 percent of the 44,000 ballots cast, and gained 65 electoral votes to 4 electoral votes for the fledgling, anti-federalist opposition wary of centralized power.

The background of Washington—a fearless, shrewd, and physically imposing man—made him the natural leader of the Federalists, with their emphasis on economic and military power and national strength. He was a plantation owner from the old tobacco tidewater region, born in Westmoreland County, Virginia, near the Potomac River about 70 miles south of today's Washington, D.C. His older brother Lawrence had co-founded, and he had surveyed, the bustling new mercantile seaport of Alexandria, Virginia. At his Mount Vernon estate, the younger Washington took on a keen interest in new crops and enterprises, from corn and wheat to whiskey distilleries. He would help sponsor the nearby Chesapeake & Ohio Canal, to spur commerce in the region.

As a ranking officer in the British colonial militia, Washington had a major combat role during the French and Indian War against the foes of Britain and its American colonies. He'd been the Commander-in-Chief of the patriot army of the American Revolution, during which he was ever frustrated by the reluctance of state and local jurisdictions to supply his men with sufficient arms, pay, and provisions.

During the post-war Articles of Confederation period of loose federal control, historians have discovered, Washington played a major, if behind-the-scenes, role. In 1785 he prodded the states of Virginia and Maryland, with the help of George Mason of the former, and Samuel Chase of the latter, into a mutual accord on trade and navigation. This led to the 1786 assembly of five states in Annapolis, Maryland, and then all the states at Philadelphia's 1787 Constitutional Convention. During this time Washington's colleagues Alexander Hamilton and John Jay of New York, and James Madison of Virginia, laid the philosophical groundwork of a vigorous central government through a series of widely published articles, *The Federalist Papers*. The Philadelphia delegates, with Washington as its presiding officer, drew up a blueprint for a new national government.

They overcame the objections of those advocating a more decentralized approach, including former Virginia Governor Patrick Henry, his fellow state planter-philosopher Mason, and ex-revolutionary stalwart Samuel Adams of Massachusetts. Such men were chary of an overreaching government that might too closely mimic the hated old British rule, and that might overtake the authority of their own powerful states. At the time perhaps a plurality or even a majority of Americans—enjoying a living standard, civic and religious privileges, and literacy rate higher than any other country—held such views.

A stage was set for the unity, and divisions, of Washington's presidency.

FIRST-TERM TRIUMPHS

In his first four years, the new President set up a strong and lasting federal enterprise, based eventually in Washington, D.C. He and his Secretary of State, Thomas Jefferson of Virginia, selected and supervised the planners and architects who established the permanent capital.

Washington brought a number of top-level statesmen to his government—Jefferson, the former war-time Governor of Virginia and ex-Minister to France under the Articles of Confederation; Hamilton, a war hero at the battle of Yorktown and a prominent attorney for major New York banks, as Treasury Secretary; and the elected Vice-President, the estimable John Adams of Massachusetts. The President's pick for the first Supreme Court Justice was Jay. John Jay was the former President of the Continental Congress as well as co-author of *The Federalist Papers*. A fellow co-author was Congressman Madison, a leader in the new federal legislature.

The first President, in his first term, strove to put the government on a sound financial footing. He and his chief advisor Hamilton set up the U.S. Treasury Department. They put in place the first federal taxes, a levy on spirits and an excise on imports, as well as custom houses, collectors, and revenue ships to gather the revenue and enforce related laws.

AN EMERGING SCHISM

In other economic actions, Washington helped bring about a split in his Cabinet, and the nation generally, which would vex him in his second term. He opted, at Hamilton's behest, to have the federal government assume the large debts, of both the nation and the states, owed from the American Revolution. This irked some states, such as Virginia, which had already paid off much of their debt, and which felt shouldn't be responsible for others who hadn't, such as Massachusetts. The debt plan also angered many veterans of the Revolutionary War, who had sold off to speculators at a steep discount the pensions owed them for their military service. In spring 1790, Rep. Madison blocked passage of the assumption plan in the House of Representatives.

According to Jefferson—who joined the Administration at that time—he and Madison then cut a "dinner party" deal with Hamilton, whereby they agreed to throw their influence behind assumption. In return, Hamilton backed their plan to place the new, permanent capital of the United States in tidewater Virginia, their home region, in the new town of Washington. They also persuaded Hamilton to much reduce the share of the debt that Virginia would have to assume for other states. Their support proved pivotal, as that July the debt plan passed the House of Representatives by a modest margin, while the plan for moving the capital was approved by just three House votes.

On another fiscal issue, Washington decided, after much deliberation, to back Hamilton's notion for a Bank of the United States, a quasi-federal financial institution. The Bank, which held deposits of federal funds, was aimed at increasing the creditworthiness of the federal government, thus allowing it to respond better to financial needs and emergencies. Like the debt assumption, the Bank, established in early 1791, tended to increase the power of the federal government relative to the states and individuals.

The Bank and the debt assumption convinced the Virginians Jefferson and Madison that Hamilton was turning the Washington Administration into a force for financial and Northern industrial interests, and even into a facsimile of the British government, with its mercantile backing of home-grown, politically connected industry.

The populace seemed ambivalent toward both of the emerging factions, in the first midterm elections, in 1790-91. (Elections to Congress then spread over parts of two consecutive years, instead of the autumn of a single, even-numbered year.) The elections were a wash, with the nascent pro-Administration group picking up two seats in the House of Representatives, for a 39-30 margin. In the Senate, the emerging anti-Administration group themselves gained two seats. Anti-Administration candidates James Monroe of Virginia, the future President and protégé of Jefferson, and Aaron Burr of New York, the future Vice-President and slayer of Hamilton, were elected. However, this block remained in the Senate minority, 17-8.

By summer 1791, Madison and Jefferson were touring the Northern states, under the guise of studying its natural history, while also quietly lining up political support for their own views. At the State Department, Jefferson hired the poet Philip Freneau, who set up the newspaper the *National Gazette*, to represent his positions and to counter those of Hamilton, which were represented by the *Gazette of the United States*, edited by publisher John Fenno of Boston. The Virginians' faction became formally known as the Anti-Federalists, for their wariness of many federal efforts, while Washington and Hamilton's faction would be dubbed the Federalists, for their support of the same. Thus was the two-party system born that has characterized American politics ever since.

Over time, to over-generalize some, the Anti-Federalists would morph into the Democrat-Republicans, and then the Democratic Party. Meantime the Federalists would change into the Whigs, then the Know-Nothing and Free Soil parties, and then the Republican Party. On a striking number of issues—such as the federal government's role on the economy, public order vs. civil liberties, public ethics vs. individual choice, "fair trade" vs. "free trade", the scale of immigration, and the proper size of the military—the topics warred over in the 1790s remain in recognizable form today.

In December 1791, Hamilton published a detailed Report on Manufactures, which called for the government, through tariffs and subsidies, to encourage U.S. industry. Southerners, and some Northern farmers, saw such measures as a tax on them to support manufacturers and urban dwellers. The powerful Treasury Secretary also helped set up a Society for Establishing Useful Manufacturing, or SEUM, a kind of laboratory for industrial innovation.

Some of the Anti-Federalists' fears seemed realized that same year when Hamilton's friend and former Assistant Treasury Secretary, William Duer of New York, secretly siphoned off monies from SEUM, in a plot to corner the market for federal bonds. This affair led that winter to a Wall Street panic, and clamped a bankrupt Duer into debtor's prison for life.

DRUMS ALONG THE FRONTIER

Another issue that burdened Washington in his first term and into his second was bloody conflict with American Indian tribes, egged on by the British, and heightened by the movement of settlers westward, on the frontier of the Old Northwest. The President, who over 30 years before had fought several dozen battles against Native-Americans during the French and Indian War, was stunned by twin setbacks.

In November 1790, Miami and Wabash tribes in present-day Indiana defeated a force of about 1,500 militia and regular Army soldiers. Washington railed at their losing, hard-drinking commander, Brigadier General Josiah Harmar, declaring, "I expected little from the moment I heard he was a drunkard!" The President then ordered the Governor of the Northwest Territory, Major General Arthur St. Clair, the former President of the Continental Congress, to even the score. But a year later, near today's Fort Wayne, Indiana, warriors from the Miami and Shawnee tribes, led by the chieftains Little

Turtle and Blue Jacket, surprised St. Clair's army of some 1,000 soldiers. In the Battle of the Thousand Slain, the demoralized, poorly supplied American army fled the field, after suffering a stunning toll of 900 killed and wounded.

The debacle led to St. Clair's ouster, the first congressional investigation into alleged Administration misconduct, and the first claim of "executive privilege", relating to War Department documents on the military campaign. It also sparked passage in Congress of national standards for state militias, and authorization for the President to call up the militias in emergencies. The defeat also led to the raising of new federal Army regiments.

Still, despite the losses in the Old Northwest and the clash over economic policy, the nation in Washington's first term was prosperous. It generally continued to recover from the Revolutionary War, and to enjoy an interregnum of peace overseas between the French and Indian Wars and the wars of the French Revolution. And the country continued to expand, as the new states of Vermont, Kentucky, and Tennessee entered the union.

THE FIRST RE-ELECTION

The split in his Cabinet caused President Washington endless headaches, as Jefferson, from within his Administration, and Speaker Madison, from without it, tried to thwart his and Hamilton's plans and to advance their own. Due to these tensions, and due to serious health problems, Washington considered retiring at the end of his first term. In the end, however, even the Anti-Federalists—fearing Hamilton and his allies would gain even more power in Washington's absence—backed the President's re-election. And both factions feared that, without his unifying presence, the new nation might split asunder.

And so, in fall 1792, Washington became the first American president to win a second term. In terms of the Electoral College, the election was unanimous, and in the popular vote, as in 1788, nearly so. The President carried all

15 states and all 132 of their electoral votes. Of the 29,000 popular votes cast, Washington took 91 percent.

At that time, before the broad extension of the franchise, only the states of Pennsylvania and Maryland cast popular votes. The remaining states cast their Electoral College votes through their legislatures. In the election, Vice-President John Adams got the second-most electoral votes, 77, and so again took the vice presidency.

In a sign of a growing partisan chasm, however, the former Governor of New York, George Clinton, a Jefferson ally and an anti-Federalist, garnered 50 electoral votes. Further, the Anti-Federalists gained support in the elections for Congress in 1792 and 1793.

Due to the additional seats added to the House of Representatives, based on the census of 1790, both factions won more seats. Yet the Anti-Federalists gained twice as many, adding 24 seats to 12 for the Federalists, to seize a majority, 54-51.

The Anti-Federalists did especially well in the Southern states of Virginia, the home base of their leaders Jefferson and Madison, and in North Carolina, gaining seven and six seats, respectively. They also performed well in Pennsylvania, adding four seats, a harbinger of trouble for Washington in his second term among the farmers of that state's western frontier. The Federalists did particularly well in Massachusetts, a bastion of their support, picking up four seats. The Senate elections were a wash, with both sides gaining one seat each, giving the Federalists an 18-11 majority.

Washington seemed prophetic about his coming second stay in office. He confided to his old Federalist ally and Revolutionary War commander, Virginia's Henry "Light Horse Harry" Lee III: "To say I feel pleasure from the prospect of commencing another tour of duty would be a departure from truth." He mulled serving for just two more years, and then turning over his office to Vice-President Adams.

FIRST IN WAR, FIRST IN PEACE, FIRST TO BATTLE THE SECOND-TERM WOES

In his second term, Washington continued to preside over a functioning federal government, if a less-talented Cabinet, and a growing economy at home. Abroad, he managed, despite many provocations from foreign powers, to mostly keep the fledgling republic out of the chaotic wars spawned by the French Revolution. In his final year, he codified this lesson of avoiding "foreign entanglements", with a strongly partisan political tilt, in a famous Farewell Address.

Still, though his second term was hardly a failure, even George Washington could not evade many second-term tribulations, in contrast to his very successful and more unblemished first term.

Immune to personal criticism, as opposed to his policies, early in his presidency, Washington became the target of personal attacks from the very start of his second term. In the *National Gazette*, Freneau mocked the President as taking on the trappings of a king. "A certain monarchial prettiness," sniffed the publisher about Washington, "levees, drawing rooms, stately nods instead of shaking hands." Another Anti-Federalist paper, the *Aurora*, run by Benjamin Franklin's grandson, Benjamin Franklin Bache, nicknamed "Lightning Rod, Jr.", painted Washington as a puppet of Britain. Franklin demanded the President "point out one single act that unequivocally proves you a friend of the independence of America." A thin-skinned President bit his lip, while raging inwardly at such gibes. The Federalist press, which controlled a large majority of newspapers, struck back. The high-profile *Gazette of the United States*, indirectly subsidized by the government, hosted anonymous articles by Hamilton and Adams, and its own hit pieces on the anti-Federalists.

Responding to the charges of having a kingly style, the President kept a low, "republican" profile at his second inaugural. He arrived by himself, took the oath of office indoors at the Senate, and delivered a barebones, 135-word inaugural statement. When any two-term president, even Washington, begins to answer his critics by bending their way, it usually reflects a loss of power and a decreasing ability to set the tone of public debate.

DISEASE AND DECONSTRUCTION

Another harbinger of trouble quickly came in the form of mankind's oldest affliction: a plague. The first summer of the second term of the first two-term President witnessed the worst epidemic to ever affect the nation's capital city. From August to November 1793, Philadelphia, then playing host to the federal government, was ravaged by a plague of yellow fever. It killed over a tenth of its population of 45,000, and sickened thousands more.

Alexander Hamilton fell ill to the mosquito-borne virus, but recovered. The wife of Washington's private secretary Tobias Lear died from it. That autumn, the entire government, from Cabinet secretaries to customs inspectors, fled the city, and the central government practically ceased to function. This delayed for a time Washington's attempts to heighten the country's military preparedness, in the face of growing conflict between France and its European foes.

Emblematic of the slowing pace at which the Administration operated were delays and disputes over the construction of the planned new capital of Washington. Work on the main federal buildings for the city went slowly. In 1792, Washington and Jefferson had dismissed Pierre L'Enfant, the capital's designer, over the expense and grandiosity of his plans, and his failure to produce a specific plan for the Capitol Building.

During the second term, one the first architects of the Capitol Building, Stephen Hallet, was also cashiered for trying to make unapproved design changes. To save money, hundreds of slaves were put to work on the President's House and the Capitol. Some, paid wages for the special work, were able to save enough funds to buy their own freedom. Late in the President's second term, the three presidentially appointed commissioners running the Capitol's construction were required to focus on just its north, or Senate, wing. The Capitol Building would be only partially finished when Congress moved in, per the Constitution's directive, in 1800.

VEXED BY FOREIGN POWERS

As in many second-term presidencies, Washington faced strong headwinds from foreign turmoil. Much of it, as in some presidencies, was not of his making, but was plain bad luck. America fell victim to wars between the British Empire, and its allies, and the other superpower of the time, Revolutionary France.

As conflict broke out between London and Paris, America had to choose between one, the other—or neutrality. The Francophile Jefferson represented parts of the country that were oriented more to the West and South, and less to Britain and the North Atlantic. He argued that America was bound to its Revolutionary War treaty with Paris that pledged a mutual defense pact. The Anglophile Hamilton as an attorney often represented the merchant houses of his adopted New York, which had revived, along with New England, its old and lucrative trade with Britain. He argued that the treaty, signed by the French King XVI, was void due to his execution by guillotine, under the French Republic, in January 1793.

Washington was sympathetic to the revolutionary cause in France, yet wary of the disorder it spawned. In April 1973, the President came out strongly, on the surface, for neutrality—for the U.S. not backing either rival power militarily, and for a willingness to trade with both. His Neutrality Proclamation forbade Americans from supplying military supplies to, or engaging in combat for, either party. In reality, this took a significant step toward Britain, as it forsook the old treaty of alliance with France, and because trade with France was difficult due to the superiority of the Royal Navy, which often interrupted France's commerce with the outside world.

Anti-Federalists howled at this decision's anti-French slant, and what they saw as its unconstitutional nature. After all, they reasoned, if the Constitution gave the Senate the power to approve treaties, didn't it also grant the Senate the right to disapprove them? But President Washington's views won out, and in so doing he set down a major marker for the executive branch's prerogative over foreign policy, which extends strongly to this day.

On the same month of the Neutrality Proclamation, the U.S. envoy for the radical government in Paris, Edward Charles "Citizen" Genêt, arrived in America. Dubbed *Citoyen*, as aristocratic titles had become fatal in France, his mission was to push the American people into war with Britain and its allies. The polar opposite of neutrality, Genêt would be a great headache for President Washington.

The envoy's strategy was indirect, and outrageous. Instead of proceeding directly to his diplomatic perch in Philadelphia, Genêt landed in South Carolina. There he encouraged the outfitting of American ships as French privateers, and urged locals to ignite a rebellion in Florida, then part of Spain, then an ally of Britain. He also backed a plan by George Rogers Clark of Virginia—the older brother of William Clark of later Lewis & Clark fame—to lead an American force to seize the Mississippi Valley from Spain, which was impeding U.S. riverine commerce there. On his journey to the U.S. capital, Genêt spoke to raucous, pro-French rallies, and helped set up pro-French societies that called themselves "Democratic-Republican", the new moniker of the Anti-Federalist party.

President Washington was enraged at this attempt to refashion American foreign policy behind his back. Eager to maintain neutrality and avoid war, and increasingly partial to Britain and to the prosperous trade with London, he received Genêt coolly. This angered the French government, pro-French elements in America, and the President's France-inclined Secretary of State, Jefferson.

After a French ship brought a captured British vessel into Philadelphia, the Washington Administration forbade Genêt to send the refitted vessel, re-christened *Le Petite Démocrate*, back out to sea as a French privateer. With a wink from Genêt, the ship sailed out anyway. Meantime, thousands of Americans and French exiles marched in protest outside the President's mansion, demanding Washington take the side of Paris. Vice-President Adams feared an uprising might topple the government. The acerbic Genêt condemned Washington's Federalists as the party of kings, and threatened to completely undercut the President's authority with further direct appeals to the American public.

But the envoy's over-the-top tactics finally backfired. He lost the support of his American sympathizers, even Jefferson. Public opinion swung against him. The Administration forbade any more seized ships from entering U.S. ports, or the outfitting of ships as armed privateers. At this time, an even more radical French government took over in Paris, and demanded Genêt's recall, probably to face the guillotine. At that point, ironically, the foes of the mercurial diplomat, Washington and Hamilton, saved his neck by granting him asylum. After one of the wildest episodes in U.S. diplomatic history, Genêt retired from public life, and later wed the daughter of New York's Democratic-Republican Governor, Jefferson ally George Clinton!

At this time, Washington's neutralist course and pro-British tilt seemed proven correct, as the French Revolution fell into a frenzied blood lust. France was run by a "Committee of Public Safety", led by Robespierre and St. Just, democrats turned blood-soaked dictators. They consigned to the blade, mass drownings, and other means of execution perhaps 40,000 foes, and suspected foes, of the Revolution, about one out of 100 Frenchmen.

Even the President's, and America's, great friend from the American Revolution, the Marquis de Lafayette, fell prey to the turmoil. At the start of the French Revolution, with diplomat Jefferson's help, he'd authored—echoing the Declaration of Independence and the U.S. Constitution—the landmark Declaration of the Rights of Man. As head of the French National Guard, he helped set up a tentative constitutional monarchy, with the king the executive, yet limited by the rights and delegates of the people.

But Lafayette fell out of favor when he opposed the detention and subsequent execution of the King, and his wife and Queen, Marie Antoinette. Accused of sympathy for the Old Regime, the gallant revolutionary was thrown into prison with his wife and son, George Washington de La Lafayette. U.S. envoys to France, New York's Gouverneur Morris, as well as Virginia's James Monroe, and his courageous wife Elizabeth Kortright Monroe, intervened to save the necks of the Lafayette family.

But after escaping from France, the Marquis was accused of revolutionary sympathies by the monarchial powers at war with Paris. In Austria and Prussia, the ruling authorities clamped him in jail, fettered in dank cellars full of lice and filth. His situation presented President Washington with a dilemma.

If he publicly pushed for Lafayette's release, the President might alienate the European powers with whom his Administration was striving to maintain peaceful ties. If he did nothing, he would be spurning an old friend. So, behind the scenes, Washington employed quiet diplomacy to free Lafayette. Instrumental in this was James Marshall, the brother of John Marshall, formerly Washington's top Army lawyer in the Revolution, and later the noted Supreme Court Chief Justice. In 1797, Lafayette was finally released.

The excesses of the French Revolution probably helped the President's Federalist Party in the 1794 congressional elections. This occurred even as political trends, including the nation's expansion westward, began favoring the Anti-Federalists, now formally known as the Democrat-Republicans.

In the contests for the Senate, which were then held in the state legislatures, the Federalists and their pro-Administration allies did well. They gained five seats, and much increased their majority, to 20-10. The Federalists even won in the generally anti-federalist South and West, picking up seats in Georgia and Kentucky. Democrat-Republican gains were limited to the House, where they picked up five seats, increasing their majority to 59-47.

AN ENEMY, TURNED AN ALLY OF SORTS

Along with deepening the rift in the Cabinet, the revolution in Paris led to major difficulties with Britain, at the end of Washington's first term and at the start of his second. As Genêt departed, the old English enemy reared its head again.

In 1793-1794 the Royal Navy, as part of a blockade of France, seized hundreds of American ships, and many U.S. sailors, acts of war that provoked outrage and calls for a formal declaration of war. Britain also refused to evacuate forts in the Old Northwest frontier, as stipulated by the 1783 Treaty of Paris ending the Revolutionary War. The forts blocked American expansion, and the officers within them urged on Indians to attack American settlers. Now it almost seemed Jefferson was right, and Washington wrong, in their approach to foreign relations, in the wild tempest of the French Revolutionary wars.

In response to London's acts, Congress and the Washington Administration approved and began construction of a small but powerful and expensive fleet of six frigates, to be completed in the John Adams Administration. The construction included world-class ships that would become legend, such as the *USS Constitution*, or "Old Ironsides", and the 36-gun *USS Constellation*. Congress also voted for a trade embargo on Britain, which upset many

American merchants in New England and the Mid-Atlantic states whose businesses depended on commerce with London.

But the President held out a laurel leaf of peace, and a concession to the North's businessmen. In 1794 he sent to Britain, for negotiations, his Anglophile Supreme Court Chief Justice, John Jay. Jay could play hooky. In the early years of the republic, the Supreme Court was far less powerful than today, its work load considerably less, and intervals between sessions much longer.

His resulting Jay Treaty, signed by Washington in November 1794, enraged many by failing to stop the impressments, or kidnapping, of American seamen by the Royal Navy. The Treaty granted most-favored-nation trade status to Britain, while Britain failed to grant the same to America. Anti-Federalists saw the accord as stepping on commercial matters that Congress had theretofore handled. Southerners were angered by the Treaty's failure to provide compensation for slaves who'd escaped to British lands during the Revolution. And Britain was hardly gracious in its follow-up, when it prevented U.S. ships from carrying foodstuffs to France.

As a result, Jay was burned in effigy by riotous throngs, and in Philadelphia surging crowds surrounded the presidential mansion in protest. The schism widened between Washington's Federalists and Jefferson's Democrat-Republicans. The President was ground down from the resulting dissension and personal attacks. He told Edmund Pendleton, the Chief Justice of Virginia's high court: "I can religiously aver that no man was ever more tired of public life, and more devoutly wished for retirement."

Under the Jay Treaty, Britain did agree to pay much restitution, about $10 million worth, or approximately $140 million in 2015 dollars, to U.S. ship owners whose goods and vessels the British Navy had seized. And Britain made the major concession of closing, by 1796, its Great Lake forts. Both political parties managed to strip from the treaty a disliked provision that kept larger American ships out of British West Indies ports. Above all, outright war with London was averted, allowing the U.S. to continue to grow and prosper in relative peace. Still, the Senate approved the Treaty in June 1795 by the bare two-thirds minimum required, 20-10.

Better received was the subsequent Pinckney's Treaty with Spain, which Madrid and the U.S. agreed to in November 1795. For a period of three years, it pried open the Mississippi River for the unfettered passage of American commerce to New Orleans. It also clarified the border between Spanish Florida and the U.S. The Jay Treaty, by bringing America closer to Britain, pushed Spain, which feared an Anglo-American alliance, closer to America via the Pinckney accord.

CONFLICT FROM THE MEDITERRANEAN TO THE OLD NORTHWEST

Along with the depredations of the Royal Navy, President Washington was pestered by attacks on U.S. ships by Mediterranean pirates, operating out of Tripoli and Algiers in North Africa. In November 1794, the President, with his warship construction not yet begun, settled for the embarrassing Treaty of Tripoli. With Senate backing, the Administration agreed to pay the pasha of Tripoli a modest tribute each year to secure the safety of American shipping.

Ironically, future President Jefferson, though reluctant to engage in military and naval buildups, would use Washington's warships to wage war on the Tripoli pirates during his first term of office.

During the Administration of Washington's successor, President Adams, the French government, still angry over the Jay Treaty, would seize U.S. ships heading for Britain, and would try to coerce the U.S. into granting it loans to stop the seizures. The French Prime Minister Charles Talleyrand even demanded a $250,000 payoff for himself. Angry Americans would respond with cries of "Millions for defense, but not one cent for tribute."

At home, in 1794, Washington's government did win a major military victory. For three years the Administration had worked to avenge the disastrous defeat of General St. Clair near the Wabash River of Indiana and Illinois. This time, the Americans had a competent commander, General "Mad" Anthony Wayne, famed for his service at the battles of Yorktown and Stony Point during the American Revolution. They also had a disciplined federal force of 3,500, dubbed the "Legion of the United States".

On August 20, 1794, Wayne and his men crushed an Indian army and ransacked Indian villages during the Battle of Fallen Timbers. Among the few managing to escape Wayne's wrath was a young Indian warrior, named Tecumseh, destined for future glory. The lopsided victory near today's Toledo, Ohio broke Native-American power in the region, and ended British support for the tribes there.

A SPIRITED REVOLT

As in many presidencies to follow, some of the offshoots of trouble in Washington's second term were sowed during the first. In his initial four years, to finance the new government, Washington and chief aide Hamilton had set up a system of national taxation. One impost was a 1791 levy on whiskey, a prized product among the nation's grain farmers, particularly those on the western frontier. The tax, and the power granted federal investigators to search farmers' properties without permission, reminded some settlers of British outrages during the Revolution.

In Washington's second term, frontier farmers' affection for their "moonshine" took the form of a growing Whiskey Rebellion, with growers and distillers in western Pennsylvania moving to open revolt against federal tax collectors. In summer 1794, the issue reached the fever pitch of crisis, and led to the only large-scale deployment of U.S. troops, other than the Civil War, against American citizens in U.S. history.

Outside Pittsburgh, near where Washington and British Gen. Braddock had fought the French and Indians back in 1755, some 6,000 tax protestors, many of them veterans from the American Revolution, and many of them armed, held a raucous rally denouncing the government. A large force of armed rebels attacked and burnt down the house of a tax inspector, and violently threatened others.

Washington was adamant in his response. He saw the enforcement of the tax as a test of whether the new government could uphold the law and enforce his authority. "If a minority…is to dictate to a majority," he noted, "there is an end put at one stroke to republican government." The President angrily noted his policy was taxation *with* representation.

Pennsylvania itself was split. Its legislature declared federal excise taxes unconstitutional, while its Governor Thomas Mifflin, a major general in the Revolution who'd also been a delegate to the Constitutional Convention, allowed federal agents to collect the tax.

In his approach, President Washington was influenced by the populist terror then reaching its height in France, and by the Daniel Shay's Rebellion of seven years' prior, a farmers and debtors' revolt in western Massachusetts. And Washington had pushed for the Constitution and had agreed to become President under it, after all, to establish a strong and respected federal government.

The President decided to call up over 12,000 soldiers from state militias. Critics like Madison and Jefferson thought this a considerable overreach, and a justification for a large standing army that the Federalists desired. For his part Washington saw the rebels in league with Genêt's radical, pro-French societies, and said so. His criticism in turn made Anti-Federalists think he was trying to suppress dissent by linking them to the rebels. The Pennsylvania farmers were in fact rebelling for their own reasons, but some in other parts of the West, men such as George Rogers Clark, were conspiring with Genêt.

Again donning a military uniform, Washington led the militia deep into Pennsylvania toward the rebels. At this time his Secretary of War, Henry Knox, took for personal reasons a lengthy leave of absence. The President was bitter about what he saw as an old comrade from the Revolution deserting him during a crisis.

From Philadelphia, Washington rode out toward Pittsburgh with Hamilton, appointed as a fill-in for Knox. The President chose as the formal head of the military forces Light Horse Harry Lee. With great irony, Lee's son, Robert Edward Lee, would 70 years thence lead a far greater rebellion against federal authority. The elder Lee, and Hamilton even more, handled the details of administering the federalized militia.

The show of force had its effect. In October the revolt dissolved, fortunately with only three rebel deaths. This was partly through the mediation of anti-Federalist Rep. Albert Gallatin from Pennsylvania. And partly due to rebel envoys who urged a temperate response from Washington.

Washington acceded to their entreaties. He urged his soldiers against undue violence. Scores of rebels were taken prisoner, but eventually released. Two men were condemned to death, but the President pardoned them. The government had established its authority. The excise tax that had touched off the whole matter went largely uncollected.

But the Whiskey Rebellion led to growing support for the Anti-Federalists opposed to the Washington Administration, and to what they saw as the overweening power of the new government. This in turn helped lead to their eventual electoral victory, under Jefferson, in 1800, over Washington's successor

John Adams. Gallatin, as Jefferson's Treasury Secretary, would formally revoke the whiskey tax.

HEALTH AND HEARTH

Theretofore an extremely active man, Washington's health suffered from the sedentary nature of the presidency, and its endless rounds of meetings and social gatherings. In his first year in office, in 1789, he nearly died from an anthrax infection in his leg, and was confined to bed for more than a month. In 1790 he was stricken by severe pneumonia. Further, he was going increasingly deaf, which complicated the innumerable social functions over which he presided. He also was plagued, famously, by his chronically bad teeth.

By the time of his presidency, he had only one original tooth left, which was used to help hold together his ungainly dentures of hippopotamus tusk. Other teeth were purchased from slaves and others who had had their own extracted. The dentures caused the President's upper lip to visibly protrude, as captured in an unflattering portrait by the Danish artist Christian Gullager.

The condition much embarrassed the President. In his second term, Washington wrote coded letters to his dentist seeking palliatives. At times he was forced to take laudanum and opiates to still the pressure and pain of the unnatural dentures upon his gums.

Washington was even bedeviled in his second four years by his household slaves and personal servants. This was because he was President from 1790 to 1797 in the temporary federal capital of Philadelphia, a city founded by Quakers and inimical to slavery.

In 1780, Pennsylvania had passed an Act for the Gradual Abolition of Slavery. Under this law, anyone born after 1780 in the state, including anyone with slave parents, was declared free. Further, any slave brought in from another state who stayed in Pennsylvania for six consecutive months was also free. Amazingly, the President's Attorney General, Edmund Randolph of Virginia, misinterpreted this law, and was forced to give up the slaves he had taken with him to Philadelphia, and who had stayed past the half-year deadline.

Randolph subsequently advised the President to rotate his nine slaves who were residing in Philadelphia in and out of the capital, to avoid the six-month limit. This led to the sad farce of George and Martha Washington sending their servants to and from Mt. Vernon and other locales outside of Pennsylvania.

One slave who wasn't fooled was Martha's formidable personal servant, Oney Judge. 23 years old, of light complexion, she was the child of an enslaved seamstress and an indentured servant of British ancestry. She was horrified to learn Mrs. Washington was going to make a wedding gift of her to granddaughter Nelly Custis. So, one evening, while the Washingtons were preoccupied with packing for a trip to Virginia, Judge slipped away, and boarded a ship sailing up to the free state of New Hampshire.

The First Lady was shaken and angered at what she saw as Judge's disloyalty, and the President took extraordinary steps to try to get her back. While cloaking his intentions—which might have touched off protests in the North—he discussed with then-Treasury Secretary Oliver Wolcott, Jr. of Connecticut, the possibility of someone waylaying Judge, and carrying her back to Mt. Vernon.

Through intermediaries, Washington also informed Judge she would be treated well and freed upon his death, if only she returned to Virginia. The President also took an ad in *The Pennsylvania Gazette*, which read in part: "Absconded from the household of the President of the United States, ONEY JUDGE, a light mulatto girl, much freckled, with very black eyes and bushy hair... Ten dollars will be paid to any person who will bring her home." Probably to avoid political embarrassment, Washington declined to legally and publicly force the return of Judge under the Fugitive Slave Act he had signed into law in 1793.

Judge refused the President's wishes, and stayed put. She went on to marry and have three children with a free African-American. She resided in New Hampshire until her death in 1848. In interviews, she continued to express fondness toward the Washingtons.

As the personal servant to Martha, Judge had been one of the Washington's favorite slaves. Another was Mt. Vernon's skilled chef, a flamboyant man named Hercules. He too surreptitiously slipped away to freedom while in Philadelphia. The President bore him less ill will, and eventually formally freed him in his final testament, whereby he freed, and provided schooling for, all the slaves in his inheritance.

DEPARTURE OF KEY AIDES, WHILE OTHERS DECLINE TO SERVE

The Washington Administration was also the first to witness a common indicator of second-term trouble, the departure of key aides from an Administration. All of Washington's top Cabinet officials left in the first and second year of his second term. Jefferson left on the last day of 1793, and Hamilton and Knox departed the following year. Their replacements did not reach the level of the President's original, redoubtable staff.

The irreplaceable Hamilton's spot at Treasury by taken by Wolcott of the Oney Judge affair; he was formerly Connecticut's comptroller, and later Comptroller of the U.S. Treasury. Knox at War was replaced by the Postmaster General, the dour Anglophile Timothy Pickering.

The worldly Jefferson's replacement at State was his cousin and former Attorney General Randolph, the lawyer who'd misread Pennsylvania's slavery laws. Randolph would provide a bitter shock for Washington.

In autumn 1795, the British Navy intercepted a letter from Jean-Antoine Fauchet, the French Minister to the U.S., outlining secret conversations Fauchet had had with Randolph about the Whiskey Rebellion. The letter revealed Randolph as a partisan Democrat-Republican, and hinted he might accept bribes in exchange for blaming the revolt on the British. The British, eager to sour Franco-American relations, handed the missive over to the Washington Administration. The President confronted his Secretary of State with it.

Randolph largely cleared himself of the corruption charge. But he quit in a huff, literally running out of the presidential mansion, then publishing a bitter pamphlet against the President. He also likely leaked the fact that the President had been overdrawing his salary. This was hardly scandalous: Washington literally lost a fortune in spending so much time, in public service, away from his estates. But it was embarrassing to the President's reputation, and the whole Randolph episode left Washington with a bitter feeling of betrayal.

It got worse. Washington had much trouble finding a fill-in for Randolph. Five prospects turned him down, including Patrick Henry, the former Virginia Governor, and the stirring war-time orator of "Give me liberty or give me death" fame.

Washington aimed high. The others whom he asked, and who turned down the job were: William Paterson, New Jersey's first Attorney General and U.S. Senator and the state's former Governor; Thomas Johnson, Maryland's first Governor and a Supreme Court Justice; Charles Cotesworth Pinckney, a Revolutionary War general from South Carolina, a delegate to the Constitutional Convention, and later the Federalist Party's candidate for President; and New York's Rufus King, another Constitutional Convention delegate, later Washington's Minister to Britain, and in time the Federalists' Vice-Presidential and Presidential candidate. King declined the job due to the "foul and venomous shafts of calumny" that Washington had borne, and that he too might have to bear.

After all these eminent men rejected his offer, the President wanly wrote to Hamilton, "What am I to do for a Secretary of State?" The former Treasury Secretary glumly replied: "A first-rate character is not attainable. A second-rate must be taken with good dispositions and barely decent qualifications…'Tis a sad omen for the government."

In the end, the President moved Timothy Pickering over from the War Department to the State Department. A delay then ensued at filling the Secretary of War spot, as three men turned Washington down for that position! Finally, physician James McHenry of Maryland accepted the role. Yet he failed to impress his boss.

"I early discovered," the President commented, "his talents were unequal to great exertions or deep resources." McHenry would become known not for anything he did, but for something named after him: Baltimore's Fort McHenry, whose defense in 1814 inspired "The Star-Spangled Banner".

In addition to their generally less-than-stellar talents, McHenry, Pickering, and Wolcott were dyed-in-the-wool Federalists, robbing Washington of contrary views and convincing the Anti-Federalists of the President's Federalism, thus contributing to the hyper-partisanship of the Washington Administration's final years.

"The offices are once more filled," Vice-President Adams commented. "But how differently then when Jefferson, Hamilton, Jay, etc., were here!"

One plus from the turnover in all the President's men was the President leaned more on the irascible yet canny Adams. He even made the Vice-President's precocious, 26-year-old son, future President John Quincy Adams, the U.S. Minister to the Netherlands. Adams would engage in far-reaching diplomatic work for future two-term Presidents Madison and Monroe.

ABSENCES ON THE BENCH

At this time, President Washington's legal and judicial picks were also marked by woe. Attorney General William Bradford of Philadelphia had replaced Randolph as head of the Justice Department when the latter moved over to State. In fall 1795, Bradford died in office. Again aiming high, Washington offered the position of Attorney General to the formidable John Marshall of Virginia. Marshall had been the President's chief military attorney in the Revolutionary War, and later his biographer, and would be the most powerful Chief Justice in Supreme Court history.

But Marshall declined, so Washington was forced to turn to former federal judge Harry Innes of Kentucky, despite the man's well-known reputation for laziness. Yet even Innes rejected the President's offer. So Washington chose lawyer Charles Lee, his personal attorney, some would say crony, from his hometown of Alexandria, Virginia, and brother of Light Horse Harry Lee. Charles Lee would become known for his frequent absences from the job.

A vacancy, and an almost comic-opera set of embarrassments, also occurred in summer 1795, for Chief Justice of the Supreme Court, when John Jay resigned his position to successfully run for Governor of New York.

First, Hamilton, busy with work and family in New York City, declined the President's offer to head the Court. Next, the Senate threw out his recess appointment of Supreme Court Justice John Rutledge of South Carolina, formerly that state's war-time Governor. Astonishingly, three weeks after his selection, Rutledge publicly denounced Washington's signature foreign policy effort, the Jay Treaty. An angry reaction in the Senate forced him out of office. John Rutledge remains the only Supreme Court Justice ever removed from office. Deeply troubled, Rutledge returned to South Carolina, and attempted to kill himself in Charleston Harbor.

The President then chose William Cushing of Massachusetts, the former Chief Justice of that state's court, and then a Justice of the U.S. Supreme Court. But six days after the Supreme Court unanimously approved the pick, Cushing, citing age and illness, declined to serve. Finally, a full eight months after the Chief Justice vacancy opened up, the Senate unanimously confirmed Washington's pick of Oliver Ellsworth of Connecticut. He had been a Constitutional Convention delegate. As one of Connecticut's first U.S. Senators, he'd authored the Judiciary Act, giving the Supreme Court the authority to veto state laws it deemed constitutional. Ellsworth was a well-regarded pick who served to the end of the John Adams presidency.

Ever since Washington, two-term presidents have typically seen important staff, with their eyes on future employment and administrations, head out for greener pastures. This usually has a negative effect on the efficiency and efficacy of the Administration in question.

FAREWELL PARTING SHOTS

For the entire presidential campaign year of 1796, Washington stayed officially neutral, and rhetorically so for most of it. The standard bearer for the Federalists was his Vice-President, John Adams. For regional balance, the Quincy, Massachusetts denizen had as his vice-presidential running mate Thomas Pinckney of South Carolina. He had negotiated the Pinckney Treaty with Spain that had for a period secured America's borders with Spanish Florida and its freedom of navigation along the Mississippi River.

Adams's opponent was his former, and future, friend, and now bitter political foe, Jefferson. The Virginian also picked his running mate out of regional balance: New York's slippery Aaron Burr, that state's U.S. Senator and a prominent attorney.

The issues of the campaign reflected the bitter partisanship of Washington's second term. The Adams camp accused the

Jeffersonians of being in league with France and of undermining Washington. The Jeffersonians attacked Adams as on the side of Britain, and slammed the Federalists as "monocrats", supposed royalists in disguise.

Washington's "Farewell Address" of September 1796 can be seen in large part as his entry into the campaign. The Address, actually a letter published by many newspapers, came out just two months before the election. Modern Americans tend to see it, with some justification, as enduring and sage advice from a Founding Father. However, crafted with help from Hamilton, most of it was a justification of Washington's contemporary views, and thus a criticism of the Anti-Federalists and their presidential candidate.

It was in effect the first campaign speech by a two-term President at the end of his presidency, in quiet support of his successor, Adams, and even more of Hamilton, his former right-hand man.

The heart of the address was a defense, in Washington's formal, deliberate style, of his foreign policy of neutrality, with a tilt toward Britain. This was the issue that had dominated his second term.

"Our detached and distant situation invites and enables us to pursue a different course," Washington stated. "It is our true policy to steer clear of permanent alliances with any portion of the foreign world."

He took a clear shot at the Jeffersonians who favored France. "Permanent, inveterate antipathies against particular nations, and passionate attachments for others, should be excluded; and that, in place of them, just and amicable feelings towards all should be cultivated." The President even linked such an approach to religion, and a benevolent, Christian approach to all nations.

Washington also made what was in effect a personal attack on candidate Jefferson, who was both a Francophile and Anglophobic: "The nation which indulges towards another a habitual hatred or a habitual fondness is in some degree a slave. And it gives to ambitious, corrupted, or deluded citizens (who devote themselves to the favorite nation), facility to betray or sacrifice the interests of their own country." This statement could have also been a dig at the President's former, pro-French Secretary of State, Edmund Randolph.

The Chief Executive indulged in some bitterness about the attacks he had endured: "Real patriots who may resist the intrigues of the favorite [nation] are liable to become suspected and odious."

The President backed his neutrality decree outright: "Our country...was bound in duty and interest to take, a neutral position." He noted a solid reason for staying out of Europe's broils, to buy time for America to build its strength: "A predominant motive has been...to gain time to our country to settle and mature its yet recent institutions, and to progress without interruption to that degree of strength and consistency...necessary to give it...the command of its own fortunes."

He seemed to undermine his argument, however, and enraged his foes, by claiming his approach had been purely neutral, when it had favored commerce with Britain: "Our commercial policy should hold an equal and impartial hand; neither seeking nor granting exclusive favors or preferences." Further, he overreached when claiming the Jay Treaty with Britain had solved all commercial disputes with London, when it fact ignored continuing English impressments of U.S. sailors and other disputes. He stated the treaty had secured for the nation's regions "everything they could desire...towards confirming their prosperity."

In the address, Washington also famously attacked political partisanship, and couched this as a means of favoring France, and agents of it like Citizen Genêt: "[Faction] opens the door to foreign influence and corruption...Thus the policy and the will of one country are subjected to the policy and will of another."

Composing the address after a five-man Directorate, a dictatorship, had seized control of a revolutionary France in turmoil, Washington warned that extreme partisanship could lead to despotism. He noted the "alternate domination of one faction over another, sharpened by the spirit of revenge...The disorders and miseries which result gradually incline the minds of men to seek security and repose in the absolute power of an individual." In this the President seemed to anticipate the French Emperor, and despot, Napoleon, who would take power in Paris three years later.

Having put down the Whiskey Rebellion of western farmers, a group strongly Anti-Federalist, President Washington also cautioned against regional faction, noting the economic and military advantages "the West" gained from a political union with "the East".

Stung by the attacks on his Administration, Washington dismayed his critics, by chiding vigorous partisan dissent against a duly elected government: "There is an opinion that parties in free countries are useful checks upon the administration of the government and serve to keep alive the spirit of liberty," he stated. "But in those of the popular character, in governments purely elective, it is a spirit not to be encouraged." In this he may have somewhat anticipated the Alien and Sedition Acts of his successor Adams, measures that placed some political opponents in jail.

At the same time, the President warned of government over-reach, stating federal officials should "confine themselves within their respective constitutional spheres, avoiding in the exercise of the powers of one department to encroach upon another. The spirit of encroachment tends to consolidate the powers of all the departments in one, and thus to create, whatever the form of government, a real despotism." However, in this he may have had in mind in part the desire of congressional opponents to impinge upon what he saw as his prerogative in setting foreign policy.

Then he defended the controversial revenues he and Hamilton had raised to help pay off the debt from the Revolution, one of the main issues of his first term. In this, he tried something difficult for any politician, even George Washington, to do, namely: defend raising taxes. Washington stated that "towards the payment of debts there must be revenue; that to have revenue there must be taxes; that no taxes can be devised which are not more or less inconvenient and unpleasant". Perhaps overestimating the patience of the taxpayer, he added that in "the measures for obtaining revenue" the people should have a "spirit of acquiescence".

Like the other Founders, Washington firmly believed that religion and ethics were a binding glue for any republic. He stated: "Of all the dispositions and habits which lead to political prosperity, religion and morality are indispensable supports." Further, he asked, "Where is the security for property, for reputation, for life, if the sense of religious obligation desert"? Yet even here he seemed to take a dig at the erudite Jefferson, whom Federalists criticized for his rather more freethinking philosophy: "Whatever may be conceded to the influence of refined education on minds of peculiar structure," Washington stated, "reason and experience both forbid us to expect that national morality can prevail in exclusion of religious principle."

THE PRESIDENTIAL COATTAILS AT PRESIDENCY'S END

An indicator of a two-term president's enduring popularity is how well his "successor" does—in this case Washington's Vice President—in the election at the end of his second term. In this case Adams won, narrowly. He took the limited popular vote of the time 53 percent to 47 percent, and the Electoral College 71-68. He achieved the latter by picking off one electoral vote each in three states that otherwise went strongly for Jefferson: Pennsylvania, North Carolina, and Virginia. Some electoral votes for a state were then determined by district or by the state legislature, instead of a winner-take-all.

Along with Pennsylvania, Jefferson took every state south of Maryland, while Adams won every state north of Pennsylvania, plus New Jersey. With the 1796 election—the first truly competitive one, as Washington had twice run essentially unopposed—the North-South divide that would dominate presidential politics for generations became clear. The Virginian would come back to win in 1800, and overwhelmingly so in 1804.

Although barely holding the President's House, the Federalists did well in the congressional races. In the House of Representatives, they picked up 10 seats to flip the House, going from a 47-59 minority to 57-49 majority. They evinced nearly unanimous support in New Jersey, Delaware, Connecticut, and New Hampshire.

In the Senate, they gained one seat in New York, to increase their large margin to 20-10. In New York Philip Schuyler, the scion of a prominent old Dutch family, beat Aaron Burr, who was running for the Senate. Later the Vice-President under President Jefferson, Burr would in 1804 slay the arch-Federalist Alexander Hamilton in an infamous duel, leaving behind a widow, Elizabeth Schuyler Hamilton, Philip Schuyler's daughter.

EVALUATING WASHINGTON'S SECOND TERM

Personally, George Washington had a very trying second term. He was the target of incessant personal and political attacks. His political party began to lose influence. Two of his most important slaves ran away to freedom. His health was poor. He genuinely wanted to retire to Mt. Vernon instead of serving out another four years.

Politically, Washington's second term was also troubled, but it had successes too.

He had to lead a force of thousands of militia to browbeat into submission a tax revolt of American farmers. His signing of the Fugitive Slave Act, which bolstered the ability of slave owners to recapture escaped servants, set a bad precedent for an issue that would vex the nation for seven decades.

He was plagued by British and French interference with American shipping that effectively reached the level of war, albeit undeclared. He was nettled by the French envoy Genêt, and his attempts to tangle the U.S. in France's wars. His Administration also suffered through a literal plague, the worst in American history, the yellow fever epidemic of 1793.

He was hurt by remarkably bad personnel problems, as his original, well-regarded Cabinet members and other high appointments departed. Their places were taken by men of lesser talent, several of whom, Randolph, Knox, and Rutledge, badly let him down.

The split between his Federalists and the opposition Anti-Federalists widened into a formal, and rancorous, two-party competition. Washington exhibited at times a tone deafness to the fears that some of his actions helped create, such as calling up troops against citizens, or criticizing dissent as almost unpatriotic. The political wars of his second term helped set the table for the great success of his Anti-Federalist foes in future years.

Still, the division of American politics into competing parties was probably inevitable, as similar divisions had existed before his Administration took office. Prior to the establishment of the new federal government, after all, there were vigorous debates over whether the states should approve the Constitution, the legal basis for that government. A greater number of Americans may have wished to continue under the loose, post-Revolutionary association of the Articles of Confederation. The Constitution was barely approved by Virginia, and was likely approved in Pennsylvania only through suspect voting practices. Widespread anti-federal sentiment naturally carried over into the Anti-Federalist Party.

On the foreign affairs front, the Anglo-Franco wars continued, but without the U.S. involved in an all-out shooting war, partly due to Washington's Neutrality Act. Citizen Genêt was dismissed by his own government, and the turmoil he stirred up settled down for the time being.

The Spanish agreed for a while to allow U.S. navigation down the Mississippi River, and at the same time the British withdrew from their Old Northwest forts. At the President's direction, Gen. "Mad Anthony" Wayne put an end in the same region to the threat of the Indian tribes. Also, Washington put into motion plans for constructing what would become over time the world's great maritime force, the U.S. Navy.

At home, the Whiskey Rebellion ended with little loss of life, while strengthening Washington's authority, even as it may have cut into his personal popularity. The Wall St. financial panic of 1791-1792 was short-lived; prosperity continued throughout the second term. On the slavery issue, given the nascent state of the abolitionist movement at the time, there was probably little Washington could do on the matter politically, even if he had been so inclined.

In addition, by declining to run for the highest office a third time, Washington sent a powerful message of peaceful, democratic transition of power for the new republic. When King George III learned of his old adversary's intent to retire—like the Roman dictator Cincinnatus, to his farm, instead of retaining power for life—the monarch remarked: "If he does that, then he will be the greatest man in the world".

As this book will show, elections are a key indicator of second-term failure or success. Washington's party picked up seats in the midterm elections of his second term, which has rarely happened for any president since, and did relatively well during the 1796 "successor election" of John Adams. The President's partisan Farewell Address may have played a role.

Given the steady continuance, despite many partisan fights, of the experiment in federal, constitutional government, and given the general peace and prosperity of the nation, Washington's second term, despite many personal and some political troubles, can be judged a slight success.

SURPRISING TROUBLE
AFTER A STERLING START
THOMAS JEFFERSON, 1805-1809

In the 1800s, and into the early twentieth century, there were some surprising second-term falls, involving some presidents held in very high esteem today. Most historians highly rate the presidency of Thomas Jefferson. Yet he, like Washington, had a trying second term, especially toward its end.

A VIRGINIAN'S ROOTS

Jefferson was born in 1743 near today's Charlottesville, Virginia, to a planter family possessing about 10,000 acres of land, as well as considerable debt. Reared near the Appalachians, Jefferson's outlook would be more toward the freewheeling frontier, and less toward the largest plantations, and their more traditionalist owners, near the tidewater shores.

Tall, lean, personally charismatic, he had the benefit of superb teachers. As a teenager, under the Rev. James Maury, the grandfather of Matthew Maury, a founder of oceanography and atmospheric science. As a law student, under the abolitionist George Wythe, of the College of William and Mary. Wythe was also the instructor for James Monroe, John Marshall, and future presidential candidate Henry Clay. Jefferson would become perhaps the nation's most influential proponent of religious and civil liberties.

At the Continental Congress in summer 1776, where publisher Ben Franklin might have been the natural choice to pen the Declaration of Independence, John Adams chose Jefferson, a writer of soaring prose from the then-largest state. As Virginia's war-time Governor, Jefferson had difficulty defending the Commonwealth from British incursions, given the weakness of the Governor's office, his own lack of military experience, and the deployment of Virginia's soldiers to other embattled states. He barely escaped capture at his estate of Monticello, from marauding British Col. Banastre Tarleton.

After independence, he became a prominent member in 1783 of the legislature under the pre-Constitution Articles of Confederation. He pushed for anti-slavery measures, and had a major role in crafting the county system of government for America's new territories, put into practice under the 1787 Northwest Ordinance. In 1784, he took over Franklin's post as Minister Plenipotentiary to France, and became an obvious choice for the nation's first Secretary of State in the Washington Administration.

As noted, with James Madison he became leader of the opposition Anti-Federalists to Washington's and Hamilton's Federalists, and 1796 narrowly lost the presidency to Washington's successor, Vice-President Adams.

A WILD ELECTION CAMPAIGN, AND A POST-ELECTION DEADLOCK

Jefferson had one of the most successful presidential first terms, after his very narrow and bitterly fought election win in 1800 over his former, and future, friend, President Adams.

The election of 1800 revolved around President Adams' perceived alliance with Great Britain, and Vice-President Jefferson's perceived sympathy for France, during the French Revolution era's savage wars between those twin superpowers. A major campaign issue was the undeclared naval war with France during Adams' last two years. To prepare for a possible outright war, Adams had approved an unpopular tax that raised funds for the new U.S. Navy fleet and for a larger Army.

A related issue was Adam's Alien and Sedition Acts of 1798. These were aimed in part, during the "Quasi War" with France, at suppressing pro-French immigrants from Europe and anti-war foes of the President. The Acts gave the government authority to arrest critics of the government.

Among those detained were the partisan Democrat-Republican Congressman Matthew Lyon of Vermont, and two prominent anti-Federalist writers—Bache, the *Aurora* editor who'd made personal attacks on George Washington, and the Scottish-born anti-Federalist muckraker, James Callender. In response to the Acts, Jefferson and Madison secretly wrote the Kentucky and Virginia Resolutions. These justified the refusal of states to enforce or even recognize federal laws they deem unjust or unconstitutional.

Another dividing issue was the regional and commercial split between the New England of Adams, which looked to its strong trade ties across the Atlantic to Britain, and the Southern and Western states that favored Jefferson, and which were more oriented toward the inland frontiers.

While President Adams prepared for open war with France, he also sought out peace. Just prior to the election, he managed, through Secretary of State John Marshall, the future Supreme Court Chief Justice, to secure an agreement with France to end the undeclared naval war. However, news of the accord reached America after the election, and was thus too late to affect it.

The campaign itself was one of the most vicious in American history. Jefferson was accused of atheism and of being in the pocket of France. Adams was accused of being a closet monarchist and a British puppet. Retired President Washington was dragged through the mud. The factions hired writers to mount slanderous attacks, the most notorious being Callender, jailed under the Sedition Act for scurrilous putdowns of prominent Federalists such as Adams.

In the election campaign President Adams' running mate, selected in part for regional balance, was South Carolina's Charles Cotesworth Pinckney. The plantation owner and former delegate to the Constitutional Convention was the brother of Thomas Pinckney, who'd negotiated the Mississippi River navigation treaty with Spain.

But the Federalists entered the election split, between Adams and his political rival Hamilton. A long letter from the latter that scathingly attacked Adams became public during the campaign. Hamilton himself was under a cloud after Callender published stories, later admitted to by the ex-Treasury Secretary, that he'd had an affair with a married woman, 23-year-old Maria Reynolds, and had been blackmailed by her husband.

On the other side, the anti-Federalist Democrat-Republicans were unified behind Jefferson, and his running mate Aaron Burr, also chosen for regional balance. A highly intelligent man of hard-to-fathom motivations, Burr was the grandson of noted theologian Jonathan Edwards. A lieutenant colonel of note in the Revolutionary War, Burr had also been New York's Attorney General and U.S. Senator.

The balloting, in voting that then stretched from spring to fall among the different states, gave the Virginian a big edge. In the 67,000 popular ballots cast, Jefferson handily beat Adams 61 percent to 39 percent. He took all the Southern states, plus New York, the tidewater border state of Maryland, and did well in Pennsylvania. However, his Electoral College tally was rather narrow, 73 to 65.

Under the voting process of the time, Jefferson and Burr received the same number of Electoral College votes. A Democrat-Republican elector who was supposed to vote for a third candidate instead of Burr, thus assuring Jefferson's win, mistakenly voted for the New Yorker, causing a tie. Astonishingly, Burr, instead of throwing his support behind his running mate at the top of the ticket, tried to take the presidency for himself.

A tense deadlock followed, and 35 tied votes in the outgoing, Federalist-dominated House of Representatives, charged by the Constitution with deciding the presidency by the vote of congressmen in each state. Finally, on the 36th ballot, Jefferson gained a majority of the 16 state delegations. Federalist chieftain Hamilton, believing Jefferson the lesser of evils, and having his own bitter, home-state rivalry with Burr, strongly backed the Virginian, thus swaying critical votes. Burr would not forget, nor forgive, Hamilton's slight. Nor would Jefferson forgive Burr's betrayal. For four years, the capital would witness the bizarre sight of a President and Vice-President estranged.

Along with Jefferson's victory, the Democratic-Republicans won big in the congressional elections. They picked up 22 seats in the 106-seat House of Representatives to go from the minority to the majority party there, 68 to 38. The Federalist Party would never regain control of the House. Its foes even did well in way up North, carrying districts in New York, New Jersey, and Rhode Island. They picked up five seats in Adams' home state of Massachusetts. In Georgia, the two Federalist congressmen there won only after switching their party affiliation to the other side.

In the Senate contests, which included special elections that spilled into 1801, Jefferson's party gained an impressive seven seats, to narrowly take control of the Senate, 17-15. These included pickups in the New England states of Rhode Island and Vermont. The shift was especially dramatic as the Federalists had had a more than 2-to-1 margin in the previous Senate.

Moreover, the Democratic-Republicans staged big gains in the state legislatures. The state, congressional, and presidential elections made up what historians called the "Jeffersonian Revolution of 1800". It signaled the decline and eventual demise of the Federalist Party, the domination of the anti-Federalists, and a trend to the enfranchisement of more and more voters.

AN ACCOMPLISHED FIRST TERM, AND A SCANDAL SIDESTEPPED

From the new President's House, which he had helped design, located in the new City of Washington, Jefferson pulled off a series of early triumphs. In the first use of U.S. military might overseas, in 1801 he sent the U.S. Navy and Marines off in a multi-year campaign against the Muslim Barbary Pirates of North Africa, to the shores of Tripoli. He bloodlessly increased the country's extent, by 140 percent, through the 1803 Louisiana Purchase. In 1804 he sent protégé Meriwether Lewis and Army Capt. William Clark on a famous, 29-month journey of exploration through the far western Louisiana territories.

He and Treasury Secretary Albert Gallatin, originally from a French-speaking part of Switzerland, and formerly the Congressman who'd helped defuse the Whiskey Rebellion, performed their feats while cutting taxes and reducing the federal debt by 40 percent.

The Sage of Monticello also presided over the first peaceful transition of power maybe anywhere, as his newly elected Democrat-Republican party took over from the Federalist party of Adams and Hamilton. His faction, later to morph into the Democratic Party, would dominate national politics through the 1840s, even as the Federalists began a sharp decline into dissolution, and replacement by the Whig Party and, eventually, the Republicans.

To his credit, Jefferson revoked the prior Administration's practice of jailing some dissenting Americans via the Alien and Sedition Acts, and pardoning those imprisoned. To his discredit, he backed the use of similar, local laws against some of his own political enemies, though such legislation faded away in time.

He won a short-term victory, but suffered a long-term defeat politically, over another Adams' initiative—the latter's appointment in his final days in office of 23 new federal circuit-court judgeships, the so-called "Midnight Judges". This was an effort by the outgoing President to thwart the incoming one through the enduring power of the judiciary.

A landmark legal case ensued, *Marbury vs. Madison*. The Supreme Court of Chief Justice John Marshall, appointed by Adams, ruled that the Court, contrary to Jefferson's view, could overrule laws signed by the President, or passed by the people's representatives in Congress, thus setting a precedent of lasting impact.

Still, Congress in 1802 repealed the Adams Judiciary Act of the previous year, thus eliminating the circuit court judgeships. A new Judiciary Act made the Court's justices preside over the circuit court cases in the states, much adding to the justices' work load.

Meantime, the President faced scandalous allegations. After Jefferson had pardoned the journalist Callender, and paid off part of his fine for sedition, the muckraker had demanded more, namely a lucrative federal post of postmaster general in Richmond, Virginia. Jefferson and his top advisor, Secretary of State Madison, concluded the President was being blackmailed. Jefferson also saw a political need for the new Administration to distance itself from the savagery of the campaign. He refused Callender's job request, and told James Monroe that Callender "knows nothing of me which I am not willing to declare to the world myself."

The irate Scotchman's response was to publish letters showing Jefferson's support for Callender's attacks on Adams. Of greater import, after conducting research near Monticello, he drew up charges, spread with glee by Jefferson's enemies, that the plantation-owning President had fathered children with one of his slaves, Sally Hemings. A Boston newspaper printed a wicked doggerel on the matter to the tune of Yankee Doodle Dandy: "When pressed by loads of state affairs/I seek to sport and sally/The sweetest solace of my cares/Is in the lap of Sally..." The Chief Executive maintained a discreet silence, and the allegations faded with word of the spectacular Louisiana Purchase.

Two centuries later, descendants of Hemings, who had in their family's oral history attested to an "Uncle Jefferson" as a progenitor—and employing the new technology of DNA analysis—showed that someone in the Jefferson family had fathered some of Hemings' children. Most historians think the father was Thomas Jefferson, while some maintain it was another male relative—an uncle, nephew or, perhaps, the President's rather wayward brother, Randolph Jefferson, who had a fondness for dancing, fiddling, and drinking at Monticello festivities. The matter remains one of the most intriguing, unanswered questions in American history. Regarding Callender, it was a case of Jefferson playing with fire, and getting burned.

Still, the President maintained great popularity through his first term. This was reflected in landslide congressional contests stretching from February 1802 to December 1803, with some special elections taking place after the seating of the new Congress. The Democrat-Republicans won an eye-catching 35 new seats to just one for the Federalists, to build a greater than 2-to-1 majority, 103-39.

Many seats were new ones resulting from the 1800 census, and the new Southern and Western districts in Tennessee and Kentucky, and rural ones in western New York and Pennsylvania, places which were strongly anti-Federalist.

The Democrat-Republicans picked up eight seats in Pennsylvania, six in New York, and five in North Carolina. In Kentucky they won all of the four new seats. In Massachusetts, they defeated the former Secretary of State for President Adams, then-Rep. Timothy Pickering, as well as Adams son, John Quincy. (Placing aside his political antipathy to Jefferson, the younger Adams would join the President's political party, and often dine with his father's old ally at the Executive Mansion. There, to the admiration and bafflement of other guests, the two cultured men would at times converse in ancient Greek.)

The election results were similarly lopsided in the Senate, with the Federalists losing six seats, as the Democrat-Republicans built a greater than 2-to-1 majority, 22-9. Their gains included the two seats in the new state of Ohio.

One group where Jefferson lost support was the most fervent among his own faction. The President's strong and sometimes constitutionally dubious executive actions—the retention of Hamilton's national bank, for instance, and the Louisiana Purchase and the debt incurred for it—angered some ardent anti-Federalists.

Two of the most prominent, John Randolph of Roanoke, Virginia, and John Taylor of Caroline County, Virginia, openly broke with Jefferson. Anti-war, anti-tax and anti-tariff, pro-states' rights, and deeply suspicious of central authority, including federal efforts to regulate slavery, they formed a faction called the Tertium Quids, roughly, "the Third Way". They urged a return to the "Principles of '98", namely, the states-oriented Virginia and Kentucky Resolutions that Jefferson and Madison had penned. (Through his will, Randolph would free his slaves in 1821, and provide them with land in Ohio.)

Randolph and Taylor helped lay the foundation of the modern libertarian movement, the cause championed by Ayn Rand. And after them, leaders in the major political parties would be often challenged by "true believers" within their own group.

A TRIUMPHANT RE-ELECTION

In the re-election year of 1804, Jefferson, and his party again turned in a dominating performance. With the volatile Aaron Burr off the ticket—after his slaying of Alexander Hamilton in their duel that year, and his bid to displace Jefferson four years prior—the President ran with the popular Governor George Clinton of New York. Like Burr, Clinton was an outreach to Northern voters, but without the baggage.

The Federalists had a solid ticket of their own, but a year after the very popular Louisiana Purchase, and at a time of expansion, prosperity, and peace, they stood little chance. They again nominated South Carolina's Charles Cotesworth Pinckney, and for Vice President tapped powerful New York statesman Rufus King. He had been an important player at the Constitutional Convention as well as Minister to Great Britain for Presidents Washington and Adams, and for Jefferson too.

The Jefferson-Clinton ticket won one of the largest landslides in American political history. Strong in the North as well as South, it carried every state except New England's Connecticut and the Mid-Atlantic's Delaware, taking the electoral vote, 162-14. It won the popular votes cast 73 percent to 27 percent, the highest margin of any contested national election ever. With Richard Nixon of California, Jefferson is the only former Vice President to win re-election as President. He remains one of the greatest vote getters in presidential history.

The congressional contests, held from April 1804 through August 1805, echoed the presidential results. In the House, the Democrat-Republicans gained 11 seats to build a 4-to-1 margin, 114-28. As a sign of their strength, they took three seats in the old Federalist stronghold of Massachusetts.

In the Senate, Jefferson's party built to an almost 3-to-1 majority, gaining two more seats. After pickups in New Hampshire and New Jersey, their Senate margin stood at 27-7.

Given these electoral results, and the President's first-term achievements, it might seem puzzling that the second term of the Virginia polymath proved such a trial.

A JUDICIAL OVERREACH

After overturning the Alien and Sedition Acts, and dispensing with the Federalist "midnight judges", Jefferson might have been content with his judicial wins. Instead, late in his first term and into his second he overreached, and suffered a stinging political defeat, by trying to impeach a dissenting and famous Federalist judge.

Samuel Chase was a prominent jurist from Maryland, a signer of the Declaration of Independence, appointed to the Supreme Court by President Washington. It was Chase, along with George Mason of Virginia, and with an assist from Washington, who had forged the 1785 commercial union between Maryland and Virginia, leading to the Constitutional Convention of all the states two years later.

Chase was a strident Federalist, supportive of strict property qualifications for voting. He'd presided, per the Alien and Seditions Acts, over the high-profile trial and conviction of Democrat-Republicans, including Callender. Another of his court cases involved John Fries, a Pennsylvanian who's spurred protestors to harass and detain federal agents collecting a land tax to pay for the Quasi War with France. Chase's court convicted Fries, and sentenced him to death—to much criticism, before Adams pardoned the man. In these proceedings Chase was openly partisan and dismissive toward the defendants, even if staying within the letter of the law.

His behavior induced President Jefferson to suggest Chase be impeached. Rep. Randolph, the Quids leader and foe of anything Federalist, brought up impeachment proceedings in the House. Presiding over the trial was Vice

President Burr, under indictment up North for killing Hamilton, and still in office until Clinton was sworn in as Vice President.

But even Jefferson's allies thought judicial partisanship, as opposed to misconduct, was not enough to warrant eviction from office. Further, Burr conducted the proceedings to aid Chase, and his defense attorney, Luther Martin of New Jersey. Martin, a strident anti-Federalist, defended Chase, the most partisan of Federalist. And Burr was to hire Martin as his lawyer in his own, later trial for treason!

In March 1805, the vote to impeach in the overwhelmingly pro-Jefferson Congress failed, on all eight counts. The President suffered an embarrassing and avoidable defeat. And a precedent was set, of a high legal bar for ousting federal judges—though thereafter they were usually kept their political views to themselves.

ENEMIES WITHIN

The Chase trial was a harbinger of a much more serious judicial matter. Toward the end of his first term, and for much of his second, Jefferson suffered the shock of his disgraced, former Vice-President Burr committing actions tantamount to treason, and then being acquitted of his crime. Moreover, a top official in Jefferson's War Department aided Burr. And foiling the President's attempt to punish the traitor were his old Federalist foes in the judiciary.

The ambitious Burr had become political poison to both parties, due to his falling out with Jefferson and his slaying of Hamilton. In spring 1805, as he left the vice presidency, Burr headed West.

He began assembling soldiers and supplies in the Ohio River basin, with the intent of moving down the Mississippi to New Orleans, some of whose businessmen longed to annex territory from Spanish Mexico. He bought boats from a future President, Andrew Jackson of Tennessee, who was unaware of Burr's intent. He recruited to his cause the Governor of Northern Louisiana, and Commander-in-Chief of the U.S. Army, the disloyal General James Wilkinson, of Benedict, Maryland. During the Articles of Confederation period of the 1780s, Wilkinson had favored secession for Tennessee and Kentucky, and warmed to a similar scheme.

While still Vice President, Burr had secretly asked the British Ambassador to the United States, Anthony Merry, for $500,000 in cash and warships to further his purpose. Merry, of a naturally sour disposition, despised Jefferson for making him sit at White House dinners with the rival French ambassador. He gave Burr a small sum, $1,500. The Spanish Ambassador, hoping to wound an expanding U.S., gave him several thousand more. Former Speaker of the House Jonathan Dayton of Ohio, after whom the city of Dayton is named, afforded Burr a personal loan.

It seems Burr's intent was to help instigate, and perhaps head up, a war with Spain. Or perhaps get Wilkinson, and Commander-in-Chief Jefferson, to do his work for him, by waging war on Spanish territory. Then he could make himself head of a new nation carved from Mexico and America's western territories. In that region, federal control was loose, and more than a few desired a new and independent nation of their own.

It was a wild era of vast territorial acquisitions, of ambitious men, shifting ideals, and of powerful foreign enemies on the nation's borders. America was up for grabs.

For a while, Jefferson was deaf to officials who warned him of Burr's activities. On three occasions, a federal court in Kentucky investigated Burr, and charged him of plotting against the government. However, he got off with the help of lawyer Henry Clay, the future House Speaker and Secretary of State. In spring and summer 1806, the U.S. District Attorney for Kentucky wrote to the President about a secession plot, but Jefferson, thinking partisan politics at play, dismissed the warning.

Yet newspapers were full of rumors of Burr's movements, and Jefferson's Cabinet began to grow alarmed. That October, the plot began to fall apart. Gen. Wilkinson panicked, and decided to save his own skin. He sent Jefferson a coded letter, possibly transcribed into code by Dayton, which Burr had authored and sent to Wilkinson. The letter read in part:

"…final orders are given to my friends and followers. It will be a host of choice spirits. Wilkinson shall be second to Burr only… By your messenger send me 4 or 5 of the commissions of your officers which you can borrow under any pretence you please… Our project my dear friend is brought to the point so long desired…The gods invite us to glory and fortune. It remains to be seen whether we deserve the boons…"

Finally aroused to action, Jefferson drafted a cease-and-desist order against the plotters. In December, militia rounded up many of Burr's men and equipment. The ring leader was arrested north of New Orleans, escaped into the wilderness, was caught and arrested anew.

In February 1807, the "trial of the century" began, at the federal circuit court in Richmond, Virginia. The Jefferson Administration brought charges of treason, punishable by hanging, against the President's former political ally.

Yet presiding over the court was Jefferson's foe and staunch Federalist, John Marshall. Though a skillful, even great, man, Marshall had conflicts of interest. He'd been placed on the court by Adams, Jefferson's rival, and he'd ruled against Jefferson's Secretary of State, James Madison, in the *Marbury vs. Madison* case. He was now having arduously to "ride circuit", due to Jefferson's termination of the extra Federalist judgeships. And long before, Marshall and

Jefferson had been romantic rivals over Polly Ambler, Marshall's wife and mother of his 10 children.

Burr's lawyer was Luther Martin, the attorney who'd successfully defended Judge Chase from impeachment by Jefferson's Congress. At a time when most Americans distrusted Spain, and even expected a war with it, Martin insisted Burr only intended to attack Spanish, not U.S., territory.

The prosecutors could not produce, as the Constitution requires, two major witnesses to testify to Burr's alleged treason. Although Burr was very likely guilty, much of the evidence against him was given by Gen. Wilkinson—whom historians now know was then a paid spy for the Spanish Empire. In fact, evidence of Wilkinson's double-dealing came out at the trial, further embarrassing the Administration which had appointed him. (Amazingly, Presidents Washington, Adams, Jefferson, and Madison all kept Wilkinson on, until Madison finally brought court-martial charges against the scoundrel in 1811. He beat the charges and, though a military failure in the War of 1812, was later made an envoy to Mexico by President Monroe!)

Burr was also helped by Marshall's narrow definition of treason. To the judge, treason consisted of an actual act of war, and not simply a conspiracy to wage it. Burr was acquitted.

Still wanted for alleged crimes in several states, and his reputation ruined, Burr fled to Europe. Jefferson had finally ridden himself of one of his two top rivals, who had ridden Jefferson of the other, Hamilton.

But the President's lawyers had lost their case against Burr. In addition, the President had moved against the treasonous plot very late in the game. Jefferson also bore some responsibility for selecting Burr as his Vice President in the first place. Further, the disloyal Wilkinson retained his slot at the War Department. The Burr affair was a rough way to start a second term.

The second-term midterms occurred in the shadow of the Burr conspiracy, in 1806-1807. Jefferson's Democratic-Republicans showed slight gains, as the great momentum they had generated in the elections of 1800 and the landslide congressional elections of 1804-1805 began to slow.

In the Senate, Jefferson's party picked up one seat, in New Hampshire, to keep their overwhelming majority at 28-6. Of note was the election, as Senator from Kentucky, of Henry Clay, as a Democratic-Republican, though he would serve as a lawyer for Burr. Clay would later switch allegiances, and lead for decades the party that replaced the Federalists, the Whigs. In the House, Jefferson's party picked up two seats overall, including five seats in New Hampshire, to maintain their commanding tally of 116-26.

Given their huge majorities, it would have been hard for Jefferson's party to gain more seats. In fact, it was a very unusual election in that, in the President's second term, his party actually gained seats, which has almost never happened in U.S. presidential history. (An exception was President Bill Clinton's Democratic Party in 1998.) A modest decline in the popularity of President Jefferson and his party was to come later in 1807 and into 1808-1809. Still, the election results of 1806 probably more reflect the weakness of the Federalist Party than any movement toward the Democrat-Republicans.

ENEMIES WITHOUT

Jefferson's worst woes were telescoped into his final year in office, and came about due to the wars between Britain and France that so nettled his predecessors Washington and Adams, and would plague his successor Madison.

In his first term, a shaky peace had mostly prevailed between the two superpowers. But the situation changed drastically in late 1805, during the first year of his second term. Napoleon, at the height of his military might, won an overwhelming victory over the combined Russian and Austrian armies at Austerlitz in the Austrian Empire. Britain, under its legendary Admiral

Horatio Nelson, won a smashing win over the French and Spanish fleets at the battle of Trafalgar, off the coast of Spain. With France now utterly dominant on the continent, and Britain on the high seas, both turned to commercial warfare to try to strangle the other.

In 1806-1807 Napoleon issued the Milan and Berlin Decrees, which forbade foreign nations from trading with Britain, and ordered French warships to attack American vessels attempting to trade with it. Great Britain retaliated with its Orders in Council. It forced any foreign ships trading with Napoleon's Empire to first pay a tax in British ports, and forbade any such commerce in military supplies. As before, British vessels also seized hundreds of Americans ships, and many American sailors. From 1803 to 1815, the British impressed about 9,000 American seamen. And about 1,000 British sailors jumped ship for service aboard U.S. merchant vessels.

The Administration and Congress focused its ire on Britain. A law was passed banning English manufactures that might instead be made in the U.S. This legislation was delayed while the two U.S. Ministers to Britain, Monroe and former Maryland Attorney General William Pinkney, embarked on a mission to London. Their role was to renegotiate the Jay Treaty and attempt to end the impressments. They succeeded in the former, but failed in the latter. As a result, in March 1807 the President rejected their Monroe-Pinkney Treaty.

Meantime the U.S. had even less leverage with the foreign superpowers than during the previous undeclared wars with Britain and France. This was because Jefferson and Gallatin, to cut costs and the size of the military, had slashed the Army and the small but potent Navy.

On June 22, 1807, four months after shelving the Monroe-Pinkney Treaty, Jefferson faced the probability of open war with London. The precipitating incident came off of Norfolk, Virginia, then as now a center of the U.S. Navy. The British warship *HMS Leopard*, after a brief firefight that killed three Americans, forced the surrender of the warship the *USS Chesapeake*. It then seized four American sailors off their own boat. Outraged Americans cried for war.

Virginia militia managed to capture the *Leopard* and its crew. Jefferson, hoping to avoid war against a much superior foreign military, allowed the British sailors on the ship to return to Britain. He also declined to call Congress into session, lest it declare war, although he did order all British ships out of American ports. The President noted: "This country has never been in such a state of excitement since the Battle of Lexington."

With war still possible, Jefferson took steps to boost preparedness, despite the strong opposition of his own party to a robust federal military. These included increasing the federal Army from 2,800 to 8,000 men or more, strengthening shoreline fortifications, and building a large fleet of relatively cheap, 70-foot-long gunboats armed with one or two heavy-caliber cannon. Disliked by some Navy officers, who yearned for battle aboard powerful warships like the *USS Constitution*, these "mosquito" craft or "Jeffs" had crews of militiamen. They were limited to protecting the nation's coasts, as opposed to taking on the formidable Royal Navy on the open sea.

But the President's economic responses were far more forceful. His strategy was unusual. He proposed, and the House and Senate passed in December 1807, the landmark Embargo Act. This put into effect the ban on English manufactures. But it also forbade U.S. merchants from trading, not just with Britain or France, but with any nation! This unprecedented, and possibly unconstitutional, Act, was aimed at preventing even indirect trade with Britain or France via other nations. The President calculated the two countries, stung by a falloff in trade with the U.S., would cease their depredations on U.S. shipping.

Instead France, already blockaded, shrugged the measure off, and even welcomed it as an anti-British action. Meanwhile Britain's shippers, though losing some business, found markets in Latin America to supplant their U.S. customers.

In America, a sharp recession resulted. In 1808, gross domestic product fell about 10 percent. The value of exports plummeted from $108 million to $22 million, while imports fell by half. New England's stricken merchants much ignored the embargo through smuggling, especially along Vermont and Maine's British-Canadian border. Some New Englanders, echoing Jefferson's Kentucky and Virginia resolutions, spoke of secession and nullification of federal laws. In the President's base of support in the South, farmers were unable to export their timber, foodstuffs, and cotton.

Supplemental laws to enforce the Act only heightened anger over it. Privateers were banned, although privately outfitted warships were the best way, in lieu of a strong Navy, of striking back at hostile warships. Further, under the Act federal authorities could seize cargo, without a warrant, if they simply suspected a merchant of evading the embargo. Even fishermen, whalers, and owners of riverboats had to post expensive bonds, equal to the value of their ships or more, that were subject to forfeiture if they violated the law.

Some Americans were reminded of Britain's coercive actions during the Revolution, put in practice this time by the author of their Declaration of Independence. A popular cartoon mocked the Administration as a turtle—a lowly creature futilely trying to enforce the trade ban, as smugglers merrily ignored its snap to carry their illicit goods to waiting ships. The comic-strip smugglers chided: "O grab me!", a phrase that spells "embargo" backwards. During this time, the President somewhat petulantly blamed widespread smuggling on a lack of "republican virtue".

The Act was unenforceable, unpopular, and doomed. In March 1809, in his last week in office, Jefferson, along with Congress, replaced it with the Non-Intercourse Act. This lifted the trade ban on nations other than Britain and France. (Its unusual name also led to mirth for generations of schoolboys.) Many U.S. merchant ships, once they reached Britain or France, flouted this law as well. In 1810, during the Madison Administration, the trade ban on both countries was lifted. The one on Britain was put back in 1811, in the run-up to the War of 1812.

A PRESIDENT AND HIS ADVISORS' VIEWS ON ECONOMIC WARFARE

Instead of pursuing the Embargo Act, Jefferson might have followed the counsel of his friend and able diplomat, Monroe, who with Pinkney had negotiated the treaty to allow U.S.-British trade, albeit without London ending the hated practice of impressment. Yet Jefferson had fiercely opposed back in 1795 the Jay Treaty of commerce with Britain. He did this because it too failed to end British impressments; he had benefitted politically from his opposition. To accept impressments as President would have been a difficult pill to swallow.

The President also rejected the counsel of his friend and Treasury Secretary Gallatin, whose advice on the trade issue sounded like the usually liberty-oriented Jefferson himself. "Government prohibitions do always more mischief than had been calculated," counseled Gallatin, "and it is [with] much hesitation that a statesman should hazard to regulate the concerns of individuals as if he could do it better than themselves." Gallatin actually urged armed conflict over either the embargo or doing nothing: "In every point of view, privation, suffering, revenue, effect on the enemy, politics at home, I prefer war to a permanent embargo."

Jefferson harbored a deep dislike for monarchial Britain, from the Revolutionary War and its brutal occupations of his home state of Virginia, and its continuing impressments. At the same time, he had a deep distrust of armed conflict. Partly this was philosophical—he thought large standing armies and powerful navies would lead to overweening federal power, even authoritarian rule—but it was also quite personal.

During the Revolution Jefferson, as Virginia's war-time Governor, had been forced to flee the state capital of Richmond from pursuing British forces. In another British attack Jefferson had barely escaped capture and possible hanging at his Monticello estate. The following year, his beloved wife Martha Wayles Jefferson, died four months after the birth of their sixth child. Jefferson was devastated over the demise of his spouse. He locked himself in a room for several weeks, sobbing uncontrollably. Friends wrote of his black depression, and feared he might take his own life.

Jefferson has been strongly criticized, in his role of war-time Governor of Virginia, for not better protecting his state from the British invasions under the notorious cavalry leader Gen. Banastre Tarleton and the traitorous Gen. Benedict Arnold. With the post-colonial governorship granted little real power, and with much Virginia's militia fighting the British outside the state, Gov. Jefferson failed to stop the enemy's capture of Richmond. In summer 1781 the Virginia legislature began an official inquiry into the conduct of Jefferson as Governor. After the Americans victory at Yorktown, Virginia, however, the legislature had a change in mood, withdrawing any censure and publicly lauding Jefferson for his service as the state's chief executive.

Some analysts believe the trauma of the Revolutionary War made President Jefferson reluctant to go to war with Britain again, even as the former revolutionary continued to despise Britain's monarchy and empire. With the embargo, he may have let emotions and ideology get the better of him.

With other actions such as the Louisiana Purchase, whose constitutionality he doubted, or the federal government's assumption of the Revolutionary War debt, about which he was dubious, Jefferson often gave way on principle to reach a desired compromise. But in this case, he rejected the middle ground, and held to a highly unpopular, difficult-to-enforce hard line.

To be fair, during the naval crisis with Britain the President much heightened military preparedness. He even consulted with engineer Robert Fulton, the steamboat co-inventor, on a military submarine, developed and deployed over a century later with great effect.

Further, British merchants stung by lost trade from the embargo came close to convincing the British government to end the practice of kidnapping American sailors. The President staved off a war with a more powerful foe for a time. Indeed, given that the War of 1812 with Britain came about due to accident, as we shall see in the President Madison chapter, Jefferson's strategy might have avoided war with Britain altogether. Moreover, the President had to be concerned an unsuccessful war might split the nation asunder, along North and South lines or, Burr-like, between East and West.

Still, Jefferson's second-term economic failures were underscored by the policies that his colleague and successor, James Madison, following on assuming office in 1809. Madison made no effort to re-impose the reviled embargo. Then, as outright war with Britain loomed, Madison, rejecting his own and Jefferson's original approach, called for a heightened military buildup, including a larger Navy and Army, and urged the states to increase their quotas of militia. Yet Jefferson's and Treasury Secretary Gallatin's steep, first-term cuts to the military could not be rapidly restored. Thus the nation's armed forces were still weak when war did come in 1812.

Despite America's military failings in the early stages of that conflict, and his own policy of pursuing peace at great economic cost, Jefferson in retirement would approve of his friend Madison's war of 1812. At that same time, he believed erroneously that "the acquisition of Canada will be a mere matter of marching" north.

Exceptional in many fields, in his second term President Jefferson at times fell short in the arenas of military and economic administration.

OTHER JOURNEYS OF DISCOVERY DISAPPOINT

Historians and the public fondly recall the epic Lewis and Clark expedition, launched by Jefferson in his first term. But they forget that the President in his second term backed other explorations into the West that were not nearly as successful. In fact, they were bedeviled by the same traitor who was in cahoots with Burr.

In 1805, the first year of Jefferson's second term, Army Lieutenant Zebulon Pike led an expedition starting from near St. Louis and into the northern portions of the Louisiana Purchase. Gen. James Wilkinson, the foreign spy for Spain, and then Governor of the Upper Louisiana Territory, ordered Pike on the eight-month journey into present-day Minnesota, in a failed attempt to find the source of the Mississippi River.

The following year, Wilkinson commanded now-Captain Pike, along with his son James Wilkinson, to find the source of the Arkansas and Red Rivers, and to forge relations with the nearby Indian tribes. Wilkinson ordered the expedition without authorization from Jefferson, although the President retroactively approved it. This was at the time of the General's collaboration with Burr, and he may have hoped Pike's journey into territory claimed by the Spanish would spark a war with Madrid, and thus justify he and Burr's planned seizure of the Southwest.

Pike and his rough band of troops, whom he termed "a dam'd set of Rascels", did become the first persons of European descent to travel close to what became known as Pike's Peak. But that November, Pike and his rascals were captured by Spanish troops near their regional capital of Santa Fe, probably after getting lost and mistakenly crossing the Spanish border. Gen. Wilkinson had probably alerted the Spanish to the Americans' presence.

So had Pike's doctor, who convinced Pike to let him travel to Santa Fe to collect a debt, and whose presence there had made the Spaniards suspicious. In any event, the expedition was in rough shape. A number of Pike's men had become frostbitten and unable to travel, and showed their commander bits of gangrenous bone as part of a plea to call off the expedition.

The Spanish released Pike in February 1807. For a time, American officials suspected him of being part of Burr's plot, but he was cleared. And, along with Pike's Peak, he did discover the source of the Rio Grande, and he went on to write a widely read account of his journey. However, some of his men were detained in Spanish jails for several years. Jefferson himself was disappointed at how the Pike expedition ended, and in its failure to produce a scientific bonanza like that of Lewis and Clark.

Pike would die during the War of 1812, during the American seizure and burning of York (Toronto), Canada, the event that precipitated the British capture and burning in 1814 of Washington, D.C. during the Madison Administration.

Two other Jefferson Administration-backed expeditions, mostly ignored today, took place during this time. In 1806 surveyor Thomas Freeman, naturalist Peter Custis—a distant relative of Martha Custis Washington—and Army Capt. Richard Sparks led a 45-man "Great Excursion" out of Fort Adams, close to Natchez, Mississippi. Its aim was to explore the head waters of the Red River. Congress and the Administration bankrolled the expedition with $5,000 ($80,000 in 2015 dollars).

The band slogged 615 miles upriver, to Spanish Bluff, near today's New Boston, Texas. There a force of Spaniards four times as large ordered the explorers and soldiers to head back home. As with Pike's force, Wilkinson had alerted New Spain to the Freeman-Custis band. "Provoke an international confrontation for personal gain," Wilkinson informed the Spanish. Again, he longed for a firefight between the two armed forces, giving him and Burr a pretext for war. But the expedition followed Jefferson's instructions to defer to any superior foreign force.

EDWARD P. MOSER

The explorers did collect valuable information on the friendly Creek and Caddo Indian tribes. They also documented, to the scientific President's delight, some 267 animal and plants. And Spain soon allowed Americans to trade in the Red River region. However, the expedition's premature return at the behest of Spanish troops embarrassed the Administration politically. As with the Burr conspiracy, Jefferson was hurt with the Pike and the Freeman-Custis expeditions by his puzzling trust in the traitorous Wilkinson.

Another journey of discovery, the first of the three, had taken place at the end of the President's first term. From October 1804 to January 1805, two Scottish-born men—astronomer William Dunbar of Natchez and chemist Dr. George Hunter of Philadelphia—investigated the Red and Ouachita River basins of present-day northern Louisiana and Arkansas. Funded by $3,000 in federal monies, they reached the Hot Springs, which trappers and homesteaders were already using, as tourists do there today, to remedy various ailments.

However, their expedition was marred by a boat, modeled on a Chinese junk, designed by Hunter that had too deep a draft for the Red River, and by Hunter's errant discharge of a gun that blinded him for most of the journey. Winter weather forced the men's return. Yet the group of travelers, at little expense, collected valuable information on flora, fauna, soils, local homesteaders, and Indian culture.

One is struck by the President's insatiable curiosity about the natural world, a major driver of these Western treks.

A SLAVE-OWNING SKEPTIC OF SLAVERY

A grace note in his second term occurred in March 1807, when Jefferson signed legislation outlawing the slave trade from Africa—the horrific, longstanding import into America of countless Africans through the "Middle Passage" across the Atlantic. Over the centuries, myriad numbers of Africans had been kidnapped or seized as war prizes on their continent, then transported aboard

European ships across the Atlantic. A great many died during the passage, their bodies thrown overboard.

In 1788, the new Constitution, under a compromise between Southern and Northern states, forbade the abolition of the international slave trade into America for the first 20 years of the new federal government. Some believed this implied the trade should end in 1808. However, in 1803 South Carolina—which had decades before abolished the import of slaves into its state, but which was then eager to exploit the new cash crop of cotton—reinstituted the import of shackled innocents.

Instead of backtracking on the matter, President Jefferson urged and signed in 1807 an Act of Congress ending the import of slaves for all the states. He also counseled enacting the law before the constitutionally mandated timeframe. The law was imperfectly enforced, and led to smuggling, but it caused a major drop-off in the number of slaves entering the U.S.

In his State of the Union address of December 1806, the silver-tongued President had lauded the upcoming action, while coining the term "human rights", in a statement published around the nation:

"I congratulate you, fellow-citizens, on the approach of the period at which you may interpose your authority constitutionally, to withdraw the citizens of the United States from all further participation in those violations of human rights which have been so long continued on the unoffending inhabitants of Africa, and which the morality, the reputation, and the best interests of our country, have long been eager to proscribe."

Although criticized today for his ownership of slaves, Jefferson may have done as much to constrict slavery as any American until Abraham Lincoln. And without firing a shot. Earlier, the Northwest Ordinance of 1787—largely crafted by Jefferson during the Articles of Confederation period—forbade slavery in the new territories, and future states, north of the Mason-Dixon line. And, in one of the intriguing what-ifs of history, he urged, but the Continental Congress narrowly defeated, the outlawing of slavery in all new territories, South or North, formed west of the original 13 states. If the law had passed, and taken root, it is hard to imagine the Civil War occurring. The Virginia plantation owner also strongly supported the American Colonization Society, which set up the African nation of Liberia for free blacks. (And his original draft of the Declaration of Independence contained a strenuous condemnation of the British slave trade.)

President Jefferson had shifting views on race, and either he or a relative had children with household servant Sally Hemmings. Yet he presents perhaps a good example of why one should not read history backwards, with the values and standards of today, but instead carefully examine it through the attitudes, events, and possibilities of the time.

A SECOND-TERM ELECTORAL DECLINE

The Democrat-Republicans and their President declined in popularity before the election of 1808. This was largely due to the alienation of many in New England and the Mid-Atlantic to the embargo, and to their fear of a possible war with Britain, their main trading partner. This was clearly shown in the elections for the House of Representatives which, with its short two-year terms, reflects current public opinion more than the six-year Senate.

In the contests, held between April 1808 and May 1809, the Democratic-Republicans lost 22 seats to the resurgent Federalists. Their margin fell to 94-48, to below a 2-to-1 majority for the first time in 10 years.

The Federalists did particularly well in their New England bastion, picking up five congressional seats in New Hampshire, sweeping the state, and three in Massachusetts. But they also scored in New York, which had been trending to the other party, gaining six seats. They even overperformed in the South, picking up two seats in North Carolina and four in the President's home state of Virginia.

In the Senate, the Federalists gained slightly, winning one seat, with the Democrat-Republican margin a still-commanding 27-7.

Still, despite the steep losses in the House, and the unpopularity of Jefferson's trade actions, the President himself remained fairly popular. And the trend toward his party, though slowed, was not reversed. This was indicated by the presidential election of 1808, in which Secretary of State Madison handily won the White House.

In a contest for the Democratic-Republican nomination, Madison was challenged by Minister to Great Britain, ex-Virginia Governor, and Jefferson protégé James Monroe. Monroe had some backing from the strict constitutionalists of his party, people like John Randolph, who thought Jefferson had overly expanded the power of the federal government. Vice President Clinton also entered the contest. With party leader Jefferson making it clear he preferred Madison, however, Clinton and Monroe only got three ballots in the party nomination contest, and Madison won easily with a total of 83. Clinton then gained an overwhelming number of the vice-presidential ballots.

The Federalists again nominated South Carolina's Pinckney, with New York's Rufus King again their vice presidential choice. In the election, Pinckney improved on his landslide loss of 1804, when he had only carried Connecticut and Delaware. With New England angry over the embargo, he won every state in that region except Vermont, as well as Delaware, two of Maryland's 11 electoral votes, and three of North Carolina's 14.

Despite Pinckney's better showing, Madison-Clinton held their regions. They took all of the South, except for the portion of North Carolina, as well as the states of Pennsylvania and New Jersey, and 13 of New York's 19 electoral votes.

Madison won the electoral vote and the popular vote in landslides. The electoral tally by 122-47. Clinton got half a dozen ballots from "faithless electors", that is, Electoral College members who decline to vote for their assigned candidate. The popular margin was 65 percent to 32 percent, with Monroe getting three percent in a sort of write-in vote. In an act of party unity, President Madison would make Monroe his Secretary of State, and likely successor.

CONCLUSION

Thomas Jefferson today is usually ranked among the top presidents, often among the top five. However, this may be because people remember the spectacular accomplishments, such as the Louisiana Purchase, of his first term, and not the failures of his second, such as the Embargo Act and the eruption of the Burr conspiracy. Judgments are also influenced by the man's wide-ranging accomplishments outside the presidency, in fields as varied as architecture, horticulture, philosophy, and practical invention.

Yet his second term was one of the wildest in American history. He suffered stinging defeats in the courts and on the economy, and his personal popularity fell. The Spanish intercepted two of his expeditions to the West. His former Vice President, and his senior military man, launched a nation-shaking plot behind his back, and he was slow to respond to the threat, and failed to convict Burr of treason. Jefferson's party suffered stiff losses in the House elections of his final year. It is little wonder the President suffered from migraine headaches during his term.

It is also true that he ended the foreign import of slaves, perhaps the worst aspect of slavery. He did begin a military buildup, if belatedly, against the British threat.

Moreover, he had set up a political movement that would lord over most federal elections for two generations. His associate Madison easily won the White House race to succeed him, and his colleague Monroe would win two more terms after that.

Yet, due to the several major missteps of his second term, he is judged to have fallen to the two-term jinx.

Thomas Jefferson himself, with typical eloquence, offered a negative view of a President's departure from office. After leaving, on March 4, 1809, the burdens of the White House for his beloved Monticello, he no doubt recalled this statement of his on the presidency:

"No man leaves this position with the reputation he had on assuming it."

A REBOUND FROM WAR-TIME DEVASTATION JAMES MADISON, 1813-1817

James Madison, the fourth president, had possibly the most trying second term of any president, one that saw him fleeing his White House and capital in a time of foreign invasion. Yet those four years had strong elements of success as well as failure.

Madison was born in 1751 on a large tobacco plantation not far from George Washington's home county, on the Rappahannock River tributary of Virginia's Chesapeake. Short and scholarly, he obtained in just two years a rigorous classical education at what later became New Jersey's Princeton University. Rather unprepossessing himself, he married the vivacious widow Dolley Payne Todd of North Carolina in 1794. He was a principle author of *The Federalist Papers* that cleared the way for the new Constitution, of which he was the main author.

After serving as an influential Congressman for eight years, and as Jefferson's Secretary of State for two terms, in 1808 Madison was elected President. In the Executive Mansion, he kept on Jefferson's deft Treasury Secretary Gallatin as a key advisor. In his first two years, Madison continued the former President's practice of lower taxes and tight federal spending to reduce the federal debt. The economy rebounded from the steep recession triggered by the Embargo Act.

Napoleon and Great Britain were still in a death grip, but the U.S., with James Monroe as Secretary of State, stayed out of the broil. It also took advantage of turmoil in Spain, then under Napoleon's occupation. In 1810, the U.S. annexed the territory of Spanish West Florida, a coastal strip running from today's western Florida border clear across to Louisiana.

The country seemed to like the Administration's approach, especially with the embargo gone by 1809, and the export trade recovering. The Democrat-Republican Party gained 13 House seats in the midterm 1810-1811 elections, to build to a near 3-to-1 majority, 107-36. Madison's party even took four out of the five previously Federalist seats up in New Hampshire.

The Democrat-Republicans picked up one Senate seat, to boost their overwhelming margin to 27-7. That victory was significant, as it meant the defeat of Sen. Timothy Pickering of Massachusetts, formerly the Secretary of State for Washington and Adams. Irate at the embargo and the West Florida acquisition, he had tried to secretly build an alliance between New England and Great Britain. The Senate censured Pickering after his electoral loss.

A LEGISLATIVE SCHOLAR, NOT A WARRIOR

Many have commented that Madison, an unsurpassed constitutional scholar and a top-flight legislative strategist, was less talented as an executive and military administrator. He set himself up for second-term troubles toward the end of his first, by signing on in June 1812 to a poorly thought-out military clash with Britain—the War of 1812.

Madison's military entered the war woefully unprepared. This was partly due to cuts to the Army and Navy made by President Jefferson, when

Madison was his Secretary of State, in the preceding Administration. Also the Administration's construction of the fleet of small gunboats, as opposed to the expensive yet world-class warships favored by the opposing Federalist Party. The British were to sweep aside the gunboats prior to their occupation and burning of Washington, D.C. in 1814. (Jefferson in his last years as President had begun, and President Madison had continued, it should be noted, a significant military expansion due to the growing chance of war with Britain.)

And the government would be underfinanced, partly because Madison, against Gallatin's wishes, had let the charter for the first Bank of the United States expire in 1811, during his first term. The Bank had allowed the central government to more readily raise funds in the event of national emergencies. Then, two years into the war, Madison vetoed congressional legislation to set up a Second Bank of the United States.

Madison followed up on these decisions with very poor appointments to top military roles. His military advisor and first Secretary of State, Pennsylvania's Robert Smith, publicly attacked Madison's own foreign policy, and was fired. Madison retained, as had Jefferson (and Adams and Washington), as the senior officer in the U.S. Army, Gen. James Wilkinson, despite his incompetence and despite strong suspicions, later proven, that Wilkinson was spying for the Spanish. Further, Madison's Secretary of War during the 1814 British assault on Washington, D.C., John Armstrong of Pennsylvania, proved unequal to the task. Convinced the British would never attack the capital, he fled to Virginia after the attack began.

In a sense Madison, during his first-term run-up to war in 1811-1812, lost control of the political debate. As it had long done, London was seizing U.S. ships, and sailors, by the hundreds. And contrary to the spirit of the Jay Treaty, Britain was supplying weapons to Indian tribes, and encouraging them to attack U.S. settlers, in the Old Northwest territories such as Michigan, as well as in the American South.

Unquestionably, these were acts of war. So the original "War Hawks", bellicose young men in Madison's Democratic-Republican party, figures such as Kentucky's Henry Clay and South Carolina's John Caldwell Calhoun, bristled for a fight. The more cautious Madison gave way to them.

A STUMBLING START TO AN AVOIDABLE WAR

As with other troubled second-term presidencies, such as those of Lyndon Johnson and George W. Bush, the nation was not unified on a war, but badly split. In Madison's case, New England was mostly opposed to fighting its main trading partner, Britain. It refused its quota of militia due the national government. In that region, smuggling with Britain, and with British Canada, especially in Maine, continued unabated. Maine practically became a British possession during the conflict. Worse for Madison, Northern banks lent little money to finance the War Department's ambitious campaigns.

Taking the long view, the timing of the war couldn't have been worse. The conflict with Britain began the same week, in June 1812, that Britain's chief enemy, Napoleonic France, began its doomed invasion of Russia. The French marched off in what would be one of the coldest years of the century. By October, Bonaparte's Grand Armée was retreating from Moscow, and would soon collapse amid the snow drifts. Less than two years later, London was able to shift the best soldiers and ships of its triumphant Army and Navy to America, and invade the Mid-Atlantic states, as well as New York and Louisiana.

If Madison and Congress had merely waited until that fall before deciding whether to declare war, it might have seemed clear the French Emperor's star was fading, and the time wrong to take on his most powerful foe.

Further, at the same time the U.S. was deciding on war, the British Parliament was finally coming around to the American view on a prime cause of the conflict, namely, the Royal Navy's taking of American seamen and ships. London, realizing its interference with American commerce was hurting Britain's own industries, had decided to suspend the heinous practice. But it continued it when the Americans declared war.

As at the end of the conflict, when the Battle of New Orleans took place after a peace accord had been signed, the slow communications of the time affected the decisions of those in charge. Leaders in Washington, D.C. had to operate on information that was weeks or months out of date.

It's interesting to speculate how Presidents Jefferson, Adams, or Washington might have reacted in a similar situation. They may have temporized, or sent envoys to Britain, and might have avoided war altogether. But the pressure that Madison was under from his hawks, and from the British outrages, was considerable.

For the United States, in the conflict's first year, the War of 1812 brought military debacles—in the Old Northwest, the Canadian border, and the Mid-Atlantic.

In summer and fall 1812, a badly prepared invasion of British Canada under Gen. William Hull abjectly failed. Forced to retreat, Hull wound up surrendering Detroit to the British without a fight. To the east, at the Niagara River, a force led by Gen. Stephen Van Rensselaer, of an old New York Dutch family, was crushed. Still further east, near Lake Champlain, units under Gen. Henry Dearborn stalled when militiamen declined to fight beyond the U.S.-Canada border. That winter, General and future president William Henry Harrison of Indiana—hero of the Indian battle of Tippecanoe before the war—failed to take back Detroit, as Indians massacred a part of his militia.

A NARROW, WAR-TIME RE-ELECTION

President Madison's re-election campaign in 1812 reflected the poor start to the war, the nation's divide over it, and divisions within his own party, all signs of trouble for an incumbent. The election generated a highly unusual presidential campaign, one contested by members of the same party.

By 1812, many Northern members of the Democratic-Republican Party wanted to nominate someone who was not a Virginian, as the first three Presidents had hailed from the Old Dominion. Many of these looked to Vice-President George Clinton of New York. In April, however, the Vice-President died. Support then emerged for his nephew, DeWitt Clinton. The younger Clinton was New York City's Mayor as well as the state's Lieutenant Governor. An able executive, he would as Governor go on to push through the building of the Erie Canal.

In May, an assemblage of Democrat-Republican members of Congress made Madison their party's presidential nominee for the second time. However, 48 of the 134 Senators and Representatives in the caucus, mostly Clinton backers, declined to take part. Another gathering then selected Elbridge Gerry, a former Governor of Massachusetts who had been a major force behind the Bill of Rights, as Madison's running mate. (As Governor, Gerry had reluctantly backed the "gerrymandering" of state senate districts—redrawing their boundaries to pack them with sympathetic voters.)

The ambitious Clinton, seeing the intraparty opposition to Madison, decided to run as a rogue Democratic-Republican. In the campaign, he received the de facto support of the Federalists, after Chief Justice John Marshall of Virginia declined a bid for that party's nomination. The Federalist Party, in steep decline, figured its best chance was to go with an attractive candidate from the other side.

Candidate Clinton straddled the war issue, seeming to be in favor of it in the Democratic-Republican South, while opposing it in the more Federalist North. A Federalist gathering chose his running mate: Jared Ingersoll, the attorney general of Pennsylvania. Ingersoll failed to carry his home state, which proved the deciding state in the election.

President Madison won, but much more narrowly than in 1808. He took the popular vote by just 50 percent to 48 percent, and carried the Electoral College 128-89. The Virginian took every state south of the Mason-Dixon line, plus Pennsylvania and Ohio, as well as Vermont. Clinton carried all of New England except Vermont, as well as his home state of New York, in addition to New Jersey, Delaware, and five of Maryland's 11 electoral votes. Madison is one of three Presidents, along with Franklin Roosevelt in 1940 and 1944, and Barack Obama in 2012, to be re-elected with both a lower popular vote percentage and Electoral College tally than in their previous elections.

Although losing, DeWitt Clinton had coattails in the congressional contests. With many new districts created after the census of 1810, the Federalists made big gains in the House elections of 1812-1813. They picked up 32 new seats, including 13 seats in Clinton's New York, to just seven new seats for the Democrat-Republicans. One of their new representatives was Daniel Webster, later a noted New York Senator, orator, and abolitionist.

Hawkish Henry Clay remained House Speaker, presiding over a reduced but still large majority of 114-68. Both he and fellow pro-war Congressman John C. Calhoun were re-elected unanimously in their districts. In the Senate elections, the Federalists gained a Senate seat in Maryland and in New York, the latter won by Rufus King, their former vice-presidential nominee.

A SURGE OF SUCCESS IN NEW YORK AND THE SOUTH

Still, after the war's early debacles, the Americans, and the re-elected President Madison, showed much resilience as the sprawling conflict ground on, and surged to victories near the war's end.

In September 1813, Commodore Oliver Hazard Perry of Rhode Island won the naval Battle of Lake Erie, which gave the U.S. control of that strategic lake for the balance of the war. Perry famously wrote in a battle report: "I have met the enemy and he is ours." The following month, aided by control of the waterway, Gen. Harrison won the Battle of Thames River. There he beat British-backed Indian tribes headed by the legendary Indian chief Tecumseh, who was killed. The victory would open the Old Northwest up to massive settlement in future years.

Near Niagara, in 1813, the two sides took turns burning cities: Buffalo, New York, by the British, and York (today's Toronto), the capital of Upper Canada, by the Americans. But neither side was able to wrestle lasting control of their opponent's turf. The Americans had more success around Lake Champlain, in upstate New York, gaining control of it in fall 1814 during the Battle of Plattsburgh Bay.

In these brawls in the North, U.S. success against the mighty British Navy was impressive. The Americans were helped by both navies having to construct their own corvettes on the spot from the timber of the region's lakes. This negated the advantage of Britain's sea-going warships, which were virtually unbeatable.

In the South, even before the Battle of New Orleans, Andrew Jackson produced sweeping victories. With his friend Gen. John Coffee of Tennessee and allied Cherokees, he crushed the Creek Indians, allies of the British, and their red-colored war clubs at the March 1814 Battle of Horseshoe Bend, in Alabama. Among the U.S. wounded was a 21-year-old Tennessean, and in time Texas President, Sam Houston, shot in the groin by an Indian arrow.

Later, outside New Orleans in January 1815, the willful Jackson would employ Indian warriors, French pirates, "free men of color", Creoles, frontier sharpshooters, and a modest regular Army force—one of the most motley, and effective, armies in military history—to smash the invading British regulars who had previously vanquished Napoleon. The Americans lost about a dozen killed; British casualties: about 2,000.

HINTS OF SECESSION IN NEW ENGLAND, AND DISASTER IN THE MID-ATLANTIC

But America's Southern successes in 1814-15 were counterbalanced by dissension in New England and near disaster along the Chesapeake.

New England's Anglophile traders hated the war, and the renewed embargo it had brought. As British forces occupied and ravaged much of Maine, the region's governors, intent on defending their own states, refused to supply the numbers of militiamen Madison requested. In retaliation, the President refused to pay for the soldiers that were provided. Governor of Massachusetts Caleb Strong, formerly a strong voice at the Constitutional Convention, quietly treated with the Governor of British Nova Scotia for a separate peace accord. When Madison made motions to draft men from the states into a national force, many in New England had had enough.

From December 1814 to January 1815, delegates from the region gathered in Hartford, Connecticut. They met to try to prevent rash military or economic acts by the federal government, and to dilute the state of Virginia's considerable clout in Washington, D.C. They discussed such things as: requiring that a new President hail from different state than his predecessor; mandating a two-thirds majority vote in Congress to declare war; and modifying the "3/5ths rule", by which three out of every five slaves were counted in determining federal taxes as well as representation in the House of Representatives. A small portion of the assembly sought outright secession.

President Madison was so concerned about the nation breaking up that he moved troops away from the Canadian war frontier in case they were needed to put down a New England rebellion. From the view of modern-day Americans, who link secession with the South and the Civil War, the Hartford Convention seems startling.

Far to the south, a mighty British war fleet had sailed up the Chesapeake in August 1814, scattering small Jeffersonian gunboats, and marched on

Washington, D.C. Promised freedom by the British, several thousand slaves fled, and several hundred joined the well-regarded Corps of Colonial Marines. Madison's Secretary of War, the hapless Armstrong, fled the capital. The scholar-President bungled in redeploying the disordered American forces meeting the British just outside Washington, D.C., in Bladensburg, Maryland. Meantime the inept local commander, Gen. William Winder, for unfathomable reasons moved the Americans off of strong hilltop positions.

The British under Rear Admiral George Cockburn and Major General Robert Ross, although outnumbered two to one by the state militias and a small federal force, and lacking cannon, sent the Americans fleeing. So precipitant was the retreat the British began blowing bugles as if in a fox hunt, in a battle known ignominiously as the "Bladensburg Races".

Taking revenge for the burning of York, Canada, the Royal Marines marched into Washington, and burned the Capitol and Supreme Court, and the White House. They did so after Madison's spirited wife Dolley, servant Paul Jennings, and an aide of Secretary of State Monroe's helped save priceless artifacts, such as original copies of the Constitution and the Declaration of Independence, from the Executive Mansion. The invaders only spared the Patent Office Building, after its superintendent William Thornton persuaded them that its inventive contents belonged not to the U.S., but to the world. A beaten Mr. Madison was sent packing to Maryland and Virginia, and returned to find a burnt-out capital, and a bankrupt Treasury.

It was the low point in the President's topsy-turvy second term, and one of the nadirs in American history.

But again the Americans rallied, aided much by a ferocious storm that damaged the British fleet, delaying by weeks their approach to nearby Baltimore. There the Americans, given time to prepare, put up a valiant and skillful defense of the city, and its vast complex of Fort McHenry. From a ship nearby, Maryland attorney Francis Scott Key observed the failed British cannonade on it, and composed his nation's anthem. In the while Madison made two excellent moves. He fired Armstrong, and he made his Secretary of State, the able military veteran Monroe, the acting Secretary of War.

Today it seems inconceivable the U.S. could wage a major conflict without large central institutions like a powerful central bank. In the past, this wasn't always the case. After all, without such a financial institution the United States beat the British military to attain its independence, and fought it to at least a draw in its "second war of independence" in 1812-1815. And the same was true of the smashing victories of the Mexican-American War and the Spanish-American War.

In some regions, the much-maligned militias fought well when led ably, as with Jackson in Louisiana, and with Gen. Samuel Smith in Baltimore. And commanders in the field, like Commodore Perry and Gen. Jackson, improvised brilliantly in a peculiarly American fashion. Monroe, once taking over at the War Department, helped things considerably by strengthening fortifications along the sea coasts, raising needed funds from big municipal banks, and calling up large numbers of militia from the states.

PEACE, AND ELECTION EVALUATIONS
Still, success in the War of 1812 was a close thing, and it came late, after many reverses. In the end, Madison was content with the Treaty of Ghent peace accord. It was worked out in the Netherlands with British representatives and by U.S. diplomats, including Gallatin, Clay, and John Quincy Adams.

Britain, having achieved its main war aim of defeating the French Emperor, was also glad to make peace, and regain a major trading partner. Given the end of the Napoleonic wars, it stopped the impressing of American sailors. It also ceased its long-time incitement of the Indian tribes. Further, it compensated the U.S. for slaves who had escaped to its side with $1.2 million ($192 million in 2015 dollars).

Bolstered by Andrew Jackson's "post-war" New Orleans victory—which occurred after the peace treaty was signed—as well as naval victories on the Great Lakes and the defeats of the Indians, the Madison Administration recovered some of its popularity.

In the fall 1814 congressional midterms, Madison's Democratic-Republican party picked up five seats in the House, while losing three in the Senate.

But in the 1816-1817 congressional elections, the Democratic-Republicans gained 26 seats, giving them an insurmountable 145-40 edge. They also gained a Senate seat, adding to their almost a 2-to-1 advantage.

Americans at this time were proud at having held powerful Great Britain to a draw. The public had soured on Madison's Federalist foes who, by opposing the War of 1812, and hinting at secession, seemed to side with the British. This shift in opinion, despite Madison's many troubles, led to the easy 1816 election of Monroe, the de facto Secretary of War, as Madison's successor. The new President, a former law student of Jefferson's, would be elected nearly unanimously twice, thus continuing the White House dominance of Virginia's anti-Federalist gentry.

As many historians have noted, the public, after fighting, enduring, or even opposing, the war for three years, took on a feeling of elation, an "Era of Good Feelings", at its conclusion. Meantime the economy took off as a Europe rebuilding from its wars bought massive amounts of American goods.

With peace restored, Madison and his party, although unchallenged nationally, moved somewhat in the policy direction of the Federalists, and the Whig party of Clay's that would replace them. Chastened by the apparent need for a stronger central government that could more ably defend the country, Madison reversed positions and pushed for the Second Bank of the United States, and a much larger standing Army and Navy. He did draw the line against some local road and canal projects he judged were outside his constitutional authority, which helped shore up his support among his states-rights base.

Madison in effect returned to his roots, the main framer of the Constitution, and an advocate for a strong if somewhat constrained federal government. At the same time, by stealing some of the Federalists' issues, he helped sealed their eventual doom as a viable party.

James Madison's second term was thus a mix of abject failure and soaring success. Blunders and debacles at the start, and good fortune and solid results at the end.

His bad fortune was spectacular. Embarking on a major war that America probably could have avoided, if it had waited out events for a few months more. And a war that resulted in the only invasion of U.S. soil, other than the American Revolution, with much destruction and loss of life.

Still—given the eventually strong performance of American armies and militia against a mighty foe, the defeat of hostile Indian nations, the post-war euphoria, the bracing economic recovery, a new national consensus on an effective federal government within constitutional limits, and the great electoral success of his party as he left the presidency—Madison may be judged to have rebounded strongly enough in the later stages of his second term to have edged out a jinx.

HIGHLY RATED FOUNDER
JAMES MONROE, 1821-1825

Opinion polls and surveys of historians consistently place James Monroe among the top-ranked presidents. Such ratings are impressive, given that Monroe's presidency took place almost two hundred years ago, and that Monroe tends to be overshadowed by contemporaries like Madison and Washington.

In 2010, Siena College's Siena Institute survey placed Monroe seventh out of 43 presidents. A C-SPAN opinion poll in 2000 placed him at ninth. And a C-SPAN polling of historians in 2009 put Monroe at 14th. Based on his record, he should be ranked higher.

FROM FRONTIER STUDENT TO FRONT-LINE SOLDIER

Raised in Virginia's rustic tidewater, Monroe grew up frontier-tough. Although from fairly modest farming roots, from age 11 to 17 he attended—along with fellow student John Marshall, the future Supreme Court Chief Justice—a Virginia county school steeped in classical education. Its learned instructor, the Rev. Archibald Campbell, taught Monroe advanced mathematics and foreign languages, as well as Biblical studies. Later his law teacher, and personal and political mentor, was Thomas Jefferson. Along with the law, Jefferson steeped Monroe in the writings of such thinkers as Cicero, Isaac Newton, and David Hume. He also purchased for his protégé's edification the *Encyclopédie*, the influential, 30-volume compendium of human knowledge by the French Enlightenment *philosophes*.

With the outbreak of the American Revolution, Monroe dropped his studies as an impoverished student at Virginia's College of William and Mary, and enrolled without pay as an officer in the ragged Continental Army. At his first battles, Lieutenant Monroe and fellow Virginia sharpshooters helped George Washington's beaten Colonial army escape from their doomed defense of New York City by pursuing British troops.

During the Revolution's blackest hours, in the winter of 1776-1777, he crossed the Delaware with Washington's men. At the subsequent, pivotal battle of Trenton he led a daring end-around the lines of the Hessian mercenaries, and captured the foe's artillery, a deed critical to the battle's outcome. During this assault he fell grievously wounded in the chest and shoulder; he would have bled to death if not for a doctor's timely appearance.

At the 1777 battle of Brandywine in Pennsylvania, Monroe's covering fire helped save the life of a wounded and estimable French ally, Major General the Marquis de Lafayette, leading to a life-long friendship between the two. At another major fight, at Monmouth, New Jersey, he led a daring mission to scout the British lines. Washington himself issued a commendation stating "the high opinion I have of (Captain Monroe's) worth."

A CAREER OF HIGH-LEVEL POSTS

After the war Monroe practiced law, but could never turn down a chance at public service. In 1789 he suffered a rare political defeat by narrowly losing a Virginia congressional election—to James Madison. But Monroe may have won by losing. He had run for the seat in Congress by voicing opposition to the new Constitution, Madison's brainchild, in part because it lacked a list of inalienable civic rights. The election winner, Rep. Madison, remedied that inadequacy by shepherding first 10 Amendments to the Constitution, the Bill of Rights, through the new federal legislature. The following year, Monroe was elected as a U.S. Senator from Virginia.

Monroe spent many years as a diplomat, and held his own among the astonishing array of talent—including Benjamin Franklin, John Adams, Jefferson, Madison, and John Quincy Adams—that served as America's first foreign envoys and Secretaries of State. As Minister to France in 1794-1796 during the French Revolution, he saved from the guillotine the neck of Thomas Paine, the wide-ranging Englishman turned American, then French, Revolutionary. The Minister's wife, Elizabeth Monroe, the cultured daughter of a New York merchant, valorously braved the Parisian mobs to save from the guillotine Lafayette's wife, Adrienne, and her son George Washington de La Lafayette, the godson of George Washington.

As envoy to France, Monroe had wrung important concessions from the French on trade and on the harassment of American sailors. But Secretary of State Timothy Pickering publicly berated his performance, and President Washington dismissed him. Politics was the cause: Monroe was inextricably linked to Jefferson's pro-French views as the Washington Administration was moving toward the pro-British Jay Treaty with London. (The irony of the charge of being pro-French and disloyal was considerable. As we have seen, Pickering would secretly negotiate with the British enemy during the War of 1812.)

As Monroe's diplomatic stay wound down, Alexander Hamilton falsely accused him of publishing documents on Hamilton's extramarital affair with Maria Reynolds. In response, Monroe challenged the former Treasury Secretary, like himself a brave Army veteran and a crack shot, to a duel. "I am ready; get your pistols," he angrily told Hamilton. Monroe was dissuaded from the encounter—by Aaron Burr, who later killed Hamilton in a gun fight!

Yet such as rash reaction was out of character for Monroe. Almost universally, people saw him as affable, cautious, even-tempered. His Secretary of War, John C. Calhoun, remarked: "He had a wonderful intellectual patience; and could above all men…when called on to decide an important point, hold the subject immovably fixed under his attention, until he had mastered it."

In his long career before the presidency, Monroe had a huge impact on Virginia, during his three one-year terms as the state's Governor, in 1800, 1801, and 1811. The landed aristocracy that then controlled the Commonwealth was jealous of its power, and fearful of an overly strong executive like Britain's Royal Governor of old. So it rendered the position of Governor practically powerless. (This had caused Gov. Jefferson endless trouble in trying to raise and outfit state militia during the Revolution.)

But upon taking office, Gov. Monroe transformed the executive office of the country's then-largest state into the most powerful in the nation. Transferring authority from localities to the State House, he set up new systems of state schools and of public roads, regular training for Virginia's militia, and the first state prison, one that did away with many cruel and unusual punishments. His approach was copied by governors throughout the nation, and was a springboard to higher federal office.

Back in Paris in 1803, with New York's Robert Livingston, he skillfully negotiated the greatest land deal in human history—the Purchase of the Louisiana territories. As Minister, or ambassador, to France the following year, he was charged to undertake a dangerous side mission to Spain. He traveled over the Pyrenees Mountains, pistol at the ready, hardly sleeping for a week, along paths where brigands had previously robbed passing dignitaries.

President Jefferson moved Monroe over to the post of Minister to Britain. His chief mission was to end or reduce London's attacks on U.S. sailors and shipping. Monroe's proposed 1806 trade treaty was not enacted, somewhat diminishing his diplomatic reputation as the architect of the Louisiana Purchase. Yet here Monroe again fell prey to partisan politics, this time from within his own party.

It seems the Secretary of State, James Madison, was reluctant to allow Monroe a diplomatic triumph going into the 1808 presidential election, with Monroe being Madison's only serious possible rival for his party's nomination. In any event President Jefferson, for political and personal reasons, could not accept the terms of a treaty Monroe negotiated with the British, because the accord would not stop the British from impressing U.S. seamen. As previously discussed, Jefferson soon opted for a trade embargo on Britain, which failed miserably, being largely ignored by New England's merchants. In the light of history, Monroe's more tempered and realistic approach to trade with Britain was correct.

The War of 1812, which took place when Secretary of State Monroe was in charge of foreign relations, proved deeply unpopular with large segments of the public. But Monroe, who was lukewarm about the conflict, especially compared to hawks like Henry Clay, dodged blamed for what became known as "Mr. Madison's War". The fact that he was seen vigorously pursuing the administration of the war near its end, at the time of the great victories at Baltimore and New Orleans, also aided the public's positive perception of him.

Some of Monroe's best moments came at the worst of times, as after the 1814 British burning of Washington. Secretary of War Armstrong had ignored Madison's and Monroe's repeated urgings to prepare the capital against invasion. After British troops sacked the city, Madison sacked Armstrong, and placed Monroe in his stead. Along with Commodore John Rogers, he swiftly fortified the capital in case of another incursion by the British. He ordered troops and cannon placed on bluffs overlooking a secondary British fleet near Alexandria, Virginia. The guns peppered the ships with fire, helping delay the Royal Navy's assault on Baltimore.

He then tried to transform the stumbling U.S. military as he had the Virginia governorship. To get the bankrupt Treasury on its feet, he twisted the arms of cities and banks for $5 million in war loans. He increased to 40,000 the number of troops the president could call up from the states during emergencies. With generous bounties of land, he encouraged thousands of militiamen to enlist, and head to New Orleans, to help Gen. Andrew Jackson in his overwhelming victory there over the British. After the war, Monroe persuaded Congress to keep the peace-time size of the Army at 20,000, to fortify waterways throughout the country, and finance the military preparations with a new Second Bank of the United States.

REALPOLITIK

Monroe's career-long successes in foreign policy would be marked by a very practical assessment of the goals and power of the United States, and of the foreign powers it faced. Over time, he became much more of a realist in foreign affairs, as well as in those domestic matters that seemed to boost the power of a nation.

He had started out as an idealist in the mold of his mentor Jefferson, opposing a standing army, firmly supporting revolutionary France over monarchial Britain, even believing national borders in a democratic world would wither away. But a major change came during his frustrating years in France and Britain, in trying to stop those twin powers from interfering with seaborne U.S. commerce, which it was very much in the interest of both countries, then in vicious wars with each other, to do.

Indeed, in 1803, to set the stage for the Louisiana Purchase negotiations, Monroe, with Secretary of State Madison, was willing to threaten France with war if it did not agree to sell New Orleans to the U.S. This tough, pragmatic approach helped persuade even the hard-nosed Napoleon, faced with the prospect of thousands of American militia marching on New Orleans, to sell off all of Louisiana.

In 1807, then-Minister to Britain Monroe wrote to President Jefferson: "Nothing will be gained of any (foreign power)...should they conclude that they have nothing to fear from us." He had come to believe these belligerent countries pursued their own interests, often through military force or the threat of it, and only respected those nations who did likewise.

Later, as Secretary of State, and Acting Secretary of War, under President Madison, and as President himself, Monroe much altered the policies of his mentor Jefferson, and his own prior views. He called for a standing, permanent national army, and a national bank to finance it in the event of war. (Jefferson himself for practical reasons moved in these directions.)

By his presidency, on both economic and military matters Monroe seemed at least as much a Hamiltonian as a Jeffersonian. In his first inaugural address in 1817, he stated: "We ought not to depend in the degree we have done on supplies from other countries...The capital which nourishes our manufactures should be domestic...our coast and inland frontiers should be fortified, our Army and Navy...be kept in perfect order."

AN UNIMPEDED PATH TO THE PRESIDENCY

Some unsuccessful two-term and one-term Presidents have faced fierce opposition, even primary challenges, from within their own party. The opposite was true of Monroe.

James Monroe had little competition for his Democrat-Republican party's 1816 presidential nomination. More importantly, Monroe faced no real partisan opposition. The Federalists, viewed negatively by most Americans as the party of privilege and restricted suffrage, had been steadily declining in popularity since at least the John Adams Administration of the late 1790s. Or even by Washington's second term, as indicated in 1796 by the

Anti-Federalist Jefferson's close, second-place finish to Adams (68 electoral votes to 71). By 1816, the Federalists were deeply unpopular, due to their perceived disloyalty in their opposition to the War of 1812. They were on their way to extinction during Monroe's terms of office.

In autumn 1816 Monroe breezily won the White House, garnering a crushing 68 percent of the popular vote, and tallying 183 electoral votes to just 34 for his opponent, New York's Rufus King. With the election outcome assured, neither Monroe nor King bothered to campaign!

BEST AND THE BRIGHTEST, WITH REGIONAL BALANCE

On entering the White House in March 1817, President Monroe took pains, like President Washington, to foster national unity by shrewdly selecting Cabinet members from the country's various regions.

From the South he picked as Treasury Secretary Georgia's William Harris Crawford, a former Minister to France, and an ex-Secretary of War who had worked with Monroe to reorganize the battered U.S. military towards the end of the War of 1812. For Attorney General Monroe kept, from the Mid-Atlantic region, Pennsylvania's Richard Rush, son of the esteemed scientist Dr. Benjamin Rush. The younger Rush would later serve as Treasury Secretary and Minister to Great Britain, and secure the endowment for the Smithsonian Institution.

For Secretary of the Navy, deemed a vital post in the aftermath of the naval wars with Britain and France, Monroe also retained the grandly named Benjamin Crowninshield, scion of a Boston shipping family—his brother had been Jefferson's Navy Secretary. Also from New England came the highly skilled diplomat John Quincy Adams. The younger Adams, the future Chief Executive who literary research indicates may have had the highest IQ of any President, had been Minister to Britain and the first U.S.

Minister to Russia. He would fashion with Monroe a lasting string of diplomatic triumphs.

For Secretary of War, Monroe wooed the nation's most prominent Western politician, Kentucky's Henry Clay. His legal defense of Burr long behind him, Clay was then House Speaker. When he declined the offer, Monroe picked Clay's fellow war hawk from the 1812 conflict, then-Congressman Calhoun, later a Vice-President, Secretary of State, and a very influential U.S. Senator. To all these appointments Monroe delegated broad responsibility for their departments, while firmly retaining the final say, and responsibility, for the big decisions.

TOUR DE FORCE

Monroe's desire to unify America after the divisions of the war with Britain also took form, in 1817, with exhausting tours of all the nation's regions. He was the first president since Washington, and on a far bigger canvas, to undertake such journeys, and one of the last to do so before modern transport rendered such tours far more practicable.

On the most memorable part of his journeying, he traveled for 16 weeks by horse, carriage, and steamboat from Washington, D.C. to New Jersey and New York, and then throughout New England. He was welcomed as a hero, most dramatically among the Revolutionary War veterans of New Jersey. At one gathering, old soldiers tersely and emotionally greeted Monroe with the single words "Monmouth", "Brandywine", and other bloody fights where they'd jointly served.

The President met surprising acclaim in Boston, the center of the opposition Federalists. There old John Adams, the arch foe of Monroe's Democrat-Republicans, hosted him at a banquet. Crowds in New England sported red and white roses, the symbols of both competing parties. For a while, a peaceful and prosperous nation forgot its differences. A Boston Federalist newspaper crowed that Monroe's visit marked a new "Era of Good Feelings", and the catchphrase stuck.

THE LUCK OF A BOOM

Monroe took office during one of the great economic and demographic booms in the nation's history. The War of 1812 had ended the threat, from British troops and Indian warriors, to the Old Northwest's states and territories of Ohio, Michigan, Indiana, and Illinois. After the war, Americans poured into those places, clearing land for countless farms and villages. In fact, Indiana and Illinois, burgeoning with new settlers, both became states within two years of Monroe taking office.

The same dynamic happened in the South, as Americans swarmed into Florida, the Deep South, and the Louisiana Territories. These were lands where, largely due to Gen. Jackson, the threat from the British, French, and Spanish empires had lessened, as had the menace of the Creek and other Indian tribes. Alabama and Mississippi also came into the Union on Monroe's watch. So did Maine, the latter as part of the congressional Compromise of 1820 which also brought in Missouri the year of his re-election.

This geographic and demographic expansion was accompanied, and aided, by a spurt of technical breakthroughs and economic trends. During this era the steamboat became the conveyance of choice along America's rivers and coasts, furthering the speed and ease of transport. The number of steamboats on America's waters had risen rapidly to about 70 by the middle of Monroe's presidency, and would grow to about 700 over the next 35 years.

In this era of new modes of transit, and during Monroe's presidency, workers in New York State built the Erie Canal linking the state capital of Albany with the Great Lakes. And further work was done on the Cumberland Road, the so-called National Road from Wheeling, West Virginia to Illinois. Both projects supplied swift means of transporting goods from the Ohio River valley to East Coast ports, and both ignited more trade and growth.

A double-edged technology was the cotton "engine" of inventor Eli Whitney from Westborough, Massachusetts, a town much later a center of the office computer revolution. Whitney would popularize mass assembly manufacturing, which helped lead in time to the industrial dominance of Northern factories. But his cotton gin fueled the South's economy too, as it was much applied to the new plantations of Alabama, Mississippi, and soon, East Texas. Supplanting the old cash crop of tobacco, cotton markedly raised the profits for Southern agriculture, and for related shipping and manufacturing in many Northern cities. It also much deepened the commercial appeal of slavery, which would trigger a political crisis and a moral quandary in the middle of Monroe's presidency.

Cotton, along with American lumber, furs, tobacco, and other products, helped fuel an export boom of products to Europe. After Napoleon met his Waterloo in 1814, the continent went on a five-year binge of rebuilding itself from the deposed Emperor's and French Revolution's 25-year stretch of destructive wars. American farms and forests supplied much of the material for reconstruction.

The post-war commercial surge let the Monroe Administration swiftly pay off the nation's debts from the War of 1812. So flush was the federal treasury that Monroe ended federal taxes on income. He was able to generate all of his government's revenues from import tariffs and from excise taxes on products.

NORTHERN BOUNDARIES

There had long been a foreign threat north of the Canadian border, given the longstanding disputes between America and British Canada, bloody adversaries in the War of 1812 and the American Revolution. But Napoleon's fall had quelled the tensions between the two. Early in his first term, Monroe seized on this diplomatic possibility to settle outstanding disputes with Canada—through the Rush-Bagot Disarmament Treaty of 1817, and the Anglo-American Accord of 1818.

The Rush-Bagot negotiations yielded a lasting boundary line between the U.S. and Canada, at the 49th parallel. A remarkable demilitarization was also set. Both parties pledged to station no more than one warship and one cannon each on their mutual, watery border of Lake Ontario and Lake Champlain. The treaty led to the longest, and longest-lasting, peaceful border in modern history.

The Anglo-American Accord, meanwhile, set up joint control of the Oregon Territory for a decade, and put an end to disputes over fisheries off of the Canadian coasts.

Monroe appointed two skilled emissaries to negotiate these agreements. For Rush-Bagot, the lead envoy was Attorney General Richard Rush. For the Anglo-American Accord, the envoys were Rush again, who had become Minister to Britain, and Minister to France Albert Gallatin. The wide-ranging Gallatin would go on to co-found New York University, and become the nation's leading authority on the languages and origins of the American Indian. Monroe's diplomats were the brightest and best.

SOUTH BY NORTHWEST

Spanish Florida had long posed a worry to the new nation expanding rapidly to its South and West. On his 1807 mission to Spain, and even before as diplomat to Paris for the Louisiana Purchase, Monroe had offered to purchase Florida from Spain. (As far back as 1784, as delegate to the Continental Congress, Monroe was greatly concerned about the possibility of Spain chocking off American commerce at the critical port of New Orleans.) Now, during the Monroe Administration, a new concern sprung up, from the Seminole Indian tribes in Spanish Florida. Bolstered by slaves escaped from Georgia, the Seminoles launched a series of raids into Georgia.

Monroe wrote to the highly aggressive U.S. Army commander on the scene, Gen. Andrew Jackson, to "adopt the necessary measures to terminate a conflict…made necessary by their settled hostilities."

The hero of New Orleans took his instructions and ran with them. With a thousand troops, he made in 1818 a punitive expedition deep into Florida, leveling or burning Seminole villages. Jackson also ignited a diplomatic crisis by executing two British traders he suspected of helping incite the cross-border raids—killing one by firing squad, and hanging the other.

Some U.S. officials were enraged, including Secretary of War Calhoun, who was steamed at what he saw as Jackson's insubordination. House Speaker and opposition leader Henry Clay drummed up criticism from his congressional committee. Monroe, the leader of a political party with its base in the South and West, where Jackson's incursion was wildly popular, was more politically savvy. Monroe publicly supported Jackson, calling his incursion an "act of patriotism", as he privately conceded the U.S. might have to withdraw its troops to avoid war. Clay, shaken by the people's support for Jackson, was forced to try to apologize to the General. Much later, Monroe would distance himself from Jackson's invasion, saying he had never granted the General permission for it.

Yet what mattered at the time was Spain realized it could not hold onto Florida against an aggressive, expanding United States. In 1819, it accepted Secretary Adams' proposal that Spain cede Florida to the U.S., in return for the U.S. picking up $5 million in financial claims by Americans against the Spanish government.

As part of the deal, Spain gave up any right of possession to the distant Oregon Territory, while the U.S. renounced its claims to Texas. A declining Spain kept its pledge—two decades later, a rising America would renege on its.

In the President's second term, Monroe and Adams followed up on their Oregon maneuver. They eliminated a rival to eventual American supremacy in the central and northern Pacific coast. Russia had begun settling Alaska in the 1740s, and in 1812 had set up California's Fort Ross, laying claim to part of the Oregon Territory.

In response, President Monroe spoke harshly and wielded a modest stick. He had two warships assemble off Oregon, and had Adams, per the Monroe Doctrine, warn Czar Alexander I that any new European settlements in North America were unacceptable. Adams' experience as Minister to Russia during the War of 1812 proved valuable. Moscow backed down, moving its claims to a point well north of Oregon.

THE FIRST "TEFLON" PRESIDENT

A secret to Monroe's success was he was usually not blamed for his few failures. He was a 19th-century "Teflon President". The prime example of this was the Panic of 1819, a major economic contraction that happened during his third year in office.

The Panic, as depressions or recessions were then called, resulted, as they often do, then and since, from overinvestment. In 1819, as in the Great Recession starting in 2007, the fault was overinvestment in real estate.

The surge in the economy after the War of 1812 derived in part from the rapid development of vast new lands in the western United States. Speculators fueled the boom. So did the federal Bank of the United States, with too much money, and state banks, with money and with loans of questionable value. One example: a New England bank issued $800,000 in bonds backed by just $45 of capital.

In 1818, Congress and the Second Bank of the United States, fearing inflation caused by the overinvestment, cut back on lending. At the same time, cheap goods from Britain's factories undercut much of American industry. As has often happened in America after a war and subsequent recovery, the boom that followed the War of 1812 became a bust.

Numerous state-registered banks went belly up. Others called in mortgages on the overvalued properties. The value of property plunged in the western territories and in East Coast cities—by 80 percent in Philadelphia alone. Hundreds of thousands were thrown out of work: for the first time, long bread lines formed in the United States. So many people were thrown into debtors' prisons that a successful movement to abolish such jails sprung up.

Some economic historians think the severe impact of the Panic lasted into the early 1820s; others believe the impact was short, and limited mostly to the banks, speculators, and farmers who placed bets on the riskiest and most directly affected properties. Yet everyone agrees the Panic little affected Monroe's popularity. Although the downturn began just one year before his re-election, the President won re-election with no opposition and with every Electoral College ballot save one.

One reason was Monroe's personal popularity. Another was that, in the early 19th century, people did not think the federal government could, or should, do much about a business downturn. The "Spoils System" of handing out large numbers of federal jobs to political supporters was still a decade away. And the Welfare State and the Keynesian economics of "pump priming" the economy was a century off. Instead, most banks were regulated by the states, and many actions, such as debt relief and relief of the poor, to alleviate the Panic's effects, took place locally.

Today, Washington, D.C. would likely react to such a recession with more spending and greater debt. Then, Treasury Secretary Crawford pursued a "tight money" approach, vigorously collecting on debts owed the national treasury. And he demanded payments in gold and silver, not devalued paper. In a bow to his constituents, many of them down-on-their-luck farmers, Monroe did consent—through the 1821 Relief for Public Land Debtors Act—to give debtors more time to pay back what was owed on indebted federal properties. The same Act let defaulters keep that part of federal lands they had already paid off. States in the South and West took similar measures; New England's flinty legislatures demurred.

But otherwise Monroe reflected, in this case, Jefferson's Democratic-Republican philosophy. Namely, that economic matters were the prerogative of the states and of individuals, who were responsible for fortunes gained, or lost. Few expected differently from the President, and therefore he lost little support over his economics.

CRISIS AND COMPROMISE IN 1820

Monroe has usually been portrayed as aloof during the 1820 imbroglio over the admission of Missouri into the United States as a slave state, which many in the North feared would tip the balance of national might to the "slave power". At the time, Secretary of State John Quincy Adams said the President believed Congress would simply "wink" away the dispute. In fact, Monroe was well aware the sectional dispute could rend the Union, later writing to Jefferson, "I have never known a question so menacing to the tranquility and even the continuance of our Union. All other subjects have given way to it." This was when the former President remarked, in a presage of the Civil War: "This momentous question, like a fire bell in the night, awakened and filled me with terror. I considered it at once as the knell of the Union. It is hushed indeed for the moment. but this is a reprieve only, not a final sentence."

Behind the scenes, Monroe worked to coax influential Virginia politicians to temper talk of secession, and to accept the deal by which the free state of Maine entered the United States along with Missouri. (Maine became a state after *seceding* from Massachusetts, which it felt hadn't properly defended it during the War of 1812.) Meantime, in an echo of Jefferson's old attempt to ban slavery in the new territories, the Compromise forbade it in any new lands north of latitude 36°30'. Here "luck" played a role for Monroe, as slavery, although an important issue, was not yet the almost irreconcilable matter it would become by 1850. (And in the years beyond, especially north of 36°30', in the strife-torn territories of Kansas and Nebraska).

SLAVE REBELLIONS, AND MISSED OPPORTUNITIES

President Monroe had had personal, and unsavory, experience with slavery as a political issue. In 1800, after his election as Virginia governor, a major slave revolt, Gabriel's Rebellion, made him its target. Gabriel Prosser, the leader of the planned rebellion, and his band of slaves aimed to take Gov. Monroe hostage at the Richmond state house. A slave revealed the plot before it began, however, and Monroe responded decisively, even brutally. Memories of the great 1790s slave revolt in Saint-Domingue, now Haiti, were fresh in the minds of white, and black, Southerners. That insurrection had massacred thousands of whites, along with bringing on the deaths of thousands of blacks, while forcing French planters and soldiers off of the island. Many Virginians were terrified of a repeat.

Ignoring Virginia's Executive Council, which had jurisdiction on such matters, Gov. Monroe called up the state militia. He sent it on roaming patrols of the roads and on unannounced raids of slaves living quarters. He made blacks carry travel passes, and blocked blacks from traveling at night. "It is unquestionably the most serious and formidable conspiracy we have ever known of the kind," Monroe noted to Jefferson.

Twenty-eight members of the rebellion were sentenced to hang, with Monroe commuting several of the death sentences. The rebellion and the response threatened to reverse a previous trend in the tidewater region, whereby thousands of slaves were manumitted, or freed, by their owners, or through wage earnings bought their own freedom.

By 1820, in fact, about half of the African-Americans in the District of Columbia, and a significant percentage in Maryland and Virginia, a region with a great concentration of slaves, were free blacks. But by 1831, with Nat Turner's slave rebellion in Virginia, this positive movement would reverse itself. The influential state placed more onerous restrictions on the freedom of slaves, and blacks generally, to travel and work outside their towns and farms, as well as to educate themselves. The chance that the Old Dominion, the South's most populous state, might gradually abolish slavery, which its legislature at the time seriously considered, went by the boards, as did a chance of avoiding a future war between the states.

Oddly, by the standards of that distant time and place, Monroe was relatively enlightened on this key issue. Like his mentor Jefferson, and his colleague Madison, he owned slaves, while taking some steps to alleviate slavery. In the wake of Gabriel's Prosser's revolt, he asked President Jefferson to consider a western territory in which free blacks might settle. Like other Virginia gentry he was a leading member of the movement to "repatriate" freed slaves in Africa, leading to the establishment of the African nation of Liberia, with its capital of Monrovia named after its champion. In retirement, at an 1829 convention to amend Virginia's constitution, he angered slaveholders by backing an idea to let federal authorities purchase, free, and send slaves to other nations. But the proponents of restricting and diluting involuntary servitude were eventually drowned out by the proponents of cotton and slavery's expansion.

To be sure, Monroe's compromises on slavery were mild. He never made a sweeping appeal like a gradual yet complete abolition of slavery, perhaps by buying out all slaveholders, as the British Empire did in 1833. A later congressman, Abraham Lincoln, would advance such a notion with a proposal to buy out the slaves from their owners. Monroe might have been one of the few figures with the prestige and power, and appeal to both North and South, to pull off such a scheme. Perhaps it was a great opportunity missed, as the issue went from terrible to much worse. More probably, it was never in the cards, given the politics of the day, the lack of voting rights and thus political clout by most blacks, and the vast wealth thrown off by King Cotton.

A RELAXED RE-ELECTION

For his re-election in 1820, two remarkable things happened. Monroe's political party, the Democrat-Republicans, didn't even formally nominate him at the party convention, so assured was his eventual triumph in the fall election. Moreover, the Federalist opposition didn't officially nominate anyone to run against him.

Like Washington in both his elections, Monroe in his re-election would have gained a unanimous vote of the Electoral College, but for New Hampshire. Its Governor, William Plumer, who had wanted New England to secede over the Louisiana Purchase negotiated by Monroe, cast his vote for New England's favorite son, John Quincy Adams. (Yet even Adams' father, former President John Adams, voted for Monroe, as an elector of the Electoral College.)

President Monroe was thus the only Chief Executive, with Washington, of having almost no serious political opposition from within his own party or from another political faction. There was no other game in town.

HIS DOCTRINE ON FOREIGN AFFAIRS

Monroe is best and justly known for his prowess on foreign policy, and for his Monroe Doctrine of strong national interest. Announced at his seventh State of the Union speech in 1823, in an address composed with Secretary of State Adams, Monroe proclaimed to the world that European interference and colonization in the Americas would no longer be tolerated. The immediate impetus for the declaration were rumblings from monarchial Spain and France to reinstate European control over the Spain's Latin American colonies. Most of them had recently freed themselves from Spanish rule, in good part due to the rebellions led by Venezuelan Simón Bolívar.

The Doctrine was, in part, but a reflection of new power realities among the states of Europe and the Americas. Spain was a declining empire. France had fallen from its heights under Louis XIV and Napoleon. A Britain triumphant from the Napoleonic wars had no reason to tangle, and much reason to trade, with a stronger and more assertive United States. In fact, Britain's implicit guarantee that its pre-eminent Royal Navy would block any Spanish or French attempt to reestablish its authority in Latin America, with whom a commercially oriented Britain wished to do business, supplied the muscle behind Monroe's proclamation.

Still, Monroe and Adams had skillfully laid the groundwork for their Doctrine, both by taking advantage of the new balance of power in Europe, and by eliminating real foreign threats to America's borders with their prior diplomacy toward Florida, Canada, and Oregon.

POST-MORTEM FORTUNE, AND A BIT OF THE JINX

Monroe and his reputation were lucky even in death. Like Jefferson and John Adams, he died on the most patriotic of days, the Fourth of July. And his posthumous appeal was boosted by the famous 1850 painting of "Washington Crossing the Delaware". The depiction shows Lieutenant James Monroe, on Christmas Night 1776, gripping the American flag, and standing in the center of General Washington's very own boat.

Although Monroe did cross the Delaware, he in fact traversed the icy river on a different vessel than Washington's. The iconic image of the future first and fifth presidents crossing together was a patriotic invention of the artist, Emanuel Gottlieb Leutze. (In his painting, Leutze was nostalgically recalling the attempted 1848 democratic revolution in his native German Confederation, as well as warning Americans, during the year of the Compromise of 1850 over slavery, of the dangers of disunion.)

Despite many successes and remarkable popularity, President Monroe did not completely escape the second-term jinx. Serious sickness struck his family and friends. His wife Elizabeth, his granddaughter Hortensia, and his daughter Eliza—the wife of his chief political advisor, George Hay of Williamsburg, Virginia—all fell very ill from influenza. Elizabeth's illness caused her to curtail her First Lady social duties. Her performance could not match her convivial predecessor, Dolley Madison. Combined with the Monroes' more formal style, this led some to complain the First Family was transforming the White House receptions of a simple republic into ones akin to monarchial Europe. This was the same charge that Monroe's party had made of President Washington! Meantime, Monroe's dissolute brother Joseph caused him much heartache by quitting his White House job, and moving to Missouri, to die just two years after departing.

The President's second term was also marked, despite his solid personnel selections, by bitter Cabinet infighting. This partly stemmed from Monroe's very political success. His popularity, and the unpopularity of the Federalists, had practically banished partisan opposition. But this in turn undercut party discipline among his Democrat-Republicans, and especially so among the Cabinet members. They spent much of his final years in office vying with one another to succeed Monroe. This was particularly true of Treasury Secretary Crawford, and it led to a near-violent confrontation within the White House.

After reelection, Monroe wanted to accelerate his program of constructing military defenses to protect the nation's borders. Secretary of War Calhoun was charged with this task, which required a lot of funding. Yet Calhoun was a rival for the presidency with the Treasury Secretary, who announced, apparently to embarrass Calhoun, a swelling budget deficit. Crawford said the funding shortfall was largely the result of the War Department's overspending on military construction.

Crawford, despite his apparent fiscal probity, later visited Monroe at the White House to request that several of his colleagues receive plum patronage appointments as customs inspectors. According to Navy Secretary Samuel Southard, who witnessed the meeting, Monroe told his Treasury Secretary: "Sir that is none of your damn business." Crawford then rushed the President and, raising his cane, shouted, "You infernal scoundrel!" Monroe, the old war veteran, grabbed hot tongs from the White House fireplace to defend himself. After things calmed down, Crawford apologized, but relations between the two were poisoned.

Monroe's unwise decision to announce, early in his second term, his intention not to run for a third time also undercut his authority. It helped trigger a wild scramble to succeed him in the 1824 election.

By then, Crawford had suffered a massive heart attack and drew little support. Monroe's tempestuous general, Andrew Jackson, handily beat his erudite diplomat, John Quincy Adams, in the popular vote. However, Henry Clay threw his Electoral College support to Adams, ensuring his election, as well as the bitter enmity of the volatile Jackson. An "era of bad feelings" would mark inter-party politics during Adams' unpopular administration.

President Monroe himself—after a lifetime of public service in which he had paid for many of his expenses out of his own pocket—left the White House $75,000 in debt, or $1,875,000 in 2015 dollars. Adding to his financial woes, the Second Bank of the United States, who very reconstitution he'd championed with Madison, moved to sue Monroe over $25,000 he owed it. The legal action forced him to sell off 40,000 acres of western lands, and his beloved Ash Lawn-Highland property near Monticello. Like Jefferson and the Madisons, Monroe would end up deeply in the red after leaving Washington. In 1831 Congress paid off $30,000 of his remaining debts. Back in the day, it seems, some statesmen would actually leave Washington, D.C. with less money than when they entered it.

SUMMARIZING MONROE

By most criteria, Monroe's second term was successful. On his watch the nation continued to experience peace, a steady westward expansion, and widespread prosperity. He helped forged a tentative compromise over slavery. His foreign policy successes were many. It's interesting to note that even some of the first classics of American culture and literature—including Washington Irving's "Rip Van Winkle"—appeared during his presidency. And despite the Panic of 1819 and the "Inside Washington" wrangling of his Cabinet, his popularity in the country at large remained strong.

Jefferson's appraisal of him, at the time of Monroe's appointment to negotiate the Louisiana Purchase, seem on the mark:

"Some men are born for the public. Nature, by fitting them for the service of the human race on a broad scale, has stamped them with the evidences of her destination and their duty."

FULLY ACHIEVING HIS AGENDA
ANDREW JACKSON, 1833-1837

A ndrew Jackson has been generally regarded by historians and the public as one of the most successful presidents. Various polls over the decades have placed him among the top 15, and often the top 10, of Chief Executives.

Yet he is seen by many today, in the 21st century—because of his views on removal of Indian tribes, slavery, opposition to a federal bank, and his "Spoils System" of rewarding supporters—as one of the most controversial. There has even been a movement to remove him from the $20 bill, and replace him with abolitionist Harriet Tubman of Maryland. He is viewed more favorably on his expansion of the franchise, thus permitting more Americans to vote, and on his strong support for federal union.

Still, on all the above issues, he generally got his way, and at the time had considerable public support for them. Further, economic woes that he might have helped cause only erupted after he had left the presidency. Therefore, judging by the standards of his time and by the criteria of this book, Jackson clearly dodged the second-term curse.

BORN TO BATTLE

The book has mentioned Andrew Jackson's military actions, which won him a nation-wide reputation, and in time the White House. His victories in the War of 1812 over the Creek Indians of Alabama, and over the British at New Orleans, and later his raid into Florida which led to its acquisition by Monroe and Quincy Adams.

"Old Hickory" proved as ferocious on the dueling ground as the battle-field. He carried into the Executive Mansion three bullets from duels, a common practice of the time for a gentleman striving to maintain his honor.

The most astonishing of these firefights was the 1806 face-off with Charles Dickinson of Kentucky, that state's finest gunman. So fine, in fact, that Jackson and his "seconds", his friends who accompanied to the confrontation, were convinced Jackson couldn't win it. Instead of disgracing his name by backing out, he determined on an astonishing strategy: take the first bullet. At the duel, Jackson presented a more difficult target by wearing a loose coat, and by standing obliquely toward his opponent. Then he deliberately held his fire, took Dickinson's shot in the abdomen, steadied himself with an iron will, and coldly shot his shocked rival to death.

Andrew Jackson was born in 1767 on remote borderland between North and South Carolina. Like many famous American warriors, such as Winfield Scott and Thomas Jonathan "Stonewall" Jackson, he was of Scotch-Irish ancestry. Descended from men who were "born fighting" over the millennia, having battled the Romans, then the English, then the Catholic Irish of Ireland, when not feuding with their own clans.

In the American Revolution, Andy Jackson lost one brother killed in a battle with the British, and a second who died in a British Army prison. His mother died of cholera while caring for sick American soldiers. Jackson himself was scarred on head and hand for life by a British major named Coffin, who sabered the teenage militiaman for refusing to scrub his boots.

Moving to the western territory of North Carolina that became the state of Tennessee, he helped found Memphis, and built up a large plantation near Nashville. He was made major general of the new state's militia as well as its U.S. Senator.

A ZIG-ZAG PATH TO THE WHITE HOUSE

In the wild scramble of 1824 to succeed the popular President Monroe, four candidates from the dominant Democratic-Republican Party ran in the autumn election. The contenders were Tennessee's Jackson, Secretary of State Adams from Massachusetts, the sickly Treasury Secretary, Georgia's William Crawford, the man who'd nearly come to blows with Monroe, and the ubiquitous House Speaker, Kentucky's Henry Clay.

Jackson came out ahead in the popular vote and the Electoral College. The voting percentages, respectively, for Jackson-Adams-Clay-Crawford, were: 41%-31%-13%-11%. Their electoral totals were: 99-84-37-41. John C. Calhoun of South Carolina won the balloting for Vice President by a large margin.

With no presidential candidate taking a majority of the electoral votes, it fell to the House of Representatives to decide the election. Its Speaker, Henry Clay, hated the bellicose Jackson over his Florida incursion, and even demeaned his greatest military triumph, writing, "I cannot believe that killing 2,500 [sic] Englishmen at New Orleans qualifies for the various, difficult, and complicated duties of the Chief Magistracy." Like Adams, Clay had quasi-Federalist views on a high federal tariff and federal financing of roads and canals. He threw his considerable support behind the New Englander.

Quincy Adams thus won the House vote, which took place by state: 13 for him, seven for Jackson, and four for Crawford. He went on to select Clay as his Secretary of State, and thus his likely successor. This so-called "Corrupt Bargain"—Adams picking Clay for Secretary of State, after winning his backing—enraged Jackson, and kept his political base energized throughout the Adams presidency.

The result was an 1828 rematch, with a thumping Jackson victory over the incumbent, first-term President. That November, the Tennessean won handily, with 178 electoral votes to 83, with a popular vote margin of 56 percent to 44 percent. Jackson took every state south and west of Maryland, plus Pennsylvania, a chunk of New York's electoral votes, and even one in Maine.

At the same time, Jackson's newly named Democratic Party, the successor to the Democrat-Republican Party, gained 23 seats in the House over the rival National Republicans. The latter were a kind of successor to John Adams' and Alexander Hamilton's Federalists, a stepping stone to the Whig Party, and a precursor of the Republican Party. The gains gave the Democrats a 136-72 margin, with 5 seats for the Anti-Masonic Party. (The Anti-Masons were a kind of throwback to the old Federalist distrust of the supposedly atheistic Anti-Federalists; they were loosely aligned with the National Republicans, and their successors the Whigs and the Know Nothings.) In the Senate, the National Republicans gained one seat, as the Democrats retained a 26-22 edge.

JACKSONIAN DEMOCRACY

An area where historians typically accord Andrew Jackson much credit is the great increase in voter participation during his time, due to the expansion of the suffrage to almost all white male voters. His time has been called the era of "Jacksonian Democracy". In fact, he was more its beneficiary than the cause, as the phenomenon mostly occurred nation-wide before he was elected president.

Throughout the 1810s and 1820s, property and other restrictions for voting disappeared throughout America, and coincided with the collapse of the anti-Jefferson and anti-Jackson Federalist Party. Popular votes became the norm for choosing state and local legislative offices. By 1828, when Jackson was first elected, almost every white male could vote. And most did vote, with turnouts reaching 80 percent in some cases, a remarkable rate of participation compared to today.

Jackson did support and encourage the expansion of the vote to many more Americans. But he was more a major symbol, than the cause, of the trend. In the long run, the vote would be extended to all women, all blacks, all citizens. President Jackson was an important way station in this movement.

A SEX SCANDAL UPTURNS THE CABINET

On March 4, 1829, Jackson survived a scare during his wild first inaugural, when thousands of rowdy supporters knocked down the fence outside the White House, and swarmed inside to greet their hero. As drunken revelers from the backwoods smashed china and elegant French furniture, the new President's terrified aides and servants formed a human chain to allow him to escape through a back window of the mansion. An opposition judge commented sardonically: "The reign of King Mob seemed triumphant." The new President scrambled on his horse down to Gadsby's Tavern, 10 miles south in Alexandria, Virginia, where he spent the remaining hours of his first evening as President.

Early in Jackson's presidency, it emerged that Vice President Calhoun had secretly criticized then-Gen. Jackson for exceeding President Monroe's orders back in 1818, during Jackson's raid into Florida. At that time, Calhoun was Jackson's boss at the War Department, and displeased at one of his generals making Department policy on the fly.

The animosity grew much worse with the so-called "Petticoat Affair", which also emerged early in President Jackson's first year in office. It was probably the most consequential sex scandal in D.C. history, which is saying a lot.

Jackson's Secretary of War, John Eaton—a fellow war hero, Tennessean, and friend—had allegedly had an affair with a Georgetown woman, Peggy O'Neale Timberlake, while she was married to a purser in the U.S Navy. According to historian Samuel Eliot Morrison, the lady was "luscious brunette with a perfect figure and a come-hither look in her blue eyes that drove the young men of Washington wild, and some of the old ones too." Eaton wed the beguiling woman after the death of her husband, either from drink or, some said, from a broken heart.

Vice-President Calhoun's wife, and most of Jackson's Cabinet, subsequently refused to have anything to do with "that hussy". The animosity toward Mrs. Eaton reminded the President of the mostly unfair campaign attacks on his recently deceased wife, Rachel Donelson Jackson, who'd been accused of bigamy. Jackson rose to the defense of his friend's wife, even claiming that Mrs. Eaton had preserved her virginity. This led the President's arch rival, Clay, to pronounce sarcastically that, "Age cannot wither, nor time stale, her infinite virginity."

The Cabinet infighting disrupted the Administration's agenda. The matter was resolved only after almost the entire Cabinet, and Calhoun, were forced out, and replaced with men more loyal to the President. The new Vice President was one of Mrs. Eaton's few defenders, Jackson's cunning, former Minister to the United Kingdom and former Secretary of State, Martin Van Buren of New York.

SLAVERY'S STATUS QUO

Jackson was President during a time of a growing movement in the North to abolish slavery, and of actions in the South to fiercely defend the peculiar institution.

In 1831, during his first term, a major slave revolt, Nat Turner's Rebellion, took place in Virginia's Southhampton County, west of the seaport town of

Norfolk. Turner, a preacher inspired by the story of Moses, rose up against slavery with a band of followers, and killed 57 whites. In suppressing the revolt, whites and the state militia killed about 200 slaves. In 1832 the Virginia legislature shunned a proposed bill to abolish slavery in the state. The abolition would have occurred over time, with compensation to slave owners. At the time, the British Empire was moving to abolish slavery under such a plan.

The same year as the slave insurrection, William Lloyd Garrison of Massachusetts founded the influential abolitionist periodical, *The Liberator*, and co-founded the American Anti-Slavery Society. Garrison's supporters called for the immediate end of slavery as a moral blight, and without compensation to slave owners. They sent thousands of anti-slavery tracts to Southern officials and ministers. The missives were often met with censorship and violence.

As President, Jackson generally supported the status quo on the issue. He condemned "sectional fanaticism" in both the North and the South. However, he skirted the law by letting his powerful Postmaster General and advisor, Amos Kendall, let some Southern postal officers block the mailing of abolitionist writings. Further, during the Jackson years, the House and Senate put in place a gag order forbidding petitions on abolition. Thus was official debate suppressed, in the legislature of a democratic republic, on one of the great issues of the time.

In his lifetime, Jackson much increased his own slave holdings, from 9 in 1809 to about 155 on his death in 1845. Most of the slaves were at his Hermitage estate, outside Nashville, where cotton was the cash crop. Jackson permitted the whipping of escaped slaves. At the same time, he defended his own slaves in courts of law.

He represented a transition from the old Virginia gentry like Monroe, Jefferson, and Washington, with their advocacy of modest restrictions on or reductions in slavery, to the Southern firebrands of the 1850s, in the run-up to the War Between the States, with their unabashed calls for slavery's expansion.

As the ownership of slaves did not become a paramount national issue again until the late 1840s, Jackson's tolerance for human servitude, and support to block the efforts of abolitionists to publicize their cause, did not impinge upon his general popularity nation-wide, and even helped him politically in some areas of the nation. Although the morality of his stance is whole another matter.

INDIAN REMOVAL

An issue that Jackson largely settled in his first term, but which played out in his second, and beyond, was the mass removal of American Indian tribes from various Southern states. The tribes in question were the Choctaw, Chickasaw, Creek, Cherokee, and Seminole. At the time, they dwelled in scattered settlements throughout the states of Kentucky, Tennessee, Mississippi, North Carolina, Georgia, and Florida. They were known as the "Five Civilized Tribes", as some of the Indians had adopted white customs such as tending farms, building houses and schools, even owning slaves.

The issue involved a fundamental clash between the state governments, which claimed sovereignty over the tribes and their lands, and the tribes themselves, which claimed treaties they'd signed with the federal government gave them the status of sovereign nations, with all attendant rights and authority.

Before becoming President, Jackson, as an Army officer, had a long history of fighting against, and negotiating with, tribes in the South. His successful war against the Creeks in 1813-14 had opened up to settlement more than 20 million acres of Alabama and Georgia. He'd also waged war in 1818 against Florida's Seminole Indians, after their raids into Georgia. Moreover, Jackson had put together treaties, not yet enacted when he took office, with a number of tribes that were promised lands in the West in exchange for their existing lands in the South and East.

Andrew Jackson had Native-Americans as friends, and raised an Indian orphan as his own son. But, like the vast majority of Americans, he looked down on Indian culture. He was adamant the tribes should either bow to the power of the state governments, and American culture, and fully assimilate, or move outside the boundaries of the United States. An advocate of states' rights, President Jackson usually came down strongly on the side of the state governments, even when other federal authorities ruled otherwise.

In 1830, Jackson pushed through Congress the Indian Removal Act, and visited his home state of Tennessee to start putting it into effect. The Act offered the tribes new lands west of the Mississippi, funds for moving there, and compensation for their current land and buildings. Believing removal was inevitable, the Choctaws and Chickasaws agreed to the Treaty terms. In 1832, the Creeks yielded much of their land through a treaty, then watched settlers grab much of the rest. Some of the Creeks struck back with arson and murder. The Army intervened and, in 1836-37, about 15,000 Creeks were compelled to head West.

In 1832, Jackson pressured a faction within the Cherokees to accede to removal to the West. But the majority of the tribe balked. At this time the Supreme Court, with 78-year-old John Marshall still its Chief Justice, issued rulings in support of the Cherokees, declaring them a sovereign state. Jackson purportedly replied: "John Marshall has made his decision; now let him enforce it!" The President got his way, both with the Cherokees, and the Court.

In 1836, Jackson replaced the retiring Marshall with Attorney General Roger Taney, a firm states' rights supporter. (Taney was later the author of the dreaded Dred Scott decision that denied citizenship rights to African-Americans.) Also in 1836, the Cherokees agreed to leave their lands within two years. Then they balked again at departing.

In 1838, under Jackson's successor, President Van Buren, the Army forcibly evicted the tribe. The Cherokees were unable to secure proper food or clothing for their long journey to Oklahoma, and perhaps 4,000 died on the resulting, tragic "Trail of Tears".

A bit of justice: the descendants of some Indians expelled from Georgia, due to the suspicion they were sitting on gold-laden property, got rich in Oklahoma, where the new lands sat atop large oil and gas deposits. But those seizing their ancestral lands in Georgia never found a nugget.

In Florida, the hardy Seminoles not only stayed, but took up arms, leading to the Second Seminole War of 1835-1842. The conflict was bloody, leading to almost 1,500 U.S. Army deaths. It was also expensive, costing the War Department an estimated $35 million in 1840 dollars, slowing Jackson's successful effort to pay off the federal debt.

The Jackson Administration typically offered pledges of protection and support for the migrating tribes, but often didn't follow through on them, or fund them adequately. And it turned a blind eye when local contractors or settlers reneged upon the agreements.

The result of Jackson's actions removed, or led to treaties to remove, tens of thousands of Indians to the Western plains. Tens of millions of acres of land were opened up to settlement, and to slave agriculture. The actions also set a precedent of sorts for President Franklin Roosevelt's movement of Japanese-Americans to internment camps during the Second World War.

Indian removal was popular in the Southern states, less so elsewhere. New England, where Native Americans had been largely pushed out generations prior, protested against the seizure of the Indians' lands. Congressman and frontiersman Davy Crockett of Tennessee opposed removal, lost his House seat because of it, and moved to Texas, and his fate at The Alamo, as a result.

With much blood, great cost, and inconsiderable injustice, Jackson forever settled the Indian issue east of the Mississippi. Today, it has damaged his presidential reputation. At the time, however, much of the public, and most of his political base, backed the removal, and he did not suffer politically for it.

THE BANK OF THE UNITED STATES

Another major issue reared up at the end of Jackson's first term and colored his second. This was the longstanding matter of the Second Bank of the United States.

This successor to Hamilton's original Bank of the United States was a powerful federal bank, supported by proponents of a stronger government role in the economy, men such as Clay and then-Sen. Daniel Webster, as well as many bankers and merchants. And, as we have seen, by some previous opponents-turned-proponents, such as President Monroe.

The Bank was opposed by many Southerners, Westerners, and farmers, all constituents of Jackson's party. People from the President's regions of the country tended to be workers of the soil eager to obtain cheap financing for their lands, and wary of banks intent on prompt repayment of loans or quick confiscation of property in the event of default.

The topic of whether the U.S. government should have its own bank with major influence over the economy dated back to the great fault line of American politics, in the 1790s between Jefferson and Hamilton, over agricultural versus financial interests, and over state governments and individual rights versus federal authority.

President Madison, eager to bolster federal finances after the trauma of the War of 1812, had in 1816 chartered the Second Bank, for a term of 20 years. In July 1832, as Jackson's re-election campaign got underway, the President's political foe Clay, and the Bank president, the able but combative Nicolas Biddle of Philadelphia, proposed to re-charter the Bank four years in advance through an Act of Congress.

The Bank had grown corrupt in the 1820s, before Biddle's tenure had cleaned things up. And in Jackson's first term, the President had had a major run-in with Clay, vetoing a bill to federally fund a major roadway in Clay's home state of Kentucky.

Now Jackson vetoed the bank bill, and attacked the interests behind it. He bracketed his action with elegant words, penned by aide Amos Kendall, that appealed to the small farmers and skilled artisans, far from Washington's power centers, who made up much of his election coalition:

"In the full enjoyment of the gifts of Heaven and the fruits of superior industry, economy, and virtue, every man is equally entitled to protection by law; but when the laws undertake to add to these natural and just advantages artificial distinctions, to grant titles, gratuities, and exclusive privileges, to make the rich richer and the potent more powerful, the humble members of society—the farmers, mechanics, and laborers—who have neither the time nor the means of securing like favors to themselves, have a right to complain of the injustice of their Government."

Congress failed to override Jackson's veto. The Bank became a major, and winning, issue for the President in his re-election.

In the 1832 election, Jackson easily won a second term against the National Republican party candidate, then-Sen. Henry Clay of Tennessee, and the Anti-Masonic Party candidate, William Wirt of Maryland. (Yes, even back then some believed in a masonic conspiracy.) The President gained 55 percent of the vote to 37 percent for Clay. Eight percent voted for Wirt who, although standing against Masonic organizations that some viewed as elitist, was a prominent Mason himself. The Nullifier Party, which believed states could void federal laws it found illegal, nominated Virginia Gov. John Floyd, and carried South Carolina.

The Electoral Tally for Jackson, Clay, Floyd, and Wirt, respectively, was 219-49-11-7. Jackson ran strongly throughout the North and South.

President Jackson's coattails were strong in the House, with the Democrats gaining 17 seats to build up their majority to 143-63. The surprisingly strong Anti-Masonic Party won eight seats for a total of 25. The Nullifier Party, strong in South Carolina, picked up five seats for a total of nine. In the Senate, however, the National Republicans opposed to Jackson gained a seat to take control of that body, 23-21. The Nullifiers hurt the President's Democratic Party by winning two seats. The Nullifier Party would prove a continuing burr in Jackson's side.

In 1833, the first year of Jackson's second term, the Bank issue heated up even more, and triggered a crisis that threatened to derail his presidency. The President acted in effect to gut the institution, by transferring its federal deposits to state-chartered banks. He did this against a large majority of the House, which preferred the status quo. Further, his own Treasury Secretary, William Duane, refused to make the transfers. This compelled Jackson to replace Duane with his Attorney General, Maryland's Roger Taney, later the President's pick to head the Supreme Court.

Meantime Biddle, punching back at the President, called in many of the Bank's loans, hoping a resulting financial downturn would make the President reverse course. This just reinforced Jackson's Jeffersonian belief that the Bank, and centralized money interests, were inherently corrupt.

In turn, Congress was enraged by what it saw as the President's high-handed actions. Many of its National Republican members, some hailing from the old Federalist party, some simply enemies of Jackson, formed a new Whig Party. It was named after a group of British Parliamentarians that opposed a corrupt king and his Tory supporters. The American Whigs rejected Jackson's proposed appointees to the Bank.

Next, in March 1834, a frustrated Senate—for the first and only time in American history—passed a resolution, of Clay's, to formally censure the President. The Senate action noted Jackson's "derogation" of "power and authority not conferred by the Constitution". (The upper chamber rescinded its censure just before Andrew Jackson left office in 1837, after his backers had gained control of the Senate in the 1836-1837 elections.)

More serious than a temporary censure, according to many economic historians, was the effect that crippling the Bank had on the U.S. economy. State-chartered banks, laden with new deposits, inflated the economy with easy credit, fueling a land boom in the Western territories. The bubble burst with the Panic of 1837. Fortunately for Jackson, this steep recession took place just after he left office. However, his handpicked successor, Van Buren, had a presidency saddled with economic woes. This was a factor in Van Buren losing his 1840 re-election bid.

Some historians note that, after the Bank's defunding, the remnants of the federal financial institutions also artificially pumped up the economy in Jackson's second term. (At least until his Specie Circular of 1836, which required gold or silver for land transactions, which also helped trigger the bust.)

Moreover, a decentralized banking system, following up on Jacksonian and Jeffersonian notions, and created by President James K. Polk in the 1840s, oversaw general prosperity until 1913, with the creation of the powerful central bank the Federal Reserve. The issue of the extent of federal banking power over the economy remains an important and unsettled one today.

TARIFFS AND A WHIFF OF SECESSION

Just at the time of his 1832 re-election, Jackson faced another major crisis, one that threatened the nation with disunion, and the Chief Executive with a second-term disaster. That November, a South Carolina convention adopted the Ordinance of Nullification, by which a state could nullify or void a federal law it found unjust or unconstitutional. The issue in question was the federal tariff, or tax, on imported goods.

Southern states despised the tariff, which they viewed as a bid by Northern states to protect their industries from foreign competition by imposing higher costs on the South. The latter, lacking many factories, imported many of their manufactured goods from Europe, whose costs the tariff raised. These feelings were especially marked in South Carolina, where eight of its nine U.S. Congressmen, had deserted Jackson's Democrats, and joined the Nullifiers Party.

Jackson, though a plantation owner from Tennessee who generally favored states rights and weak tariffs, was even more a ferocious proponent of Union. As noted, in the American Revolution, he'd lost his brothers and his mother during the British occupation of South Carolina, and had been literally scarred by a British officer. Jackson grew to despise foreign, or domestic, threats to American strength and unity.

As President, his antipathy to South Carolina was heightened considerably by the leader of the nullification movement, John C. Calhoun, the former Secretary of War who'd clashed with Gen. Jackson over Florida, and President Jackson's former, hostile Vice President during the "Petticoat Affair". Calhoun was then a U.S. Senator from the Palmetto State.

The tension between the President and ousted Vice-President had been on display at the 1830 Democratic Party's annual Jefferson Day Dinner. (It still exists, as the Jefferson-Jackson Dinner.) There were dueling toasts between the two former allies-turned-adversaries. Looking at Calhoun, Jackson stated testily: "Our federal Union, it must be preserved." Calhoun toasted tersely in return: "The Union, next to our Liberty, most dear."

From his home state, Calhoun had led the battle for nullification. At the 1832 state convention, South Carolina declared the tariff illegal, and readied its militia to block collection of the excise tax from federal officials.

Jackson's response was both volcanic and clever. He spoke with quiet thunder of sending the Army to occupy the wayward state, and of hanging Calhoun as a traitor. Meantime, behind the scenes, he backed efforts to diffuse matters by lowering the tariff. His unlikely, unspoken allies in this were

Calhoun, and his political rival Clay. The latter's "American System" of national strength called for higher tariffs, but at this juncture Clay was worried more at the prospect of civil war.

A deal was reached where the import tax was steadily reduced over a 10-year span; meantime South Carolina backed off nullification. The President achieved both of two key aims. Namely, federal loyalty from the South, and lower tariffs for the same.

TO THE VICTOR BELONGS

Another economic and financial issue in Jackson's second term was the President's creation of a "Spoils System" to reward his political followers. Jackson dismissed many appointees of John Quincy Adams from federal service, and put in his own men. Jackson ally Sen. William L. Marcy of New York put it famously: "To the victor belong the spoils of the enemy."

Unfortunately, Jackson often based his selections not on merit, but on partisan loyalty and political connections, and on the recommendations of cronies. This led to gross abuse, most notably in the case of Samuel Swartwout, who had back in 1806 taken part in former Vice President Aaron Burr's attempted seizure of the western United States for his own personal fiefdom. Over the protests of many officials such as Secretary of State Van Buren, Jackson made Swartwout in 1829 head of the New York City customhouse.

In an age where tariffs, not the income tax nor capital gains tax, provided most federal revenue, the customs post at the country's largest port garnered half of all federal revenue. It also offered an unmatched perch for an unscrupulous man like Swartwout to line his pockets. Which he did, raking off $1.2 million (about $30 million in 2015 dollars). In 1841, federal officers persuaded him to return much of the loot, in return for immunity from prosecution.

The Spoils System set a marker for much largesse to come, for instance during the Grant and Harding Administrations, not to mention the huge federal corporate and social welfare states of today. However, it did not particularly hurt Jackson politically at the time, and probably helped strengthen his support among some factions of his party.

HEALTH OF THE PRESIDENT

Andy Jackson dodged the second-term woes in terms of his personal health. This was no small thing for Jackson, who in his life suffered from malaria, dysentery, smallpox—and bullets lodged in his body from his duels. One pellet, which had remained in his shoulder, gave him such discomfort that in 1832 a Navy surgeon had to remove it. The physician conducted the operation at the White House, without benefit of anesthesia, or modern antiseptics. Old Hickory gritted his teeth, and bore the pain. The President's health immediately and markedly improved.

Given the fact he was suffering from the effects of lead and mercury poisoning, from the bullets in his body and from the medical potions of the time, the Chief Executive was fortunate not to have suffered even worse physical problems during his time in office.

In his second term, Jackson narrowly avoided assassination during an 1835 visit to the Capitol. A deranged man pulled two Derringers on him, but both pistols misfired. The irate President's response was to beat the fellow with his walking stick, his trusty old hickory, before Congressman Davy Crockett and others intervened to save the assailant's life.

The President was incredibly fortunate to avoid serious harm. When the Smithsonian in the 1930s conducted test firings of the two extant guns, both discharged successfully. The Institution estimated the odds of both not firing at 125,000 to 1. Luck, and the humidity of that day, which probably dampened the guns' powder, saved him.

SUMMING UP "OLD HICKORY"

Today, quite a few analysts of Jackson's presidency sharply disagree with the actions he took on matters such as Indian removal, and removal of the Bank of the United States. However, on these topics, and the other main issues of his presidency, Jackson almost always prevailed. He succeeded on the Indians' dispersal, on defunding the Bank, on quashing South Carolina's nullification, on reducing the tariff, and on putting a temporary lid on the slavery issue. On the Bank and on nullification, he acted decisively to resolve major problems, just as his strong executive action settled the Indian issue, for better or worse, far worse for the Native American.

Jackson won and retained office by large electoral majorities, based on a major expansion of the suffrage which he represented, while his Democrat Party remained the dominant political group in the land. At the same time, he appointed many of his friends to high office. His colleague and confidant Martin Van Buren managed to succeed Jackson as President. Van Buren did lose, however, his own 1840 attempt at re-election, due in part to fallout from economic policies adopted during the Jackson years.

Foreign powers feared Old Hickory, as did almost anyone encountering him, and the U.S. remained mostly peaceful and prosperous on his watch. Even as the battle over the Bank raged, Jackson paid off the entire accumulated federal debt, running an overall surplus for one of the few times in American history, a major accomplishment. And despite major medical woes, he managed to serve out his terms as an elderly and rather sickly man in the White House.

This book attempts not to "read history backwards", by current perspectives. Thus it tries not to judge a historical figure too much by the standards and fashions of today, but by the standards of yesteryears, and of having succeeded politically. Therefore, the controversial yet formidable President Jackson must be seen as having decisively avoided a second-term fall.

TRAGEDY, THEN
CONTINUED TURMOIL
(ABRAHAM LINCOLN)/ANDREW
JOHNSON, 1865-1869

President Abraham Lincoln, the Great Emancipator, was assassinated in the second month of his second term, on Good Friday evening, April 14, 1865. His murder would end hopes for a rapidly improved future for the former slaves and defeated Confederates, and a swift reconciliation of North and South, after the bloodbath of the Civil War.

This book considers Lincoln and his successor, Andrew Johnson, as the two halves of a "two-term" presidency. The slain Lincoln had a very brief second term, with Johnson serving out the rest of the second four years.

A RAIL SPLITTER'S ROOTS

Lincoln was born in 1809 on the western frontier of the border state of Kentucky. A lover of books, he was self-taught in the law. He recoiled at the slavery in his border region, and further south, from a young age. Very tall, strong, and "rail-thin", Lincoln would serve in the Illinois legislature for eight years, and would work as an attorney where he often represented the railroads.

In 1842 he bested a future political rival, future Illinois Sen. Stephen Arnold Douglas, to win the hand of Mary Todd, the daughter of a slave-owning banker's family from Kentucky. They would have four children, only one of whom, future Secretary of War Robert Todd Lincoln, would live long enough to have children of his own. Abe Lincoln was a U.S. Congressman for a term, then left in 1849 after his unpopular criticism of the Mexican-American War.

An admirer of Henry Clay's Whigs, with their support of tariffs and transportation infrastructure, he joined the new Republican Party, with its anti-slavery stance. In 1856 he finished second in the balloting for the party's vice-presidential nomination. He lost a nationally publicized Senate race to Democrat Douglas in 1858 over the issue of popular sovereignty. This was the notion the people of a new territory should decide on whether or not to permit slavery. This was contrary to President Monroe's and Henry Clay's old Compromise of 1820, which barred forced servitude in new lands north of Mason-Dixon.

Despite the Senate loss, Lincoln's words from his nomination speech that year lived on: "A house divided against itself cannot stand. I believe this government cannot endure permanently half slave and half free…It will become all one thing, or all the other." In 1860, Lincoln issued another well-received talk at Manhattan's Cooper Union college, theretofore a political bastion for two rivals and future Cabinet members, New York Sen. William Seward and Ohio Gov. Salmon Chase.

A BUMPTIOUS, PRE-WAR ELECTION RACE

By that election year, North and South were already at each other's throats. From 1854 on, armed pro- and anti-slavery bands had fought pitched battles for turf in the Kansas territory. Slave catchers grabbed escaped blacks off the streets of

Northern cities and returned them South to their owners. In 1859, John Brown of Connecticut led a raid on the federal arsenal at Harper's Ferry, Virginia (today's West Virginia), aiming to spark a slave rebellion. Federal troops led by Col. Robert E. Lee of Virginia—the son of Washington's cavalry commander Lighthorse Harry Lee—quashed Brown's effort. Regional rancor simmered on other matters such as the tariff and the North's desire to construct a transcontinental railroad. President James Buchanan of Pennsylvania, a Democrat with his political base in the South, seemed helpless to stop a rising tide of secession.

His party's April convention in Charleston, South Carolina was divided against itself. All the delegates from seven Deep South states bolted the assembly: Alabama, Arkansas, Florida, Georgia, Mississippi, South Carolina, and Texas. Leading the presidential balloting among the remaining attendees was Lincoln's former rival for the Illinois Senate seat, Sen. Douglas. However, Douglas couldn't secure the nomination, and the convention broke up. For the first and only time in American history, a major political party had failed to nominate a candidate at its convention.

In May 1860 at Chicago's Wigwam assembly hall, Lincoln received the Republican nod for President on the third ballot, over the better-known Seward and Chase. Lincoln was viewed as a moderate who opposed slavery's extension, and its abolition. His advocacy of tariffs to protect Pennsylvania's metal industries added to his support. Further, his Kentucky and Illinois roots appealed to delegates from the West.

For regional balance, the party chose Maine Sen. Hannibal Hamlin as Lincoln's running mate. Hamlin had opposed the 1854 Kansas-Nebraska Act which led to slavery's spread into the Midwest.

The Republicans had mostly superseded the old Whig Party. However, its remnants, hoping to preserve the Union while underplaying the slavery issue, met in Baltimore. They were known as the Constitutional Union Party. Its possible presidential candidates included Texas Gov. Sam Houston, formerly a driving force behind Texas' Lone Star independence, then its inclusion in the Union, and thus fiercely opposed to leaving it.

The convention ended up picking Tennessee's John Bell, formerly the U.S. Speaker of the House and Secretary of War. For regional balance, the vice-presidential choice was Edward Everett of Massachusetts, its former Governor and a former U.S. Secretary of State. When war broke out, Bell would join the Confederacy; Everett stayed with the Union.

The Democrats tried again to nominate a candidate at their second convention, that June in Baltimore. Douglas won the nomination this time, and Herschel Vespasian Johnson, a former Governor of Georgia named after a British astronomer and a Roman emperor, was his vice-presidential pick. In the campaign to come, Douglas would pledge to use force if necessary to stop rebels from leaving the Union.

But the larger number of Democrats who'd left the first party convention held their own, separate gathering in Baltimore. They renamed themselves the Southern Democratic Party. Affirming slavery and its expansion, they nominated the Vice-President of the United States, Kentucky's John Cabell Breckinridge, the grandson of Jefferson's Attorney General. Oregon's pro-slavery Sen. Joseph Lane, formerly the Governor of the Oregon Territory, received the vice-presidential nod.

ELECTION, AND POST-ELECTION CRISIS

Not surprisingly, the campaign was dominated by the "peculiar institution" and the possibility of secession. The schism among the Democrats assured a Republican victory.

Abraham Lincoln and running mater Hamlin took the weird four-way race with a modest popular vote win of 40 percent—to 30 percent for Douglas' Democrats, 18 percent for the Southern Democrats, and 13 percent for the

Constitutional Unionists. The Electoral College tally for the four parties was, respectively: 180-72-39-12, with the Republicans winning in a landslide.

Lincoln won every Northern state except Delaware which, along with Maryland and the Deep South states, went to the Southern Democrats. Lincoln's Republicans also gained the Western, free states of California and Oregon.

Douglas' Democratic Party, although second in the popular vote, was nearly shut out in the Electoral College. It only took Missouri, and three of New Jersey's seven electors. It was the Democrats' worst-ever showing in a presidential race.

Nowadays, Americans tend to think of the South of that time as monolithic, but the vote was hardly that. Although the pro-secession Southern Democrats won North Carolina, Georgia, and Louisiana, the Constitutional Unionists took over 40 percent of the ballots in all three states. The Constitutional Unionists were even stronger in the border states and the upper South, winning Kentucky, Tennessee, and Virginia.

Indeed, before taking office on March 4, 1861, Lincoln discounted the chance of the South departing the Union. But attempts at regional compromise failed. Kentucky Sen. John Crittenden, of the Constitutional Union Party, called for extending westward the Missouri Compromise's 36° 30' line of parallel dividing the slave territories from the free ones. Lincoln, whose party's founding issue was any new territory must be "free soil", rejected the idea.

By February, seven Deep South states—South Carolina, Florida, Mississippi, Alabama, Georgia, Louisiana, and Texas—had declared themselves the Confederate States of America. Jefferson Davis, a Mexican-American War hero and the former federal Secretary of War, resigned his post as Mississippi Senator to become the Confederacy's provisional, and soon official, President. His Vice President would be Alexander Stephens, once a Georgia Congressman for many years, and a former Whig, Constitutional Unionist, and Democrat. Stephens had helped push the Kansas-Nebraska Act through Congress.

In March 1861 Stephens explicitly rejected Jefferson's statement that "all men are created equal" applied to all men under the law. The Confederate Vice-President declared: "Our new Government…rests, upon the great truth that the negro is not equal to the white man; that slavery, subordination to the superior race, is his natural and normal condition." Stephens also noted that the new Confederate Constitution abolished the tariff, as well as construction of "internal improvements" such as harbors and railroads by a central government.

In his inaugural address, President Lincoln stressed he had no intent to interfere with slavery where it already existed. He appealed to the historic ties between the divided regions: "The mystic chords of memory, stretching from every battlefield, and patriot grave…will yet swell the chorus of the Union, when again touched…by the better angels of our nature." The fledgling Confederacy, however, with its Constitution declaring slavery inviolable, wanted no truck with a Northern advocate of new territories devoid of servitude.

A CIVIL WAR TAKES SHAPE

Fighting erupted on April 12, when Confederate cannons brought on the surrender of federal troops at Fort Sumter in Charleston harbor, South Carolina. War fever then seized both North and South. President Lincoln called for 75,000 volunteers from the states to preserve the Union and to protect federal installations. Meantime, Tennessee, Virginia, North Carolina, and Arkansas, angry at Lincoln's troop buildup, and fearing a Northern occupation, joined the Confederacy. All of its states contributed soldiers for a Confederate army.

The North's 21 million people, including 400,000 slaves, faced off against the nine million persons, including 3.5 million slaves, of the South.

The ensuing conflict had three main theaters. One, in the East, centered on Virginia, and the rebel capital in Richmond. The Confederate Army of Northern Virginia there would be led by Lee, the officer who'd suppressed the John Brown raid. A former Superintendent of West Point and a ranking officer of the Mexican-American War, Lee turned down Lincoln's offer of command of the Union Army.

For several years, things went badly for the Union in the East. In July 1861 a Union force was mauled in the war's first major battle at Manassas, or Bull Run, Virginia. In spring 1862, a rebel army, under the relentless Gen. "Stonewall" Jackson of Virginia, defeated three Union armies in that state's fertile Shenandoah Valley.

Meanwhile, the first of many Union attempts to take Richmond failed that spring and summer. It followed an ambitious sea-borne landing of a federal army—under Gen. George Brinton McClellan, a Democrat from Philadelphia—in a region just south of the nation's founding Virginian towns of Jamestown and Williamsburg. McClellan, an efficient, if cautious, drillmaster, reached the outskirts of the Southern capital, before Confederate counterattacks induced his withdrawal.

The second theater was in the West, and centered on Tennessee. There Union commanders such as Ulysses S. Grant of Ohio, a highly valorous officer of the Mexican-American War, had more success. In February 1862, Grant captured Fort Donelson, gaining the "unconditional surrender" of some 12,000 rebel troops, and the nickname of "U.S." However, that April at Shiloh, Tennessee, Grant's army suffered 13,000 casualties, underlining the war's mounting toll.

The third, sometimes overlooked theater, was on the waves. The overall Union commander at war's start was Virginia's Winfield Scott, a military hero stretching back to the War of 1812. Gen. Scott formulated a clever "Anaconda Plan". Its aim was to strangle like a snake the South's ability to export cotton and to sustain its economy and currency. This was to be achieved by seizing its coastal ports and Mississippi River towns. By spring 1862, a U.S. Navy fleet had captured New Orleans, the chokepoint of the Mississippi basin.

A WAR-TIME ADMINISTRATION

America had largely gained its independence during the Revolution by the military intervention of France against Britain. So both the South and the North scrambled to gain the affection, or at least the neutrality, of Paris and London, still the preeminent powers of Europe.

In December 1861, President Lincoln defused the Trent Affair, in which the U.S. Navy ship the *San Jacinto* had without authorization seized two Confederate diplomats off of the neutral British ship the *Trent*. One of the envoys was James Murray Mason, the grandson of Virginia's George Mason, the godfather of the Bill of Rights. The violation of British neutrality led London to mobilize forces in British Canada for a possible war with the U.S. Lincoln calmed matters by releasing the two men and by disavowing the actions of the American vessel.

To run his government, Lincoln appointed a generally talented set of Cabinet members and advisors. His Secretary of State was Seward. In the vital post of Minister to Britain was Charles Francis Adams, Sr., of Massachusetts, the son of President John Quincy Adams and the grandson of President John Adams, both of whom had held the same post.

Salmon Chase headed the Treasury Department, with considerable controversy. His agency began printing cheaper-money greenbacks, as opposed to gold coins, risking a debasement of the currency. Chase also put in unpopular taxes to pay for the war's expenses, and his Department incurred a record amount of national debt.

In 1862 the President chose a pro-Union Democrat, Edwin Stanton of Ohio, to shake up the War Department, and deal with war-time profiteering and inept administration there. With military expenditures exploding, fraud was rampant among suppliers of guns, meat, whale oil, and uniforms.

Lincoln's Postmaster General was Maryland's Montgomery Blair. The son of President Jackson's chief advisor, Blair had deserted the Democrat Party over Kansas-Nebraska, and over the Supreme Court's 1857 Dred Scott decision. That explosive ruling, rendered by a fellow Marylander, Chief Justice Taney, had held that African-Americans had no standing in federal courts. Another Lincoln Cabinet member who switched from the Democrat to the Republican Party, due to his distaste for slavery, was Connecticut's Gideon Welles, the able Secretary of the Navy.

The President, and his Attorney General, Missouri's Edward Bates, took controversial, even authoritarian, measures, to keep the border states in the Union and place a lid on war-time dissent. In April 1861, Maryland considered secession, which would have surrounded the federal capital of Washington with rebel territory.

Lincoln responded by ignoring "habeas corpus"—the legal requirement that authorities must produce evidence to detain a suspect—to arrest pro-Southern officials in Baltimore. He also ignored Chief Justice Taney's ruling that his action was illegal. Lincoln acted in the wake of anti-Union riots and pro-Confederate attacks on vital railroad lines in the state.

In September 1861, his War Department jailed pro-Confederate members of the state legislature, pushing Maryland into a pro-Union stance. The grandson of "Star Spangled Banner" author Francis Scott Key was also imprisoned, and kept at Fort McHenry, whose siege had inspired his grandfather to write the National Anthem. The Lincoln Administration also at times expended funds deemed necessary for the war before Congress had appropriated them.

A CALL TO END SLAVERY, AND LINCOLN'S FIRST MIDTERM

On September 17, 1862, at Antietam Creek, Maryland, a large federal army headed by Gen. McClellan blocked an attempted invasion of the North by Lee and Jackson. Antietam was the costliest day in American history, then or since, with a startling 25,000 dead, wounded, and missing on both sides. When McClellan failed to pursue the battered Confederates, Lincoln sacked him.

With the fall election approaching, Lincoln desired to boost the morale and turnout of Northern abolitionists, while giving the wavering European powers a reason to favor the North. The President used Lee's retreat into Virginia after Antietam as a reason to issue his Emancipation Proclamation.

This landmark directive, issued September 22, and taking effect on January 1, 1863, declared free the several million slaves in the Confederate states. It did not end slavery in the border states that Lincoln wished to keep in the Union. However, throughout the war Lincoln encouraged the movement of "contrabands", or escaped slaves, to save havens behind Union lines. Slaves reaching such areas were by law deemed free. The President was convinced this migration would help undermine the economic foundation of the Confederacy. Slavery would effectively end by the conclusion of the war, when the victorious Union had occupied all of the Confederacy. The Proclamation did not provide compensation for slave owners, as Lincoln's prior abolition of slavery in the District of Columbia had done.

Despite Antietam and Emancipation, the 1862-1863 midterm elections reflected strong unease with many aspects of the war—the early defeats, the immense casualties, conscription, Lincoln's frequent sacking of his generals, the corruption in military contracts, the war-time income tax, the gutting of habeas corpus, and economic and social fears over the prospect of freed, low-wage former slaves.

That November, the House Republicans lost 21 seats, falling to 87 seats, while the Democrats gained 27 seats, for a total of 72. The Democrats did very well in the Northern heartlands of New York, Ohio, Pennsylvania, and Illinois, where they won seven, six, six, and four seats, respectively. They even picked up Lincoln's home congressional seat in Springfield, Illinois. Republicans losses took place even though the overwhelmingly Democratic Southern states were out of the Union, and didn't vote in the federal elections. The Southern-leaning, but pro-war, Constitutional Union party lost three seats, leaving it a total of 25 congressmen.

The G.O.P., or Grand Old Party, still young, made small gains in the Senate. It picked up a seat to retain a commanding 32-10 majority. Unionist parties allied with the Republicans wound up with six seats. The two Senators from the new state of West Virginia, which had split off from Confederate Virginia, joined the Senate as Unionists. (During this period, 20 Senate seats in 10 Confederate states remained unfilled on Capitol Hill.)

State-wide elections went terribly for Lincoln's party. Democrats won the governorships of New York and New Jersey, and state Democratic candidates even thrived in the bedrock Republican states of Ohio, Minnesota, and Illinois.

The war would get worse, before it got better, endangering Lincoln's re-election prospects before much strengthening them.

FIELDS OF BLOOD

In March 1863, massive casualties and personnel demands led to the first conscription in the country's history. The Civil War Military Draft Act put in place enlistment quotas for each congressional district. It mandated the enrollment of every male citizen and immigrant between the ages of 20 and 45. In the same month, and not by coincidence, Lincoln signed an Act of Congress permitting him to suspend habeas corpus, for cases relating to war, espionage, or anti-draft activities, anywhere in the Union for the course of the conflict.

The draft would prove unpopular, in part because draftees were able to substitute other men to take their spots in the ranks. Many did this by hiring someone to take their place, for $300. The system was thus skewed to the well-connected or more affluent. A century later, the Vietnam War-era college deferments would allow those able to attend university to put off military service, breeding similar resentment.

The climactic fighting of the nation's bloodiest war came that year. In the West, on the Fourth of July, Grant took the besieged Mississippi river fortress town of Vicksburg. Now he and the gunboats of Tennessee-bred Admiral David Farragut controlled the entire Mississippi River, rending the Confederacy.

Yet at the same time Grant was taking Vicksburg, Lee was again invading the North. In December 1862 at Fredericksburg, Virginia, and in February 1863 at Chancellorsville, he'd won smashing victories, though at the latter fight he'd lost his daring lieutenant, Jackson. Lee then determined to enter Pennsylvania and try to crush the main Union army in the East, and perhaps force Lincoln into peace talks. His timing seemed right, as Northern cities such as New York were about to witness bloody riots against the draft.

But in the epic, three-day battle at Gettysburg, the Army of the Potomac's stout defense mangled waves of Lee's charging troops. The Northern forces were led by Pennsylvanian Gen. George Meade, a fortuitous, late-minute command choice of Lincoln's. The casualties for both sides were perhaps 48,000—roughly nine times the number of American killed, wounded, and missing during the June 6, 1944 D-Day landings in France. Later in the year, Gen. William Tecumseh Sherman of Ohio and Gen. George Thomas of Virginia won major Union victories near the Tennessee city of Chattanooga, forcing Confederate forces to retreat into Georgia.

At Gettysburg's national cemetery that fall, Lincoln offered a remarkable tribute to the fallen. In three short minutes he spun off phrase after now-famous phrase. "Four score and seven years ago," he offered, "our fathers brought forth on this continent a new nation, conceived in liberty, and dedicated to the proposition that all men are created equal. Now we are engaged in a great civil war, testing whether that nation, or any nation so conceived and so dedicated, can long endure." Noting the "honored dead" who "gave the last full measure of devotion", Lincoln asserted "that government of the people, by the people, for the people, shall not perish from the earth."

THE PROSPECTS FOR RE-ELECTION

Along with vexing concerns of the war, Lincoln was also concerned about the approaching re-election campaign. That contest figured to be tight, given the widespread dissatisfaction in the North—especially among moderates, and anti-war "Copperheads"—with the conflict's great cost in treasure, personal liberties, and lives.

At the so-called National Union Party convention in Baltimore in June, which united Republicans with pro-war Democrats, Lincoln was easily re-nominated. He won out over Gen. Grant, whose supporters had placed his name in nomination, by 494 ballots to 22. Andrew Johnson, a pro-Union, War Democrat and a former Senator and current Military Governor of Tennessee, became Lincoln's new running mate. Johnson won out after a tight ballot race with Vice President Hamlin and with former New York Senator and pro-war Democrat Daniel S. Dickinson. Lincoln, a political strategist of a high order, realized he would likely face a Democratic "peace candidate", and calculated a Democrat on his own ticket would bolster his hopes.

The President was prescient. His Democratic opponent in 1864 turned out to be Gen. McClellan. The very man who'd been Lincoln's head of the Army of the Potomac in 1861-1862.

At the Democratic convention in Chicago that August, nominee McClellan pledged to uphold the Union. However, the assemblage picked as his running mate an anti-war Democrat, Sen. George H. Pendleton of Ohio. "Gentleman George" Pendleton was also known known as a foe of waste and patronage in government. The Democratic party platform, contrary to the position of its nominee, called for peace talks with the Confederacy.

The platform reflected the views of influential, former Ohio Rep. Clement Vallandigham. An Ohio military commission had convicted him the previous year for his vociferous, anti-war views. Not wishing to make a martyr out of an ex-member of Congress, Lincoln had Vallandigham released behind Confederate lines.

McClellan, all of 37 years, seemed to be the early favorite in the 1864 presidential race. His popularity was aided by the terrible casualties the Army of the Potomac, now under Grant's command, suffered in further attempts to take Richmond. These included the June battle of Cold Harbor, a "Gettysburg in reverse" marred by calamitous frontal assaults.

With his electoral prospects bleak, Lincoln made an astonishing pledge to continue the war in the months following his defeat.

"It seems exceedingly probable," the President wrote, "that this Administration will not be re-elected. Then it will be my duty to so co-operate with the President elect, as to save the Union between the [November] election and the [March] inauguration; as he will have secured his election on such ground that he cannot possibly save it afterward." Lincoln conferred with African-American abolitionist Frederick Douglass, of New York via Maryland's Wye plantation, to ferry slaves out of the South in the event of a Union defeat.

Yet Lincoln's election campaign was buoyed in the closing months by three vital Union victories. In August, Admiral Farragut stormed Mobile Bay, Alabama, the last of the South's Gulf Coast ports, cursing aside the mined "torpedoes" in the path of his ironclad ships. In September, Gen. Sherman took Atlanta, a rare Southern industrial hub. And in September and October, Gen. Philip Sheridan's waged a "scorched earth" campaign through Virginia's Shenandoah Valley, the breadbasket of Lee's army.

LINCOLN'S SECOND BIG WIN

In the end, given the surge of military victories, President Lincoln and Vice-President Johnson gained a smashing victory. With most Southern states out of the Union, Lincoln took the Electoral College, 212 to 21. He lost just Kentucky, New Jersey, and Delaware to McClellan. The Confederate states of Tennessee and Louisiana, then under occupation by Union troops, voted for Lincoln. He was the first President to win re-election since Andy Jackson.

However, despite the electoral vote drubbing, McClellan still won 45 percent of the popular vote. If most Southern states had voted in the election, unencumbered by federal troops, McClellan would quite possibly have won.

The congressional elections of 1864-1865 also broke very strongly for the Republicans. In the House, they won a landslide, picking up 50 seats to build a huge majority, of 137 seats to 38 for the Democrats. Further, the G.O.P. gained at the expense of the Constitutional Union Party, which lost seven of its 25 seats. In the Senate, the G.O.P. picked up two seats, to build its strong majority over the Democrats to 33-9, with Unionist parties having six seats. The would-be holders of many "Democratic" seats at this time were of course in the Confederacy, and thus absent from the Capitol.

A CONFEDERACY'S COLLAPSE

The newly re-elected President continued his remarkable oratory at his second inaugural address. Meditating on slavery, he stated the war might continue "until all the wealth piled by the bond-man's 250 years of unrequited toil shall be sunk, and until every drop of blood drawn with the lash, shall be paid by another drawn with the sword". But he offered mercy as well, speaking of "malice toward none; with charity for all".

Post-war treatment of the ex-slaves and the former Confederates was much on his mind, for the Confederacy was falling apart. After taking and setting fire to Atlanta, in late 1864 Gen. Sherman's troops had stormed their way to coastal Savannah. In their path they destroyed or seized livestock, grain, and railroads, all vital to the Southern military's provisioning.

The following spring, Sherman's friend U.S. Grant finally broke Richmond's defenses, taking the Confederate capital on April 3. Lee's forces tried to escape, but were swiftly cornered. On April 9, Lee surrendered to Grant at Appomattox Courthouse. 17 days later, the last major Confederate army, based in North Carolina under Virginia's Joseph E. Johnston, surrendered its 89,000 troops to Sherman. On May 10, Union troops captured a now-ex-Confederate President Davis, who'd disbanded his Cabinet five days prior.

The great national conflagration had taken upwards of 720,000 lives, from battle and disease. But it would take one more.

AN ACCIDENTAL ASSASSINATION

According to a close friend of Lincoln, the President had narrowly escaped an unknown assassin in summer 1864. On the way to visit D.C.'s Soldier's Home, a bullet from an unseen, crouching rifleman had missed his head by inches, passing through the top of his silken stovepipe hat. Lincoln often used the retirement center for military veterans as a retreat during the capital's hot-weather months.

After the missed shot, Lincoln's horse had bolted. Then the President regained control of his mount, rode up to the Soldier's Home, and laconically told a soldier, "He got the bit in his teeth before I could draw the rein." Not wanting to sow panic, Lincoln asked the soldiers on hand to keep mum about the attempted murder.

The actual murder of the President came about due to circumstance, and played out due to chance. The pro-Confederacy band of conspirators under John Wilkes Booth of Maryland had originally planned to kidnap, not kill, Lincoln, and exchange him for Confederate prisoners of war. But in spring 1864, Gen. Grant, aware the ongoing exchanges benefitted the manpower-starved South, ended them. When Richmond fell in early April 1865, Booth, his Confederate cause in tatters, turned to violence.

The 26-year-old Booth grew particularly enraged after a Lincoln speech of April 11, 1865. The oration was delivered from the north portico of the White House to a large crowd, which included Booth and some companions. In his talk, Lincoln backed Louisiana's reconstructed state constitution, which abolished slavery in the state. And he voiced approval of granting suffrage to some former slaves. Booth blurted out: "That means nigger citizenship. That is the last speech he will ever make." The actor tried to get one of those accompanying him to shoot the President then and there.

Some historians now believe Booth's shift to violence was influenced by a possible Union Army plot, possibly authorized at the highest levels of the War Department, to raid Richmond in March 1864—and assassinate ranking Confederate officials, including President Jefferson Davis. The raid took place with the stated aim of liberating Union prisoners. Union Col. Ulrich Dahlgren, the son of Union admiral and artillery inventor John Dahlgren, died during the incursion. On Dahlgren's person were found documents laying out a plan to kill Davis and other leading officials. Davis' government promptly had the materials published, touching off a media firestorm. Secretary of War Edwin Stanton denounced the papers as a forgery and, after the Confederacy fell, ordered the originals destroyed.

However, recent scholarly and forensic evidence suggests the documents may have been authentic, and probably were written by Dahlgren. Such an effort to kill Davis and other high officials, although extreme, may make sense given the ardent desire of some on both sides to bring the terrible conflict to a resolution, by any means possible.

Booth, who closely followed the war news, knew of the highly publicized raid, and of the alleged assassination plans, and likely took some inspiration from them, whether or not the plans were authentic.

The actor-turned-assassin had often performed at Ford's Theater, a half dozen blocks from the White House. There, early on April 14, he learned of Lincoln's intent that night to attend, apparently with Gen. Grant and Mrs. Grant, a showing of the farce "Our American Cousin". Improvising, Booth decided to kill the President and Grant at Ford's that evening. He organized his plotters to kill other top-ranking officials at the same hour.

He directed co-conspirator George Atzerodt to murder Vice-President Johnson at his room at the Kirkwood House hotel, three blocks from Ford's Theater. But Atzerodt, who blanched at replacing kidnapping with murder, got drunk at the Kirkwood bar, and left without attacking Johnson. Booth instructed ex-Confederate soldier Lewis Powell to kill Secretary of State William Seward at his home across from the White House. However, after smashing his way into the house, Powell was merely able to wound Seward, as the Secretary's two sons, daughter, and several Union soldiers in the house fought him off.

On the evening of April 14, chance played a heavy role in determining who would attend the theater with the Lincolns. The First Family invited various guests to see "Our American Cousin" with them, with each but the last declining. The Grants bowed out because Mrs. Grant disliked Mrs. Lincoln; Mr. and Mrs. Grant traveled instead through Philadelphia that evening to visit their children. Confederate veteran Michael O'Laughlen, who had conspired with Booth to kidnap Lincoln, may have shadowed Grant on the train with the intent to kill the General, but Grant remained safely inside a locked compartment and behind a cordon of porters.

Secretary of War Stanton also declined an invitation. The Marquis de Chambrun, a French attorney, Lincoln friend, and devout Catholic, declined the request as he thought it unseemly to see a play on Good Friday. The

President's own son, Robert Todd Lincoln, back from an exhausting stint as a member of Grant's staff, chose to spend the night at the White House.

Finally, Mrs. Lincoln invited Major Henry Rathbone, a hero of Antietam, and his fiancé Clara Harris, the daughter of a U.S. Senator from New York. The Lincolns had become friendly with the young couple at White House functions. Rathbone and Harris accepted.

UNGUARDED MOMENTS

Unfortunate circumstance afflicted the President's security detail that fateful eve. Lincoln had made Ward Hill Lamon the U.S. Marshall of the District of Columbia as well as his personal bodyguard. In 1861, the hulking Lamon had guarded President-elect Lincoln during a secret, nerve-wracking journey through pro-Confederate Baltimore on route to the Lincoln's first inauguration. As bodyguard, Lamon had taken to sleeping in front of Lincoln's bedroom, and to patrolling the White House grounds at night. One evening in 1864, he killed an armed man with Confederate sympathies found hiding in shrubbery on the White House property.

But on the night of April 14, 1865, the resolute Lamon was absent, as he'd been dispatched on a mission to Richmond.

The lone, remaining bodyguard that night was the worst imaginable man for the job. In 1861 the Metropolitan Police Department of the District of Columbia had been created. In 1864, at Lamon's urging, it had taken on the role of protecting the President. A total of four officers were assigned that duty, with a single officer assigned to the President each day on a rotating basis. On April 14, the luck of the draw went to John Frederick Parker.

It seems remarkable Parker hadn't been thrown off the force. He'd been caught sleeping on duty, drinking on the job, verbally abusing the citizenry, and had been called out for privately visiting a house of ill repute, then lamely claiming the enterprise had requested his policeman's presence.

On Good Friday evening, after reporting three hours late, he was assigned to guard the passageway leading to the presidential box at Ford's Theater. Parker later told relatives that, after the play began, Lincoln gave him the rest of the night off.

That might be true, as Lincoln was notoriously lax about personal safety, and the procedures for bodyguards then were far more informal than today. In fact, President Lincoln, in attending 12 theatrical performances, sometimes showed up without any security. Lincoln would at times ride in public by himself, and some nights would walk alone on Pennsylvania Avenue from the White House to the nearby War Department. Indeed, as late as the Harry Truman Administration, a President could stroll the streets of downtown Washington with a handful of guards and aides, shaking hands and calling out to pedestrians. It wasn't until the assassination of President John F. Kennedy in 1963 that a cordon of security fell around the Chief Executive and family.

In any event, Parker left his assignment of guarding the President, and found a seat to watch the play. Then during intermission, he accepted a request from Lincoln's footman, or servant, Charles Forbes, to go with him and the President's coachman to the Star Saloon, next door to the theater. Booth himself had a whiskey and water at the saloon to fortify himself before entering Ford's Theater!

That the President's carriage driver asked the President's bodyguard to drinks, leaving the President unprotected, illustrates the slack attitude of the time about security, as well as the free nature of the early republic, where it was expected the powerful would jostle with the average citizen.

It's unclear if Parker returned from tippling to the play before the assassination. He may have stayed in the saloon. In any event, when Booth slipped into Lincoln's box around 10 p.m., the President of the United States had been left without a single guard in a war-time capital riddled with rebel sympathizers.

Bizarrely, despite the epochal events of that night, Parker showed up at his police station at 6 a.m. the next morning, a woman in tow, requesting she be charged with prostitution.

On May 3, 1865, Parker was brought to trial for neglect of duty, for his failure to protect Lincoln. Behind the court action was the coachman Forbes, whom Mrs. Lincoln had blamed in part, along with Parker, for her husband's death. The court's writ stated: "Said Parker allowed a man to enter the President's private Box and Shoot the President." A month later, the court threw out the charge.

Amazingly, the policeman continued to work as a security guard at the White House. There Mrs. Lincoln bitterly reproached him for "helping to murder the President." Another Lincoln bodyguard, William H. Crook, stated that had Parker "done his duty, I believe President Lincoln would not have been murdered by Booth." Parker was finally thrown out of police department in 1868, after he was caught sleeping on duty again.

It was a long chain of unfortunate events, and a vainglorious actor's violent intent, that led to the death of the President, and the sudden, violent end of his second term after it had barely begun.

INDIVIDUAL IMPACTS

President Lincoln's killing had terrible effects on those present with him that night. Mrs. Lincoln had already lost her son Edward, at age three, perhaps from tuberculosis, and Willie, at age 11, from typhoid fever, possibly contracted from the bacterial-laden White House-area swamp that became the National Mall. On July 2, 1863, while the battle of Gettysburg roared, she suffered serious head injuries from a carriage accident. She attended séances, some at the White House, in a forlorn attempt to reestablish contact with deceased loved ones. Partly from the trauma of witnessing her husband murdered, she would suffer from severe depression and eventually from madness. Her surviving son Robert Todd Lincoln had her committed to an asylum, and on her release she attempted to take her own life. Afflicted by failing vision and injuries to her spinal cord, the former First Lady died in 1882.

Major Henry Rathbone, the officer who was with the Lincolns in the presidential box, was badly wounded; Booth stabbed him after shooting the President. Rathbone recovered physically, and married his fiancée Clara Harris. But over time, afflicted by regret and paranoia over the assassination, he went insane. In Germany in 1883, he murdered Clara, and tried to kill their three children. A court pronounced him criminally insane, and he spent the rest of his years in a German asylum. He lived until 1911, and was buried in a cemetery near Hanover. Yet even in death Rathbone found no peace. In 1952 German authorities, to free up space in the overcrowded, post-war graveyard, dug up the remains of the forgotten foreign soldier and scattered his bones in a local stream.

A strange fate also befell the apparent killer of John Wilkes Booth, Union Army private Thomas "Boston" Corbett. By his own account, Corbett mortally shot Lincoln's assassin after his unit cornered the fugitive Booth inside a barn in Port Royal, Virginia, 11 days after Lincoln's death. As a hat maker before the war, Corbett had been exposed to mercury compounds for making felt hats, and had likely "gone mad as a hatter" as a result. A religious fanatic, Corbett verbally disabused his Army superiors for their swearing, then was jailed, court-martialed, and discharged for refusing to apologize. Fearful of temptation from the prostitutes hired by other soldiers, Corbett castrated himself with scissors.

Corbett reenlisted, was captured by the Rebel raider John Mosby, and nearly starved to death at the notorious Confederate prison camp in

Andersonville, Georgia. After one of the prisoner exchanges that Booth hoped to resurrect, he wound up in the regiment that cornered Booth's gang. After the assassin's death, Corbett was arrested for disobeying Secretary of War Stanton's stricture to take Booth alive. In an interview with Stanton, Corbett insisted he'd acted in self-defense. Conceding, Stanton responded: "The rebel is dead. The patriot lives; [Corbett] has spared the country expense, continued excitement and trouble. Discharge the patriot."

Some witnesses stated Booth had never raised his gun at Corbett, and that Corbett hadn't even shot Booth. But Corbett insisted a divine hand had directed his. "God avenged Abraham Lincoln," he said. In any event, famed photographer Matthew Brady took his photo, enthralled crowds demanded his autograph, and the government gave him $1,654 in reward money, worth about $25,000 today.

However, the unfortunate man fell into the life of a destitute drifter. Like Rathbone he grew paranoid, believing federal officials as well as Booth sympathizers were out to get him. As a doorkeeper at the Kansas state house, he drew his gun on officials, and was consigned to the Topeka Asylum for the Insane. He escaped. In 1894 he was wrongly reported of having died in a fire in the Minnesota town of Hinckley, ironically the same name of future, would-be Reagan presidential assassin John Hinckley, Jr. Corbett's pathetic, tragic life ended that year, when a lawman who mistook him for another fugitive shot him dead.

One happier note on the assassination involved the strangest of coincidences. In the months before Lincoln's killing, Booth's brother, fellow actor Edwin Booth, saved Robert Todd Lincoln's life. At a Jersey City train station, a crowd had pushed Lincoln between a moving train and the station platform, where he dangled helplessly, before Edwin Booth, there by chance, hoisted him to safety. The younger Lincoln went on to serve as Minister to England and Secretary of War, and lived long enough to attend the unveiling of the Lincoln Memorial in 1922. However, through two other accidents of fate, he also witnessed the assassination of President Garfield in 1881 and was present at the assassination of President McKinley in 1901.

The broader impact of Lincoln's assassination was also dire, and far more significant. Especially due to the assumption to the highest office of Vice President Andrew Johnson, who served out Lincoln's second term. The Tennessee Democrat was to be the first President impeached by the House of Representatives, and the Senate vote to oust him from office would fail by just one vote. More importantly, fierce divisions between the President and the Republican Party over the post-war Reconstruction of the South led to grid-lock over that vital issue for four years, and fallout for the nation for a century.

RECONSTRUCTING LINCOLN

Vast turmoil continued to afflict the Southern states after the war, during Reconstruction, that is, the political reunion of the South with the rest of the nation. In that light, it's interesting to examine Lincoln's plans for Reconstruction, and to what extent they contrasted with the Reconstruction that followed him.

Based on his acts and statements before his death, Lincoln planned to chart a course somewhere between the "Radical Republicans" on the one hand, and the moderate Republicans and pro-Union Southerners on the other.

The Radicals wished to punish the South for what they saw as treason, and to aggressively raise up the status of the former slaves through a political and economic transformation of the South. In general, the moderates wished to be more forgiving toward the South, to quickly get past the war and reunify the country. Other than abolition, they put less stress on the status of the freed blacks, on such issues as guaranteeing all the right to vote.

Lincoln himself favored a gradual extension of voting rights to blacks who had some education and property. At the same time, he also thought the states should have a preeminent role in the granting of voting rights. He was also a more conventional Republican on economic matters, opposing widespread seizure and redistribution of Southern lands.

Throughout the war, Lincoln tacked back and forth between his moderate Republican tendencies, and Radical Republican positions. At the start of the war, faced with the national crisis, he turned toward the Radical stalwarts of the Union.

After an antebellum career of being pro-Union but opposed to abolition, Lincoln would move slowly but steadily toward emancipation during the war. Soon after taking office, President Lincoln signed a Confiscation Act permitting the seizure and freeing of slaves employed in aiding the Confederate military.

In a middle part of the war when it seemed the Union would survive, and triumph, Lincoln moderated his views, especially on the treatment of the post-war South. An indicator of Lincoln's thinking on Reconstruction came as early as 1863, a year in which Union victories at Gettysburg and Vicksburg raised the prospect of victory, and the need for a post-war strategy. In his Amnesty Proclamation of December 1863, the President called for a lenient pardon policy, which would have rapidly reaffirmed the American citizenship of the vast majority of Southerners. Namely, those who had not held a position in the Confederate government, who had not mistreated Union prisoners, and who would swear loyalty to the United States.

In 1863-1864, Lincoln proposed, to great controversy in his party, his Ten Percent Plan. Under it, if just 10 percent of the population of a Confederate state took an oath of loyalty to the Union, the state would be accepted back into the Union. Gen. Nathaniel Banks, at Lincoln's direction, had put such a scheme into effect in occupied Louisiana. It banned from federal office only high-ranking Confederate officials, and it pledged to protect the property of Southerners.

As noted, Lincoln's Emancipation Proclamation did not immediately abolish slavery in the loyal border states or the Southern
states occupied by the Union Army. However, formal abolition was
on its way in those places. In July 1864, Louisiana, while under federal Army control, approved a new state constitution that abolished
slavery and offered the vote for some blacks. (In January 1865, the
month before Lincoln's second inaugural, Congress passed the 13th
Amendment to the Constitution that abolished slavery nation-wide.
The Amendment took effect at the end of 1865, after the required
three-fourths of the states approved it.)

The President's Ten Percent Plan came under fire from Radical
Republicans, such as Sen. Benjamin Franklin Wade of Ohio. In summer 1864, his wing of the G.O.P. in Congress passed its own far
more stringent plan, co-sponsored by Wade and by Congressman
Henry Winter Davis of Maryland.

The Wade-Davis Bill required individual Confederate states, before rejoining the United States, to pass new state constitutions that
forbade slavery. It also mandated the vote for all blacks. Further,
the Bill permitted a Confederate state to rejoin the Union only if
50 percent of its citizens swore an "ironclad oath" they had never
backed the Confederacy. This contrasted with Lincoln's 10 percent
of people taking a loyalty oath only. Majorities of the citizens in the
Confederate states had supported secession.

Moreover, the Bill stipulated that Union Army governors, subject
to Senate approval, would rule the Southern states. Some moderate Republicans worried the legislation would lead to a long-term
military occupation of the South.

Sen. Wade and Rep. Davis also wanted to block voting rights for
many Confederate officials and military officers. After the war, some
of the state governments under Reconstruction did disenfranchise

a significant fraction of former rebel soldiers for a period of years. Further, under the Bill the federal government would not assume debts taken on by Southern state governments or the Confederate government.

Wade-Davis passed both houses of Congress by modest margins. However, Lincoln "pocket vetoed" the legislation, letting it die by taking no action on it.

President Lincoln's own Reconstruction plans were in large part a response to Wade, Davis, and other Radicals, and were an attempt to maintain control over the Reconstruction debate. A factor was the longstanding tension between the executive and legislatives branches over which part of the government should predominate. Wade and Davis made this conflict explicit in a joint broadside of August 1864, when Lincoln's political status, and re-election prospects, seemed at their nadir.

They condemned what they saw as Lincoln's unconstitutional overreach of executive authority, and his "personal ambition" in attempting to put in power his own political supporters in the South. "The authority of Congress," they stated, "is paramount and must be respected." Davis later added that the Chief Executive "must confine himself to his executive duties—to obey and execute, not make the laws...and leave political reorganization to Congress".

Wade had been far more personal in his attacks. Back in 1861, believing the President too tardy about emancipation, he'd stated that Lincoln's views had "come of one born of poor white trash".

The two congressmen backed rhetoric with action. After Lincoln's quiet veto of their bill, they refused to accept the congressional elections conducted under Lincoln's military governments in Louisiana, Tennessee, and Arkansas.

This conflict would play out big time after Lincoln's death, in the ferocious battles over Reconstruction between President Johnson and the Radical Republican Congress. But the matter was already simmering.

President Lincoln objected to Wade-Davis as obstructing his own ongoing moves on reconstruction and emancipation. In theory, he thought the Confederates had little formal need to rejoin the Union, as he deemed it unconstitutional and illegal for them to have left in the first place. Lincoln was already moving on emancipation, through his Emancipation Proclamation and embrace of contraband slaves. And by his backing of state efforts toward abolition in border states like Maryland and Missouri, and occupied Confederate states like Louisiana, where the Union Army gave the President effective control of the situation.

One can overstate, during the time Lincoln was alive, the split between Republican moderates and Radicals. Lincoln was a hero to Republicans, including many of Radical inclination. To replace Supreme Court Chief Justice Roger B. Taney, author of the Dred Scott decision so hated by abolitionists, he appointed his Treasury Secretary, the Radical Republican Salmon Chase. And it was Lincoln, obviously, who directed the Grand Army of the Republic to triumph, saving the Union and abolishing slavery in the process.

At the start of his second term, Lincoln held a strong electoral mandate. It seems unlikely Lincoln, a skilled and cautious politician, would have gone completely over to Radicals like Massachusetts Sen. Charles Sumner. And, certainly, he would not have gone in the opposite direction, to take at times quasi-Confederate, pro-Southern positions like those of his successor Andrew Johnson.

It is interesting to speculate that Lincoln, post war, might have tried to build a very broad coalition, stretching from ranking ex-Confederates like Gen. James Longstreet, in his role as head of the federally backed Louisiana state militia, to black statesmen like Frederick Douglass, with his own emphasis on public service and black uplift.

Lincoln was probably the best man in 1865 to try to bridge the still yawning gaps between North and South, and whites and blacks. The greatest tragedy of his untimely murder was he never got the chance to tackle such vital matters.

A NEW PRESIDENT'S HUMBLE BEGINNINGS, AND A TRIUMPH IN TENNESSEE

After Lincoln's death, and with the South crushed, the Radical Republican wing of the triumphant North was ascendant. It soon was on a collision course with Lincoln's successor, Democrat Andrew Johnson, who had entirely different ideas of how to govern.

When he took office on April 15, 1865, the Tennessean had extremely large shoes to fill in Lincoln, who was approaching iconic status even before his assassination. Lincoln, as Secretary of War Edwin M. Stanton poetically put it, "Now belonged to the Ages." The new President would often lack the vision, flexibility, and judgment to effectively deal with the chaotic, post-war political situation. And he would face relentless political foes who evinced scarce forgiveness toward the region of rebellion, or to those they found sympathetic to it.

In 1808, Andrew Johnson was born dirt-poor, the son of a washerwoman, in Raleigh, North Carolina. Like his future boss, Abraham Lincoln, he was born in a log cabin. As with Lincoln this proved a political boon in a nation that boasted anyone could become President. With his brother, Johnson was apprenticed at a young age to a tailor, and became skilled at his craft. But he chafed at the apprenticeship's enforced servitude, and flouted the law by fleeing the job. His employer posted the following notice, akin to the ads of the time announcing runaway slaves: "Ten Dollars Reward. Ran away from the subscriber, two apprentice boys, legally bound, named William and Andrew Johnson".

Fearing arrest, Andrew Johnson headed up the Appalachians, and settled in mountainous, eastern Tennessee, in the town of Greenville. He married Eliza McCardle, and would have five children with her. The pair were wed by Mordecai Lincoln, a Justice of the Peace who was the first cousin of Johnson's future boss, Abraham Lincoln. In Greenville, Johnson set up his own prosperous tailoring company, and purchased land, and bought up to nine slaves.

Fascinated by books and a skilled orator, he entered politics. He became Mayor of Greenville, a colonel of the state militia, a U.S. Congressmen for 10 years, and in 1857 a U.S. Senator. His views were typical of the era's Southern Democrats. He pushed through measures to help tradesmen and farmers, such as public schools and free libraries, while opposing abolition and suffrage for free blacks. A fiscal conservative like the early Anti-Federalists, he was against the tariff, a large standing army, and the anti-immigrant Know-Nothings. Further, his hardscrabble upbringing made him leery of the large plantation owners who controlled the politics of the South.

When talk of secession heated up after Lincoln's election, Johnson spoke in the Senate for union: "I invite every man who is a patriot to rally around the altar of our common country…and swear by our God…that the Constitution shall be saved, and the Union preserved." Still, after the Civil War erupted, Tennessee joined the Confederacy along with 10 other Southern states. During his state's debate over secession, Johnson was ridiculed, threatened, and shot at. But he stuck to his stance like his hero and fellow Tennessean, and fellow staunch Unionist, Andy Jackson. Andrew Johnson achieved national attention as the only Senator from a Confederate state to remain in the federal Congress.

An appreciative President Lincoln made him Military Governor of Tennessee. A stern ruler, Johnson closed pro-rebel newspapers and demanded loyalty oaths from suspect citizens. Although he persuaded Lincoln to exempt his state from the Emancipation Proclamation, as war-time governor he gave up his stand against abolition. "If the institution of slavery…seeks to overthrow" the Government, Johnson stated, "then the Government has a clear right to destroy it". The war-time governor had a hand in recruiting thousands of black soldiers for the Union Army. The Confederacy for its part seized Johnson's slaves and land.

In 1862, Congress passed what had been his signature issue, the Homestead Bill, which provided 160 acres and a mule for any ploughman willing to strap on a harness. Southern Senators, fearing the legislation would encourage Free Soilers, had blocked the measure in the pre-war years.

As noted, President Lincoln faced a rough 1864 re-election. He ran with Johnson as his new vice-presidential candidate, an appeal to moderate Unionists and to the border states. Gov. Johnson aided the Lincoln campaign in Tennessee by tightening the loyalty oath, which denied the vote for some supporters of Democratic candidate McClellan.

Noted for his oratorical gifts while a Tennessee lawmaker, Johnson's rhetoric would land him in deep trouble as a Washington politician. This became noticeable at Lincoln's second inauguration, on March 4, 1865, after he'd gotten drunk at festivities the night before. On inaugural morning, a hungover Johnson asked outgoing Vice-President Hamlin for whiskey, noting, "I need all the strength for the occasion". Before Lincoln made his famous address offering "malice toward none, with charity for all", Johnson gave a meandering, incoherent talk, as the President and mortified guests looked on. Lincoln later offered: "I have known Andy Johnson for many years; he made a bad slip the other day, but you need not be scared; Andy ain't a drunkard." Embarrassed himself, the new Vice-President went into seclusion for weeks with Francis Preston Blair, Sr., President Jackson's former advisor.

A PRESIDENT VERSUS A PARTY

Instead of a term with Lincoln potentially moving toward compromise, "with malice toward none" to hopefully "heal the nation's wounds", four years of gridlock and governmental crisis ensued. And the impeachment, and near ouster, of a President.

After Lincoln's death on April 15, Johnson retained his predecessor's Cabinet. Close consultation with the Cabinet, and with Congress, might have seemed prudent for an unelected, minority-party President from a region that was still in bloody revolt. Especially given the anger in the North about the murder of the President. But with the House and Senate out of session from March until December, Johnson declined to call the legislature back to Washington. After the war ended in May, he made policy on his own, contradicting the views of many in Congress.

Indeed, the new President turned out to have views diametrically opposed to Radical Republican leaders. He acted like a representative of Southern and border-state interests, enraging the Radicals, as well as many moderate Republicans and independents, who were convinced the war's bloody sacrifices cried out for dramatic change in the former Confederacy.

In contrast, Johnson took a lenient approach to the South that Lincoln had sometimes advocated. He granted amnesties and pardons for many former rebels. He directed the ex-Confederate states to swiftly hold conventions to pass new state constitutions. Although these assemblies abolished slavery at the state level, they did not guarantee the voting or other civic rights of the freedmen. Meanwhile, many Southern states passed the so-called Black Codes, laws which curbed the ability of African-Americans to work, travel, or vote freely.

Johnson, along with his advisor and Secretary of State, Seward, believed the states should continue to determine their own voting rules. They had done this in the past, in both North and South, with both regions often blocking black suffrage. Indeed, in 1865 several states in the far North, Minnesota and Wisconsin, moved to restrict African-American voting.

Johnson would have permitted the restructured Southern governments, largely administered by former Confederates, to reenter the Union, and would have allowed their newly elected federal officials to reenter Congress. Among those elected to the Senate were Georgia's Alexander Stephens, the former

Confederate Vice-President and vocal advocate of white supremacy. Many Unionists were enraged, and pondered whether they'd taken up their terrible swift sword in vain.

In fact, after Congress finally went back into session late in 1865, it refused to seat the new Southern legislators. It also moved on the ex-slaves. Moderate Republican Sen. Lyman Trumbull of Illinois proposed an extension of the Freedmen's Bureau, a favorite federal agency of the Radical Republicans. It offered schooling to blacks, and set wages for the many former slaves still laboring on plantations. In February 1866, President Johnson vetoed the bill, which he saw as a costly federal overreach, and one favoring blacks over whites. Congress failed to override the veto.

Four days later at the White House, the President made off-the-cuff remarks to supporters that equated his Radical Republican foes to the war-time leaders of the Confederacy. He stated that "there were two parties, one for destroying the Government to preserve slavery, and the other to break up the Government to destroy slavery." He threw fuel on the fire by claiming the Radicals were plotting against his life: "I have no doubt the intention was to incite assassination". Further, he explicitly called out the supposed plotters: radical leader Sen. Sumner, an abolitionist who'd been almost beaten to death by a Southern congressman in a precipitating incident of the war; Wendell Phillips, another prominent Massachusetts abolitionist; and Pennsylvania Rep. Thaddeus Stevens, the war-time Chairman of the Ways and Means Committee, and a fierce advocate of redistributing Southern plantations to Unionists and freedmen. Most Republicans, and many Democrats, were astonished and angered at the President's remarks.

The next month, in March 1866, Johnson vetoed the Trumbull-sponsored Civil Rights Act. Intended for the former slaves, it would have granted citizenship, and full civic rights "to every race and color" in order to "make and enforce contracts, to sue, be parties, and give evidence" in courts.

But the President saw the Act as an infringement on state prerogatives. Especially as the 11 former Confederate states had yet to return any representatives to the federal Congress to vote on such a far-reaching piece of legislation. Johnson also viewed the Act as discriminatory against whites, stating the "distinction of race and color is by the bill made to operate in favor of the colored and against the white race", and that colored persons were "less informed as to the nature and character of our institutions".

Within a month, Congress overrode his veto. This was the first time in American history the House and Senate had overridden a presidential veto of a major piece of legislation. A riled House and Senate followed up by passing, against Johnson's opposition, the 14th Amendment. It declared citizens all native-born or naturalized Americans, and guaranteed them due process and equal protection of the laws. It also barred from federal office former Confederate officials, and blocked compensation to former slaveholders for their freed slaves. To the President's chagrin, after Tennessee backed the 14th Amendment, Congress seated its congressional delegation. The House and Senate then approved the Freedmen's Bureau again, and this time overrode Johnson's veto of it.

Meantime, Johnson was losing members of his own government who refused to go along with his policies. In 1866 three of his Cabinet members would quit: Attorney General James Speed of Kentucky, a proponent of African-American suffrage; Postmaster General William Dennison, Jr., a former Governor of Ohio; and Interior Secretary James Harlan, a former Free Soiler from Iowa.

A MIDTERM MISTAKE

President Johnson likely aimed to build a coalition of Southerners and moderate Northerners for his own re-election effort in 1868. He decided to personally campaign against the Radical Republicans before the midterm elections of autumn 1866. His campaign tour of August and September, dubbed the "Swing Around the Circle", traveled north to New York, then westward to Chicago, St. Louis, and other towns, then headed back through the valley of the Ohio River. The President was accompanied by war heroes such as General of the Army Grant and cavalry commander Col. George Armstrong Custer, later the doomed Indian fighter, and by Seward and Navy Secretary Welles. For their own electoral purposes, Radicals in the North were eager to thwart the President's trip. They hoped to build a coalition with blacks in the South to ensure the election of Republicans in that region.

The barnstorming was undone by hecklers planted by political foes and by Johnson losing control of his own rhetoric. The President's handlers urged him to stay on script, but he made impromptu, controversial remarks. In Cleveland, when a heckler shouted, "Hang Jeff Davis!", the President retorted: "Why don't you hang Thad Stevens and Wendell Phillips?!" When backers told Johnson such language was beneath his dignity, he muttered audibly, "I don't care about my dignity."

In other towns, irate crowds shouted the President down, and cheered Grant. In St. Louis, Johnson blamed Radical Republicans for the New Orleans riot that July that had killed scores of blacks. Further, Johnson alienated members of his own government by threatening to dismiss dissenting Cabinet members. At an Indianapolis stop, supporters and opponents of the presidential speaker rioted, killing one. The trip's bad fortune culminated in disaster at Johnstown, Pennsylvania, where a railroad bridgeway affording a view of the presidential train gave way, killing at least three and injuring at least 350.

The press vilified the presidential journey. The pro-Johnson *New York Herald* huffed that it was "mortifying to see a man occupying the lofty position of President...descend from that position and join issue with those... draggling their garments in the muddy gutters of political vituperation." An up-and-coming New York City political cartoonist, Thomas Nast, originally from the German Rhineland, lampooned Johnson as a sour Iago betraying a noble African-American Othello. Sen. Sumner retorted that the "President must be taught that usurpation and apostasy cannot prevail". Even Johnson's sympathizers down South were dismayed. Former Georgia Gov. Herschel Johnson, Stephen Douglas' Democratic running mate in 1860, stated the President had undermined "the moral power of his position".

The campaign tour against Congress backfired at the polls that autumn. The Republicans, led by Radical candidates, ended up with massive majorities in both houses. In the House of Representatives, the Republicans picked up 38 seats overall, for a more than 3-to-1 majority of 175-47. In the Senate elections of 1866-1867, the G.O.P. gained two seats for a 39-10 margin, along with three seats from Unionist parties. At this time 10 Southern states had not been formally readmitted into the Union, and did not vote in the election.

The President had badly miscalculated sentiment in the North toward treatment of the post-war South, and was burned politically and personally. Despite his long-time membership in Congress, his relationship with that body had turned to naught within a year of entering the White House. He and Congress would remain at dagger points for the balance of his term.

A PATH TO IMPEACHMENT

When suffering losses in a midterm election, most Presidents will "move to the center", and turn toward the direction of their political foes. But Johnson refused compromise, with his own party.

He may have thought the political tide would turn his way. In 1867, the Northern states of Connecticut, Ohio, and Minnesota voted down suffrage for blacks. The border states of Delaware, Maryland, and Kentucky spurned the 14th Amendment, as did every Southern state except Tennessee. As the President Grant chapter will show, the tide would eventually turn in Johnson's direction, but only after he had departed the White House for some years.

At this time, however, Congress kept punching back, as the President endured the worst legislative sessions for a Chief Executive in U.S. history. In early 1867, Rep. Thad Stevens—one of the Radicals whom the President had flippantly suggested had been plotting his assassination—took vengeance. He and his allies proposed, and Congress approved, sweeping legislation that overturned the new Southern state governments. The law further directed the Southerners to establish new state constitutions that blocked ex-Confederates from voting, while giving the freedmen the vote. Most significantly, the bill also divided the South into five districts run by military governors wielding martial law. And the military governments were to be appointed by Congress, not the Commander-in-Chief. Congress added a provision that, as a condition of re-entering the Union, each Southern state had to ratify the 14th Amendment.

A besieged and politically weakened President Johnson finally attempted compromise. He proposed an alternative bill that would grant voting rights to former Confederates and a measure of suffrage for blacks. But by then his clout had markedly diminished. Congress ignored his measure and approved its own. As it did this late in the legislative session, Johnson could have pocket-vetoed the bill, as Lincoln had done with the Wade-Davis Bill. Instead, on March 2, he decided to veto it outright—and Congress overrode his veto.

Johnson met with another stinging defeat that very same day, as Congress passed a law that would trigger his impeachment the following year. This was the Tenure of Office Act, which forbade the President from dismissing Cabinet members without Senate approval. It was likely unconstitutional, and meant to tie Johnson's hands, and he vetoed it. But Congress overrode this veto as well.

The President's legislative losses snowballed. In January 1867, Congress had overridden another of Johnson vetoes to grant black suffrage in the District of Columbia. In March, Congress overrode a veto to grant statehood to the Territory of Nebraska, paving the way for its Republican congressional delegation. Also in March, Johnson's veto pen temporarily denied statehood to the Colorado Territory, with its similar political complexion.

Congress so disliked the Chief Executive at this point, in spring 1867, that it began its first, failed effort at impeachment. It looked into the President's financial accounts, and found nothing untoward. It investigated whether he had a hand in a federal court's release on bail of Jefferson Davis, and learned he had not. A bipartisan vote threw out the impeachment allegations.

But the real donnybrook between Congress and the President occurred in the wake of the Stevens bill—over who should control the military governments acting with broad authority in the post-bellum South. In summer 1867, Congress passed a Reconstruction Act over yet another futile Johnson veto. It firmly put the Army and its military district generals, not the President, in control of the Southern states. Johnson saw this as an unconstitutional slap at his authority as Commander-in-Chief.

Now the President punched back, hard. After Congress had gone into summer recess, Johnson removed from the Texas and Louisiana military district the Army chief there, Gen. Philip Sheridan, the war-time cavalry hero, and a tough enforcer of Reconstruction. This upset Sheridan's colleague Grant, the commanding General of the Army. More significantly, in August Johnson tried to fire Secretary of War Stanton, a Radical sympathizer. The President then suspended him when Stanton, using the Tenure in Office Act as a rational, refused to vacate his job. Grant reluctantly became acting Secretary of War.

In fall 1867 there were no midterm elections. But in local elections the Democrats did well, reflecting unease over Reconstruction, a slow economy, and black suffrage in the North. Connecticut and Ohio refused voting rights for blacks. Democrats took control of the Ohio legislature, which choose the state's U.S. Senators, which meant Radical stalwart and Ohioan Sen. Wade could not win in his re-election year of 1868. There seemed a glimmer of political hope for the President.

Some on Capitol Hill, however, figured it was time for another counter-attack. In December 1867, Congress looked into impeaching Johnson for a second time. Yet after failing to find hard evidence of any "high Crimes and Misdemeanors", a House resolution to impeach was voted down, 57-108.

IMPEACHABLE OFFENSES

Congress then moved a third time toward impeachment, over the Stanton affair. In January 1868, Congress reinstated the suspended War Secretary, prompting Johnson to finally fire and replace him—despite Stanton barricading himself in his office, and having his replacement arrested!

Most of the House and Senate thought the dismissal a violation of the Tenure of Office Act, and grounds for impeachment. Some disagreed, noting the Act should apply to officials the current President appoints, and that Lincoln had originally hired Stanton. One impeachment article, later dropped, took a shot at Johnson's excessive rhetoric, stating the President did: "declare, with a loud voice certain intemperate, inflammatory, and scandalous harangues, and therein utter loud threats and bitter menaces…amid the cries, jeers and laughter of the multitudes then assembled in hearing".

The House managers of the impeachment proceedings were the Radical Rep. Stevens, who Johnson had accused of planning his assassination; Massachusetts Rep. George Boutwell, Lincoln's Commissioner of Internal Revenue and a framer of the 14th Amendment; and Massachusetts Rep. Benjamin Franklin Butler, who as a war-time general had run the Union Army's stern and sometimes corrupt occupation of New Orleans.

In February 1868, the House did impeach Johnson, by a vote of 126-47. Facing possible ouster by the Senate, the President again belatedly tried compromise. He promised moderate, Midwest Senators more sympathetic to his acquittal that he'd let the Radicals have a freer hand in Reconstruction. And he pledged to replace Stanton with a War Secretary amenable to the Republican Congress.

Chief Justice Chase presided over Johnson's subsequent Senate trial. The tribunal took place from March to May, and usually in open session before a packed gallery of spectators. As Chief Justice Marshall had done during the Burr treason trial, Chase ran the proceedings by the letter of the law, keeping the politics of it at bay. This helped President Johnson. Sen. Wade, now a lame duck, tried to gain two additional pro-impeachment votes by admitting the Colorado territory as a state, but couldn't secure enough votes.

Heading the President's defense team was Johnson's Attorney General, Henry Stanbery of Ohio, who resigned his post to argue the case. (His brother in 1832 had won a civil suit against Sam Houston for assaulting him with a hickory cane near the Capitol.) Another of Johnson's lawyers was former Supreme Court Justice Benjamin Curtis, who had resigned in 1857 over the Dred Scott decision. On his attorneys' advice, Johnson did not testify.

On May 16, 1868, the President survived the effort to remove him by a single ballot, by a vote of 35-19. The Senate then adjourned for 10 days. The Radicals hoped some lawmakers might in the interval switch their votes against the President. However, in the second vote, Johnson again survived, barely, again by 35-19.

The pivotal Nay votes were by moderate, Western-state Republicans. "I cannot agree," stated Iowa Sen. James Grimes, "to destroy the harmonious working of the Constitution, for the sake of getting rid of an Unacceptable President." The Radicals may have offered several of these Senators bribes or high government posts to flip their votes, but any such offers were declined.

Meanwhile Gen. Grant, popular throughout the Republican Party, was moving toward a presidential bid, and was the favorite the win the 1868 election. With Grant waiting in the wings, some Republican Senators voted against the President's ouster, by reasoning it was tolerable to let the President serve out the rest of his term, powerless and in impeached disgrace. Then a President Grant could become the 'true successor' to Lincoln. It was expected he would affect a sterner yet fair Reconstruction.

Another consideration was that the person next in line to be President—as President Johnson had no Vice President—was the president pro tempore of the Senate, Sen. Wade. The fact that Wade was leading the charge for impeachment was seen by some Senators as an unseemly conflict of interest. In addition, some distrusted Wade for his then-radical positions on behalf of women's suffrage, distribution of wealth, and trade unions.

In any case, Andrew Johnson was finished politically for the final 10 months of his presidency. He became the lamest of lame-duck Chief Executives. Except for Richard Nixon, never has a President been treated so hard.

His lone accomplishments were in foreign policy, through his loyal Secretary of State, Seward. In 1866 Seward had convinced the President to use persuasion, not force, in a dispute with France over its attempt to install the Austrian archduke Maximilian as the monarch of Mexico. The following year, France, facing a bloody insurrection there, withdrew its soldiers. Also in 1867, Secretary Seward acquired Alaska from Russia for $7.2 million ($119 million in 2015 dollars), a "folly" turned a fortune down the road.

HIS SUCCESSOR'S ELECTION, AND HIS FINAL YEARS

The 1868 election turned out surprisingly close. Grant won, but by a somewhat narrow popular vote margin of 53 percent to 47 percent, against Democratic nominee Horatio Seymour, the former Governor of New York. Although benefitting from some of the Southern states still being under federal occupation, and thus unable to vote, Grant was hurt by a number of scandals among his associates, a situation that would continue in his presidency. Part of the election's context was the poor economic performance of the Johnson years. Economic growth stagnated during his presidency.

Reflecting the close presidential race, and unease over how to handle Reconstruction, the Democrats did fairly well in the congressional elections. In the House, they picked up 20 seats, while the Republicans lost four seats, with the latter retaining a 171-67 margin. (The pro-Southern Conservative Party won three seats.)

In the Senate elections taking place in 1868 and 1869, however, the Republicans had major gains. Six formerly Confederate states rejoined the Union and, under Reconstruction, they all elected Republican Senators. Overall, the G.O.P. added 17 seats, including all 12 seats from the newly readmitted states, while the Democrats added five seats. The Republicans gained a huge 57-9 majority.

After leaving the White House under a cloud, Johnson returned home to Tennessee. There he failed in bids to win election to the U.S. Senate and the House.

During Grant's re-election campaign in 1872, Andrew Johnson endorsed the presidential nominee of the Democratic Party, publisher Horace Greeley of New York City. Greeley was also the nominee of the Liberal Republican Party that split off from the G.O.P. Both publisher and party opposed the Radical Republicans' strict Reconstruction. To no avail, as Grant easily beat Greeley.

Johnson's third effort at the Senate did gain him a seat in 1875. A Republican newspaper called his comeback "the most magnificent personal triumph which the history of American politics can show". As Reconstruction fell apart in the South, it almost seemed like he had been ahead of his time politically. But he died of a heart attack the year he took office.

In summary, Andrew Johnson was forced by cruel fate to take the place of Abraham Lincoln. He held views that clashed with the dominant Republican party and nation—at a time when emotions were still red-raw from the War Between the States. He poorly ran his 1866 midterm election tour, and his candidates got clobbered in that election. Further, he was inept at handling relations with Congress and within his Administration.

He compromised with Congress on Reconstruction far too late, after he had been impeached. He faced the misfortune of strident political enemies who sought to eject him from the White House. The House impeached him, and the Senate failed to oust him by only a single vote.

Johnson spent his final months as President stripped of clout. He had no chance of being renominated for another White House run. He was succeeded by a political rival, Gen. Grant, who would have a very different approach to Reconstruction and to federal power and states' rights.

President Johnson fell hard in trying to successfully fill out the remainder of Lincoln's second term.

ILLUSTRATIONS

President George Washington, left, in Masonic attire, laying the cornerstone of the U.S. Capitol Building. After Washington's first term helped establish the federal government, his second was marked by deep political divisions.

Jefferson's unpopular Embargo Act led to satires like this cartoon, where
the ban on foreign trade is depicted as a slow-moving turtle unable
to stop smugglers. Embargo spelled backwards is "Ograbme".

The Americans rallied late in the War of 1812, improving President Madison's public standing. The scholar-President was depicted as a bare-knuckled boxer bloodying "John Bull", the symbol of England and the British crown.

President Monroe, standing, presides over an 1823 Cabinet gathering.
Monroe's choice of advisors and envoys was generally excellent.

GENERAL JACKSON SLAYING THE MANY HEADED MONSTER.

President Jackson, left, slaying the multi-headed monster of the
Second Bank of the United States. Even controversial actions
like the Bank closure did not hurt Jackson politically.

Lincoln and the Union Army, besieged by anti-war "Copperhead" snakes and by fleeing slaves. President Lincoln had to deal with vexing problems of war, emancipation, and pro-South sentiment in the North.

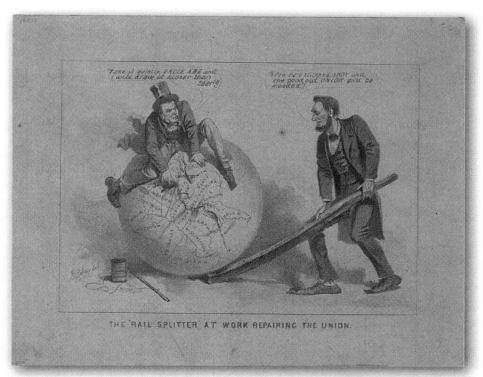

Vice-President Johnson is portrayed as aiding President Lincoln, "the rail splitter", in trying to put back together the cracked Union. After Lincoln's assassination, President Johnson's troubled Administration led to his impeachment by Congress.

Gritty equestrian statue of Grant at the U.S. Capitol. U.S. Grant performed better as a military leader than as a civilian President. Scandals and the intractable woes of Reconstruction plagued his government.

In winning his first term of office, Grover Cleveland overcame charges of fathering an out-of-wedlock child. As well as opponents' campaign cries of, "Ma ma, where's my Pa?" But his second term was wracked by a severe recession.

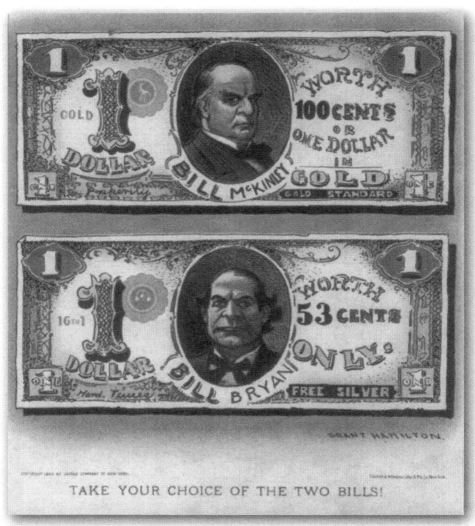

TAKE YOUR CHOICE OF THE TWO BILLS!

This cartoon contrasted William McKinley's backing of a gold standard with rival William Jennings Bryan's support for a less-valuable, silver-backed currency. After a successful first term, McKinley fell to an assassin at the start of his second.

THE BIG STICK IN THE CARIBBEAN SEA

Theodore Roosevelt's "Big Stick" diplomacy is satirically displayed as transforming the Caribbean into the President's private pond. Still, TR was generally well-regarded for his foreign and domestic policies.

BRAVE MAN, BAD ADVISORS
ULYSSES S. GRANT, 1873-1877

In 1869, America placed in the White House a military hero who embodied the nation's pro-Union beliefs. The Civil War had resurrected Hiram Ulysses S. Grant, originally from Point Pleasant, Ohio, a man who thrived in conflict as he was apt to struggle in peace.

Born in 1822, Grant had antecedents reaching back to the Puritans' Massachusetts colony and the Revolution's Battle of Bunker Hill. He attended West Point and, like George Washington, was acclaimed as the finest equestrian of his day. He became a hero of the Mexican-American War, once carrying vital messages through enemy streets, like a scene in a Wild West film, by riding dangled on the side of his horse. Afterwards, he'd been dismissed from the peace-time Army for drinking. In those quiet times, he plunged into a series of failed business ventures.

When the War Between the States broke out, Grant quickly proved a skilled commander in the battles for Tennessee; President Lincoln admired him for his aggressiveness. In the West, he won in 1863 the decisive battle at Vicksburg, Mississippi. The President made him the Commanding General of the Union Army. In the East, after many bloody stalemates, he vanquished Lee's redoubtable Confederate Army of Northern Virginia, forcing the South's 1865 surrender at Appomattox, Virginia.

Gen. Grant excelled in mobile combat, but had less success with direct assaults. Statesman Grant proved a solid vote getter, yet had trouble as a sitting President.

POST-BELLUM CONVENTIONS

During the election year of 1868, the ambitious Grant was widely expected to win the White House. The unpopular President Johnson had been impeached, and Grant, still the Army's commander, had been one of his foils.

At first, Grant had been supportive of Johnson's restrained view of Reconstruction, the federal government's attempt to reshape the politics of white and black, and rebel and loyalist, in the defeated South. Grant then moved steadily toward the stance of the Radical Republicans.

Against the President's wishes, Grant backed Congress' division of the South into military districts, each run by a federal Army general. In Louisiana, he lent support to one of those generals, his former cavalry chief Philip Sheridan. Johnson sacked Sheridan for ousting the state's Governor and Attorney General over anti-black riots, and for defending the election of black officials while limiting the franchise for whites. Grant had also opposed Johnson's effort to replace Secretary of War Stanton. Moreover, Grant, fearing the President was encouraging renewed rebellion, had ordered arsenals in Southern states transferred to the North to deny them to insurrectionists.

In May 1868, the Republican convention in Chicago, Illinois, the home state of Lincoln, unanimously selected Grant as its nominee. His running mate was House Speaker Schuyler Colfax, a Radical Republican from Indiana who beat out fellow Radical Sen. Benjamin Wade. The latter had co-authored the 1864 Wade-Davis Bill that President Lincoln had vetoed as overly harsh toward the South.

With memories of the Civil War still sharp, the ticket dripped military heritage: Grant, formerly the Union Army's chief; and Colfax, grandson of a member of George Washington's guard, and a descendant of Revolutionary War Gen. Philip Schuyler. Grant was 46 years old, and Colfax just 45. Grant was the youngest President until John F. Kennedy, age 43 when elected; and he and Colfax were the most youthful President and Vice-President until Bill Clinton and Albert Gore, Jr. in 1993.

Still, the 1868 election proved surprisingly close, and indicated that Grant would preside over a nation still far from united. The Democrats, bouncing back from the crushing defeat of the Confederacy, and their base in the Southern states, put together a powerful ticket. It had considerable appeal to a country weary of war, wary of the speedy enfranchisement of the newly freed slaves, and tired of the long governmental gridlock of the Johnson Administration and Congress.

The Democratic convention was held at New York City's Tammany Hall, with its Democratic Party machine. After 22 ballots, it chose by acclamation Horatio Seymour, the former war-time Governor of New York, the nation's most populous state. Seymour had been pro-Union, but as Governor had made statements supporting the largely Irish immigrant crowds that rioted against Civil War conscription.

His running mate was Francis Preston Blair, Jr., from the swing state of Missouri, a scene of bitter strife between pro- and anti-slave forces before and during the war. Blair was the son of President Andrew Jackson's chief advisor (and friend to President Andrew Johnson), and the brother of Lincoln's Postmaster General, Montgomery Blair. He represented the still-stark divisions in his party, and his country, over Reconstruction and race.

The younger Blair been an ardent foe of secession, and a Union General who'd ably served with Grant and Sherman at Vicksburg, and with Sherman in Georgia. However, he despised Radical Reconstruction. A vocal opponent of full civil rights for blacks, Blair inveighed against "a semi-barbarous race of blacks who are worshipers of fetishes and poligamists", desiring to "subject the white women to their unbridled lust." In their own campaign, the Republicans pledged to enforce Reconstruction and pay down the war debt.

A SURPRISINGLY TIGHT ELECTION

That November, Grant won the electoral vote 214-80, but took the popular vote by only 53 percent to 47 percent. He carried New England and the Midwest, and most Southern states. However, the latter voted under laws that disenfranchised many whites who'd served in the Confederate Army, while permitting many blacks to vote in their first presidential election. The former were embittered as the latter were ecstatic, with trouble to come. Virginia, Mississippi, and Texas hadn't been admitted back into the Union yet, and so didn't vote at all.

Gov. Seymour took his home state of New York and adjoining New Jersey, and the Southern states of Georgia and Louisiana, which were wracked by anti-black violence. By huge margins he carried the border states of Kentucky and Maryland. Republicans were so angry at losing vote-rich New York that they held a congressional inquiry into the balloting there.

Some voters were uneasy with the G.O.P.'s call for full and immediate black suffrage in the South, including former, uneducated slaves, while puzzled at the contradiction of letting Northern states decide that issue for themselves. In fact, in 1867 Rutherford Birchard Hayes, the future President, had almost lost the race for the Ohio governorship, after backing a doomed amendment to guarantee the vote to Ohio's African-Americans.

The Republicans also helped the Democrats reestablish their political base among farmers and workers. They achieved this through their "hard money" approach of using only gold, and not "greenbacks" or dollar currency, to pay off the large federal debt from the war. (The national debt had soared from $65 million in 1860 to $2.6 billion in 1865). Democrats favored a soft-money approach aimed at aiding those of lesser means during times of economic distress.

Further, the Democrats did well among immigrant voters in Northern cities. The newcomers were put off by the anti-immigrant Know-Nothing Party that had been allied with the Republicans, as well as the Republicans' support for the masses of free and newly free blacks working for relatively low wages.

In the congressional elections, the Democrats did relatively well in the House, although the G.O.P. retained a substantial margin. The Republicans did very well in the Senate races, heightening their already huge majority.

The relatively close White House election seemed shocking, coming just three years after the Confederacy's defeat. If the three Southern states kept out of the vote—and disenfranchised, white voters in Southern states had been permitted to vote—the party of Jefferson Davis might very well have won the first post-Civil War election.

It was a presage of sorts. President Grant's first, and second, terms would be ones of turmoil—marked by an attempted and eventually failed Radical Reconstruction of the South. His stay in office would also be scarred by myriad scandals, in part a product of the triumphant, and unrestrained, industrialists of the North.

REGIONAL RECONSTRUCTION

The new President faced a Southland still wracked by civil strife. The voting rights of many Confederate veterans had been suspended. Whites were trying through intimidation and violence to prevent blacks and Republicans from voting or holding office. Further, Southern states had put into effect Black Codes. Under these statutes, blacks could be fined for traveling out of state, or jailed for being out of work, thus pressuring many to continue to work on plantations. The Codes were a kind of throwback to the antebellum laws that had ended hope for a gradual elimination of slavery.

In 1870, President Grant responded by backing Congressional passage of the 15th Amendment, which forbade states or the federal government from blocking the right to vote due to "race, color, or previous condition of servitude." Also that year, Grant set up the new Justice Department, led by the existing Office of the Attorney General, with its chief role the enforcement of Reconstruction. The President firmly applied the voting rights laws, while backing the Freedman's Bureau that offered some education and economic aid to former slaves.

Grant further threw his weight behind the powerful Enforcement Acts, approved by Congress in 1870 and 1871. Along with enabling the federal government to supervise elections in the South, they permitted the President to deploy federal troops against those depriving Americans of civil liberties, or engaging in armed rebellion. Moreover, the Acts enabled citizens deprived of their rights to sue in court.

The Acts targeted the secretive vigilante group the Ku Klux Klan, which was attempting through lynching and burnings to reassert all-white rule in the South. The new laws enacted civil damages or jail time on those "going on the highway in disguise to deprive others of the exercise of constitutional rights".

These laws were aimed at protecting rights granted under the three "Freedom Amendments" to the Constitution. Along with the Fifteenth Amendment, these were the Thirteenth Amendment of 1865, which abolished slavery, and the Fourteenth Amendment of 1868, which guaranteed due process and equal protection under the law.

As a result, for the first time many black legislators took seats in Southern legislatures. However, the Administration undermined its moral clarity and political position somewhat as Northern states decided for themselves on whether to allow black suffrage.

As Lincoln had done, and also under the Enforcement Acts, Grant suspended habeas corpus, the legal requirement that authorities must produce evidence to detain a suspect. The President put aside this legal dictum in nine counties of South Carolina where whites were violently attacking black voters.

Further, the President deployed federal troops and squads of lawyers against the Klan. In a preview of somewhat similar federal actions in the 1960s, thousands of Klansmen were indicted, jailed, or sent into flight. Leading the charge on much of this were Benjamin Bristow, the first U.S. Solicitor General, and later Treasury Secretary. Seeking color-blind justice, Bristow urged that blacks be allowed to testify in court in mixed-race cases.

Bristow's superior was the resolute Attorney General Amos T. Ackerman. Originally from New Hampshire, and later a slave owner in Georgia, Ackerman had opposed secession, then fought for the Confederacy as a colonel. He joined the Republican Party after Appomattox, convinced a recovering South had to embrace Reconstruction.

One of Ackerman's and Grant's toughest challenges came in Louisiana, which by 1872 was on the verge of its own civil war between rival Democratic and Republican militias. By threatening military force, the Administration quieted the two groups for most of that election year.

President Grant performed a balancing act. Critics said he was too harsh toward the South, and he risked losing the votes of Democrats and moderate Republicans in the North. In partial response, in 1872 Grant approved the Amnesty Act. It permitted some 150,000 former Confederate soldiers to again vote and hold office, privileges denied them since the war's conclusion. Restrictions were upheld for 500 former top-ranking Confederate Army officers. Also during this period, the President backed a small-scale, if rancorous, integration of the West Point military academy, with the enrollment of black cadet James Webster Smith of South Carolina.

Grant's first-term actions in the South were largely successful. But they would be largely undone in his second term.

SCANDALOUS BEHAVIORS RINGED BY GOLD

Over time, Grant's Reconstruction was undermined in four ways. The first, by fierce resistance to it in the South. The second, by the North growing weary of the matter. The third, by a severe economic bust. The fourth, by political scandals that eroded the President's political cachet. His Administration had a remarkable number of scandals, many of them committed by Grant intimates. The misbehaviors began from the start.

The mastermind of the first major flap, which penetrated to the President's family, was the crooked financier Jay Gould of New York. Gould had started out as a speculator who bought up leather goods businesses and railroads in distress. Later he moved on to manipulate and control railway and financial concerns. He had cheated tycoon Cornelius Vanderbilt out of control of the New York's Erie Railroad, then put New York City's corrupt Boss Tweed on the company board. This "Mephistopheles of Wall Street" had a character, according to writer Henry Adams, which resembled "a family of spiders. He spun huge webs in the dark."

In 1869 Gould, a 19th-century Goldfinger, set his sights higher: control of the nation's gold supply. The fact that the entire value of the U.S. gold hoard was relatively small, about $20 million ($380 million in 2015 dollars), made manipulation of it tempting.

Gould had partnered up with a famed conniver, James "Diamond Jim" Fisk. The duo bought off Abel Corbin, a former government officer who was married to President Grant's sister, Jennie Corbin. In exchange for $1.5 million in gold, Abel Corbin helped make former Union General Daniel Butterfield, based in New York, the assistant secretary of the Treasury Department. Butterfield was himself pledged $1.5 million and a loan, in return for keeping track of the government's gold transactions in the nation's financial center.

Gould, Fisk, and Corbin then met Grant at a number of social occasions, and convinced him to hold off on any intent his government might have to sell gold, which would lower the value of the metal. They argued that a high gold price would help American's farmers, by keeping the price of commodities like wheat and cotton high. Gould and Fisk also knew high prices would hike the value of the crops transported by their Erie Railroad. The President, already a gold "hawk" who believed in keeping gold high and the dollar strong, was persuaded.

Meantime Gould and his "Gold Ring" began snapping up gold, with Fisk alone buying $7 million worth. The price of it steadily rose, from an August 1869 price of $100 to over $140. But Corbin overplayed his hand.

He was anxious to ensure the Treasury Department of his presidential in-law stayed out of the gold market. His wife wrote her sister-in-law, First Lady Julia Grant, about his concerns. When the President found the missive, he realized he'd been had. Furious, he met with his able and honest Treasury Secretary, George Boutwell, on Friday, September 24. A former Governor of Massachusetts, Boutwell had been Lincoln's Commissioner of Internal Revenue, and had reformed the Treasury Department after the disruptions of the Civil War, as well as having been one of the Senate managers of President Johnson's impeachment.

That day, "Black Friday" in Wall Street lore, rumors ran wild as the gold price shot up from $144.50 to $160. But in Washington, D.C., Grant and

Boutwell decided to smash the Gold Ring by quickly selling off $4 million in government bullion. They telegraphed their decision to the public and, as financiers realized the government's aim, the price abruptly dropped to $130. Gould, tipped off beforehand, sold off his stack of lucre and pocketed the profits.

But hundreds of speculators, many of whom had borrowed to buy gold, had nothing left to pay back their debts, and were ruined. The stock market fell by 20 percent. The price of farm commodities plummeted by about half, crippling many farmers. For months, the entire economy hurt, in the so-called Panic of 1869.

Congress launched an investigation. Rep. James Abram Garfield of Ohio, a former Union general and future President, was chairman of the House Banking Committee heading up the inquiry. Under fire, Butterfield quit the Treasury. But Congress declined to have Corbin or the First Family testify.

Gould and Fisk hired a battery of lawyers, and avoided jail. Three years later, Fisk was shot dead by a blackmailer in cahoots with his mistress. But his colleague Gould made at least $10 million through the Gold Ring. He went on to control the Union Pacific railroad of transcontinental railway fame, as well as the most important telecommunications firm of the era, Western Union Telegraph. Butterfield, after leaving government, became an executive at American Express, at the time a pony express mailing firm and, later, the credit card giant.

To author Henry Adams, great-grandson of the upright John and Abigail Adams, an "Era of Good Stealings" was underway.

The scandals were numerous enough to require a scorecard. Here's a list of some major Grant Administrations misdoings:

* The Gold Ring, attempt to corner gold market, 1869
* Western Trading Posts, contract overcharges, 1870, revealed in 1876
* Customs Houses, kickbacks, 1872

* Crédit Mobilier, railroad payoffs, 1868 and prior, revealed in 1872
* Revenue Collection, rake-offs, 1872 and 1874
* Whiskey Ring, tax evasion, 1875
* Navy Department, payoffs, 1876

MALFEASANCE IN THE WILD WEST

Out on the Western border, another scandal, which wouldn't come to light until years later, took form in 1870. William Belknap of Iowa had been a notably brave officer, and eventually a major general, in the Civil War. At the battle of Atlanta, he'd captured a Confederate colonel in Southern lines, then hauled him over ramparts back to the Union position. President Johnson appointed Belknap the Iowa Collector of Internal Revenue, and Grant made him his Secretary of War. In his new post, however, he focused too much on collecting revenue for personal gain.

Belknap persuaded Congress to grant him the authority to pick the civilian heads of the lucrative trading posts for the Army's frontier forts. In so doing Congress took the authority away from General of the Army William Sherman—Grant's, and Belknap's, old comrade-in-arms. In return for the appointments, Belknap took kickbacks. For one post, at Fort Sill, in modern-day Oklahoma, two men were appointed to the job, and Belknap and his wife got payoffs from both. Then when Belknap's wife died, he and his new wife, the sister of the deceased spouse, continued to receive payments, $6,000 a year.

Just as bad, Belknap granted monopolies to the trading posts. As a result, the posts charged exorbitant prices for their supplies. The post-war salaries of the soldiers weren't much, and the high prices impoverished many. And many of the things they bought, like guns, were shoddily made, such as breech-loading rifles prone to jamming. Further, the Indians that the soldiers sometimes had to fight were permitted to buy guns in the posts. And sometimes they were able to buy higher-quality weapons, such as repeating rifles, than the soldiers could purchase.

The trading post scandal continued throughout Grant's presidency, until Congress, as much for partisan reasons as for principle, spilled the beans in Grant's final year in office. In 1876, the House impeached Secretary of War Belknap over the matter. Testifying against him was a cavalry officer from the West, George Armstrong Custer. Grant was forced to accept Belknap's resignation. Although the Senate failed to convict him, he became, and remains, the only ex-Cabinet member impeached by the House of Representatives.

In his stead the President appointed Alphonso Taft of Ohio, who cleaned house, and directed local Army commanders to appoint the trading post managers. Taft was the progenitor of a sober Ohio political dynasty that yielded, early in the next century, President and Supreme Court Justice William Howard Taft and, in the mid-twentieth century, Senate Majority Leader Robert A. Taft.

STINGING DEFEAT IN HIS FIRST MIDTERM

Grant's party fared poorly in the congressional midterm elections of 1870-1871. With some Southern states leaving military control, and taking part again in federal elections, and with the Administration hit by scandals, the Democratic Party built on its relatively strong showing two years prior to stage a major comeback.

The Democrats seized 37 House seats, to narrow the gap in the House to 139-104. The Republicans lost big in Southern states regaining majority control of their political affairs. For instance, they dropped six seats in Tennessee and four in North Carolina. But the G.O.P. also did poorly in Northern states, losing three seats each in New Hampshire, Pennsylvania, and New York. The Empire State had been rocked by the financial woes stemming from the Gold Ring scandal.

The Republicans also lost out in the Senate, dropping six seats, one of them to the Liberal Republican Party, a G.O.P. split-off. The new faction decried the corruption in Grant's government. It also argued that federal intervention in the South should not have extended beyond the defeat of secession and the ending of slavery.

Still, the G.O.P. retained a more than 4-to-1 Senate majority, 58-14. And it could take solace in the fact the Democrats were bound to make some headway from their Civil War low point.

One Republican elected was the first African-American to Congress, an educator of mixed-race ancestry with the grand name of Reverend Hiram Rhodes Revels. At first a backer, and later a critic of Reconstruction, which he viewed as making blacks dependent on political patronage, the Mississippi Senator would later serve in that state's Democratic administrations.

UNCUSTOMARY BEHAVIOR

More Grant scandals emerged, in an era when most federal revenue came from the tariff. Vast customs houses had been set up in port cities to take in the excise tax. The most important was in lower Manhattan, the nation's busiest port and its biggest collector of revenue.

Under the spoils system prevalent since President Jackson, the local Republican political machine ran the customs house. The place had a staff of up to a thousand, and each worker was required to pay a part of his salary in political donations.

In 1871, the top job of Collector there was held by a G.O.P. lawyer, and future President, Chester Alan Arthur. Arthur was an able and generally honest man. However, like other officials in the port, he got most of his pay by "moiety"—by receiving a percentage of the fines levied on businesses found to have avoided or underpaid the tariff. This led to abuses by some officers who charged higher fines to pad their own income.

In 1872, the year of Grant's re-election campaign, congressional committees and the Treasury Department found that some merchant houses in New York were getting special treatment on imported goods stored at city warehouses. The favoritism resulted from bribing Administration officials in Washington. Charges of taking kickbacks were made against top aides to Grant, including his private secretary Orville Babcock, a Vermonter who in the Civil War had been a ranking officer and an aide-de-camp to General Grant.

Treasury Secretary Boutwell stopped the bribery and cut down on smuggling in Manhattan, while Congress ended the practice of moiety. The next Administration, under President Rutherford B. Hayes, slashed the number of patronage jobs. Throughout the reforms, however, Grant followed rather than led.

The Grant scandals, most of them financial ones, reflected in part the imbalance of political power that existed post-Civil War between the industrial North and the agrarian South and West. With the defeated South prostrate in defeat, the North's industrialists were unchecked.

Sometimes, the impact was good. Most spectacularly, with the abolition of slavery. Other times the effect was bad, as with the growing power of unscrupulous financiers such as Gould. As the South and the expanding West recovered or gained new political clout, one effect would be the rise of a populist movement aimed at curbing the power of Northeastern bankers. In a sense, the old Hamilton-Jefferson equilibrium among the different regions and sectors of the economy reasserted itself.

SUSPICIOUSLY MOBILE CREDIT

In 1872, the country was stunned by revelations about the Union Pacific railroad and its sister Crédit Mobilier firm. The scandal took place before Grant's presidency, but was closely linked to his party and the railroad and financial interests connected to it.

By 1864, construction had begun on the transcontinental railroad hooking the Midwest up to the West Coast. With the Southern states who had blocked it out of the Union, the Lincoln Administration offered mammoth subsidies to build it.

Seizing the opportunity was Thomas Durant, the head of the Union Pacific railroad, charged with building the half of the rail line running west, from Council Bluffs, Iowa to Promontory Summit in Utah. Durant, hailing from Massachusetts and formerly a surgeon, had become a railroad executive for the Mississippi and Missouri Railroad which built the first bridge over the Mississippi River. When a steamboat had run into the bridge in 1856, with the shipping company suing to demolish the span, Durant had hired none other than attorney Abraham Lincoln to successfully quash the suit. The Supreme Court had finally resolved the case in 1862, after Lincoln's election as President.

During the Civil War, Durant made a bundle by illegally selling Confederate cotton, or 'contra-bundles'. With the decline of the cotton industry due to the North's coastal blockade and military victory, the railroads became the nation's most profitable and largest industry.

As President, Lincoln was anxious to build the transcontinental railway, and tapped Union Pacific to build the eastern half of the line. But investors were less enthusiastic.

The rail to Utah would have to traverse over 1,700 miles of desert and mountain, areas subject to Indian attacks, where there were few settlers or paying customers. This was the Union Pacific of the Wild West, colorfully depicted by the recent television series "Hell on Wheels". The prospect of operating profits in a lawless frontier was scant.

So the Lincoln Administration supplied the rail line a giant helping hand: $100 million in capital, upwards of $60 million in loans, and up to $100 million worth of 20 million acres of grants of land through the territories the railroad would traverse. In all, roughly $4 billion in 2015 dollars. Each mile of rail constructed got an average of $32,000 in subsidies. It was Hamilton on steroids, and Jefferson in despair.

Previously, investors were personally liable for poor investments, and likely to lose their personal fortunes and wind up in debtors' prison if their bets failed. But Durant took advantage of the new limited liability laws. Now, someone making a bad investment only lost the investment, not his shirt or his personal liberty.

Durant also stacked the deck in favor of those investing in Union Pacific by setting up, with his aptly named business partner, George Francis Train, a shell company, called Crédit Mobilier. This company was supposedly an independent firm for building the railway. In fact, Durant and his partners secretly made up the operating board of Crédit Mobilier. They steered the federal subsidies to it, and pocketed the profits. The heads of Union Pacific paid themselves to build their own railroad, with the taxpayers taking all the risk.

The profits were even larger than might be expected from such a monopoly. Union Pacific, which was paid by the mile of track built, had Crédit Mobilier construct circular routes leading back to their points of origin, padding the revenues with unneeded tracks. Accountants cranked out invoices asking 200 percent over the norm for such work. As its engineers scratched their heads over the convoluted pathways, Union Pacific made $44 million in profits, while reporting only $23 million.

Union Pacific further greased the skids by handing in effect protection money to Congress. A co-director of Crédit Mobilier was Massachusetts Rep. Oakes Ames, brought in by Lincoln to make the railroad more efficient. On the contrary, Ames was corrupt and nepotistic, bringing in his brother Oliver Ames as director.

In 1868, Rep. Ames offered discounted stock in Crédit Mobilier to 13 members of Congress, all of whom were on committees charged with regulating the railroads and with granting any additional payments to Union Pacific. Almost all were Northern Republicans. Some of the congressmen gave the stock back, but the majority who did not reaped huge profits from the steeply rising price of their shares.

After *The New York Sun* newspaper exposed the scandal in 1872, a Justice Department inquiry found that 30 or more members of Congress might have been involved. Under suspicion were future President Garfield, then a Congressman, Massachusetts Sen. Henry Wilson, and Vice-President Colfax. The first two were cleared. Wilson wound up replacing Colfax as Grant's 1872 running mate.

Wilson had a tarnished past, though, and would have an unfortunate future. Back in 1861, he may have had an affair with famed Confederate spy "Rebel Rose" Greenough. Union officials had given her vital information bearing on the First Battle of Bull Run, the Civil War's first major fight, and a Union disaster. As Vice President in Grant's second term, he suffered a major heart attack in 1873, and a second, fatal one in November 1875. The office of Vice President remained vacant for the remainder of Grant's term. (There was then no Constitutional provision for replacing a Vice President who died in office.)

No one in Congress or the Administration was indicted or jailed over Crédit Mobilier. Congress merely censured Ames Oakes and another congressman. Oakes was branded with the moniker "Hoax Oakes".

After the boondoggle was revealed, and with its operating profit nil, Union Pacific veered on bankruptcy. Four years later, in 1876, Grant finally pressured Durant to leave Union Pacific. Taking over the company, at a steeply discounted price, was Jay Gould, the mastermind of the Gold Ring in Grant's initial year in office!

As in other scandals, the President himself did not profit. Indeed, the payoffs and money laundering took place mostly before he took office. But Crédit Mobilier tainted his political party, and tarred the President himself.

RE-ELECTION AGAINST A WEAK OPPONENT

U.S. Grant was popular enough, despite influence-peddling scandals among his associates, to win re-election in 1872. He was helped by a post-war boom that overcame the 1869 Panic. He stuck to his promise to pay down the large national debt from the war, which had grown 44-fold.

The government would steadily reduce its debt until the Spanish-American War of 1898. Like Presidents Jefferson and Monroe and their Treasury Secretary Gallatin in the early 1800s, and President Andy Jackson in the 1830s, the Grant Administration pulled off the debt reduction while cutting taxes. In its case it both reduced tariffs and abolished the war-time income tax.

After their robust ticket of 1868, the Democrats, at their Baltimore convention in the border state of Maryland, chose a fairly weak one in 1872.

Nominee Horace Greeley of New York was at first blush an odd choice for a party with a base in the old Confederacy. The famous newspaper publisher had been an ardent proponent of abolition and Union during the Civil War. He had cooled, however, to the Grant Administration due to its corruption and its embrace of Radical Reconstruction. Many Democrats found him a Johnny Come Lately to Johnny Rebel. Further, Greeley had no campaign experience.

His running mate was also something of an odd bird for his party. Benjamin Gratz Brown, the Governor of the swing state of Missouri, walked with a permanent limp from a duel he'd had with a proponent of slavery. And unlike Greeley, after backing abolition he went on to support Radical Reconstruction.

In addition to the Democratic Party nods, Brown and Greeley also received the nominations of the new Liberal Republican Party. The Democrats calculated that choosing, in effect, moderate Republicans might get them back in the White House.

The Republican convention again chose Grant as its presidential candidate, but dumped Vice President Colfax, because of, as stated, the Crédit Mobilier railroad scandal, and due to the Democratic and Liberal Republican attacks on corruption. Taking Colfax's spot was Sen. Henry Wilson of Massachusetts, like Colfax a Radical Republican, and chairman during the war of the Senate Committee on Military Affairs. With campaign funds rolling in from tycoons like New York's John Jacob Astor III, Grant's campaign much outspent Greeley's.

In the first presidential election in which every participating state chose its electors by popular vote, instead of through its state legislature, Grant won the Electoral College vote, 286-66. He also took the popular vote, 56 percent to 44 percent.

Grant won all of New England, all of the Midwest except for Missouri, the West Coast, and most of the South. Greeley, and electors casting their ballots for the Democratic Party or the Liberal Republican Party, took Texas, Georgia, and Tennessee, and the border states of Maryland, Kentucky, and Missouri.

Many Southern states that might have voted for Greeley were still under Reconstruction rule, however. And Grant's electoral votes for Louisiana and Arkansas, both wracked by violence, were tossed out due to "voter irregularities".

At campaign's end, ill fortune of the worst kind struck Greeley. His wife took sick in October, and died a week before the election. The candidate cancelled three weeks of campaigning just before the balloting to care for, and then mourn, his spouse. After the voting, he began suffering from insomnia, from grief, and from a bid to oust him from his stewardship of *The New York*

Tribune. He himself fell fatally ill, dying on November 29, just weeks after his electoral defeat.

With Grant's strong win, the Republicans performed well in the congressional contests. In the House, after major redistricting, the modest Republican margin of 137-104 soared to a more than 2-to-1 majority, 203-89, with a gain of 64 seats. The G.O.P. did particularly well in its Northeast and Midwest bastions, gaining nine seats each in New York and Pennsylvania, six in Illinois, and four each in Michigan and Indiana. The Democrats did relatively well in the Southern and border states.

Still, in the Senate, the Republican Party lost two seats to the Democrats; the Liberal Republicans retained one seat. The Republicans still had a commandeering edge over the Democrats, 54-19.

Despite his re-election, two plagues that often afflict two termers—economic turmoil and scandal—were to hit Grant especially hard. And his second term began with an embarrassing series of attempts to settle on a new Supreme Court Chief Justice that recalled President Washington's woes in that realm.

TROUBLED COURT SELECTIONS

Political infighting and White House indecisiveness led to a comedy of errors in the President's choice of a Chief Justice in May 1873, two months into Grant's second term. Chief Justice Salmon P. Chase, Lincoln's former war-time Treasury Secretary, died that month. President Grant sat on a decision until November, before asking Sen. Roscoe Conkling, head of New York's Republican machine, to take the job. Conkling demurred. The President next offered the position to Indiana Sen. Oliver Morton and to Wisconsin Sen. Timothy Howe. Both declined. He then offered the job to Secretary of State Fish, who also turned it down.

Next he asked then-Attorney General George H. Williams, but Williams fell under a cloud due to charges he and wife had drawn on government funds to pay for luxury goods. (Two years later, Williams would resign from the Justice Department when Congress found his wife had taken a $30,000 bribe.) So Grant withdrew the nomination of Williams, and dubbed ex-Attorney General Caleb Cushing. But Cushing fell under a cloud of allegations he'd been closely linked to the Confederacy and its President, Jefferson Davis.

Finally, the following January, after pressure from Buckeye state politicians, such as the scandal-tinged Interior Secretary Columbus Delano, Grant telegraphed Ohio Judge Morrison Waite that the job was his. He accepted, ending the long wait. Ex-Navy Secretary Gideon Welles commented: "It is a wonder that Grant did not pick up some old acquaintance, who was a stage driver or bartender."

Waite turned out to be a dedicated and competent jurist—in 15 years of service, his Court would rule on 3,470 cases. Despite ill health, he labored on until his death, writing about a third of the decisions. However, his narrow interpretation of the Constitution's civil rights Amendments would help end the approach to Reconstruction of the civil rights President who chose him.

ECONOMIC DISTRESS

The year after Grant won re-election, the Panic of 1873, a prolonged period of business stagnation, took hold. The Panic broke out after a major railway and brokerage house, Jay Cooke & Company—the Union's largest financier during the war—went out of business. Wall Street shut down for 10 days, touching off bankruptcies in the previously booming railway industry. The federal government's supply of massive subsidies of land and capital to the railroads had helped build a bubble which burst that year.

Grant's economic strategy prefigured that of jinxed two-term President Grover Cleveland, and his response to the Panic of 1893. In general, President Grant took a "hard-money" approach, working toward a currency backed by gold, and tightening credit to defend the U.S. dollar. Some historians believe this tact may have helped spark, and served to lengthen, the resulting "Long Depression."

Yet Grant the economic manager was rather more pragmatic than that. He and Treasury Secretary Boutwell did buy up some of the paper-money greenbacks printed to finance the Civil War. They also moved toward a gold standard where paper dollars were backed by an exact measure of gold. However, most greenbacks remained in circulation, and no limits were put on the amount of Treasury bonds in circulation. And when the 1873 Panic hit, Boutwell's successor, William Adams Richardson, circulated $26 million of paper money to pump up the markets, instead of sticking to a strict hard money policy. Grant then tacked the other way, vetoing a bill to inflate the money supply by $100 million.

After the Panic, the economy was flat for about two years, before picking up towards the end of Grant's second term. The downturn aided the resurgence of the Democratic Party, with its appeal to tradesmen and farmers through a "soft money" loosening of credit.

TAX DISINCENTIVES

In 1874, the Administration was embarrassed, and its Treasury Secretary dismissed, due to a major tax scandal. Back in 1872 the Treasury Department, as with New York's customs house, had settled on the ill-advised practice of moiety to collect taxes. Its Bureau of Internal Revenue allowed a private revenue collector, John D. Sanborn, a political operative from Massachusetts, to keep fully half of any revenues he and his associates took in. Oddly, Treasury Secretary Boutwell, while ending moiety at the New York customs house, enthusiastically backed the new approach at the revenue bureau.

At first, Sanborn focused on actual scofflaws in the spirits industry, whose products, then as now, were highly taxed, and the taxes often avoided. In time, Sanborn made up cases against companies that weren't delinquent. By 1872 his group had compiled a list of over 750 persons to target. The next year, the list rose to about 3,300 individuals and companies, including almost 600 railroad-related organizations supposedly owing estate and income levies. For his tally, Sanborn simply copied over a compendium of every railroad company in the U.S. And he never provided the required evidence of tax fraud for anyone on his lists.

Oversight from Treasury was practically nil. In fact, Sanborn enlisted Treasury agents to help him. Even if government agents ended up doing the collecting, Sanborn got 50 percent of the money, if the target was on his list. Meanwhile the Department's own inspectors independently pursued many of the same collection cases, causing confusion and delays.

In 1874, after raking in $427,000 in taxes (about $8 million in 2015 dollars), Sanborn was indicted for fraud. Treasury Secretary William Richardson told congressional investigators he had never looked into Sanborn's work. President Grant asked for Richardson's resignation, then kicked him downstairs to the U.S. Court of Claims. Sanborn was put on trial—and acquitted. According to the letter of the law, he'd mostly done what the Treasury had directed.

Congress did end tax collection by private individuals. Grant put the honest and able Solicitor General Bristow in at Treasury, and he cleaned up the revenue mess. Yet Bristow was to clash with the President over the next big pilfering of the federal purse, the 1875 Whiskey Ring.

RECONSTRUCTION ROLLERCOASTER

Along with the scandals, the economic woes contributed to a decline in public support for Reconstruction, as voters focused on joblessness, low wages, or falling demand for crops. Meanwhile, although the secretive Ku Klux Klan had been largely suppressed, some whites began to organize openly in armed, racist organizations known as the White Leagues and the Red Shirts. At the same time, funding for the Justice Department's efforts against the Klan and other groups was cut. In December 1872, a month after his re-election, Grant's Justice Department had clamped a moratorium on prosecuting civil rights cases.

A flashpoint arose in Louisiana, where Democrats and Republicans traded charges of election fraud and fought violently over control of the governorship and state house. The worst incident was the Colfax Massacre. It took place on Easter Sunday 1873, in the center of the state, in the town of Colfax in Grant Parish, named for the then-Vice-President and President, respectively. In a fallout from contested 1872 state elections, whites under Confederate veteran Christopher Columbus Nash, the local Democratic sheriff, killed over 50, and as many as 160, black Republican militia.

Nash's gunmen soon formed a fearsome vigilante group, the White League, which aimed to support a "hereditary civilization and Christianity menaced by a stupid Africanization". Chapters of the highly organized group spread to a number of Southern states.

The following year, clashes broke out in the Crescent City. In September 1874 in New Orleans, perhaps 5,000 members of the League fought over 3,000 state militia members and policemen in a pitched battle in Liberty Place, and seized the state house and mayor's office.

That December, President Grant denounced the insurgents before Congress: "White Leagues and other societies were formed; murders enough were committed to spread terror among those whose political action was to be suppressed, if possible, by these intolerant and criminal proceedings." The League retreated when Grant sent in thousands of troops and a trio of warships.

However, in 1875, frustrated by the constant disorder and by widespread resistance, Grant ordered the troops out of the Bayou State. By 1876, segregationist Democrats had taken charge of the state's politics, and the League was incorporated into the state militia.

A STINGING, SECOND MIDTERM DEFEAT

The recession, the scandals, and the violence-strewn Reconstruction were all reflected in the 1874-1875 midterm elections of Grant's second term. Grant's party and policies were sorely beaten. In the second-biggest pickup in the history of the House of Representatives, the Democrats gained 94 seats to flip control of that chamber. In a wild swing, the Republican majority of 199-89 was transformed to a Democrat majority of 183-106. A sign of the tide was how well the Democrats did in the normally Republican Northern states. They gained 12 seats in Pennsylvania, eight in New York, six in Illinois, and five each in Indiana and Massachusetts.

The story was similar in the Senate. The Democrats took nine seats, to cut the still-substantial Republican majority to 42-28. As in the House, they impressed up North, winning seats in Connecticut, Indiana, New York, and Pennsylvania.

A COURT'S DECONSTRUCTION

During this period, the legal means to enforce Reconstruction was undercut by the federal Supreme Court. In two major decisions in Grant's second term, it obviated national authority to enforce the civil rights laws.

The 1875 case *United States vs. Cruikshank* came out of an attempt to prosecute some of the militiamen who took part the Colfax Massacre in Louisiana. The Court ruled that the due process and equal protection clauses of the Constitution, and indeed its Bill of Rights, only applied to the actions of the federal government, and not the states or individuals. The Court thus threw wronged individuals on the mercy of state courts that were permitting the re-imposition of segregation and the Black Codes.

For instance, on the right to bear arms, an important privilege for someone threatened with lynching, the Court's opinion stated: "The Second

Amendment restricts only the powers of the national government, and that it does not restrict private citizens from denying other citizens the right to keep and bear arms, or any other right in the Bill of Rights."

Previously, in 1873, the Court made a similar, related decision in its Slaughterhouse Cases, which involved a slaughterhouse near New Orleans that the state of Louisiana had granted a near monopoly. Butchers in other businesses sued, claiming the monopoly denied them rights granted to all citizens by the Fourteenth Amendment. That Amendment had been designed mostly to protect the voting rights of former slaves. It reads in part: "No State shall make or enforce any law which shall abridge the privileges or immunities of citizens of the United States".

The Court ruled most of these privileges were the responsibility of the state and town governments, not the federal government. The decision was used by proponents of segregation to further undermine voting and other civil rights laws.

MAYHEM IN MISSISSIPPI

As it lost political support in Congress and the Supreme Court, the Administration's growing weakness in the South was on display in Mississippi. There former Union Major Gen. Adelbert Ames of Maine served as Governor under Reconstruction. A winner of the Congressional Medal of Honor, Ames had been in hand-to-hand fighting at Gettysburg that stopped the Confederate charge at Cemetery Hill.

In 1874-1875, his governorship came under siege form white Democrats who shot, hanged, and cannonaded black Republicans. Many joined the Red Shirts vigilante group; some wielded Colt revolvers and bolt-loading German rifles that could outgun federal troops. Red Shirt militias also emerged in the Carolinas.

In talks with Mississippi's Democrats, the Grant Administration promised not to deploy federal soldiers if they refrained from violence against blacks and Republicans during elections. Still, the Democrats intimidated enough Republicans from voting to ensure their own electoral success. In 1876, the Mississippi legislature forced the state's Reconstruction militia to disband, and pressured Gov. Ames to resign under threat of impeachment. Years later, the valiant Ames would fight at the Spanish-American War's Battle of San Juan Hill; he lived until 1933.

Grant's Civil Rights Act of 1875, landmark legislation on its surface, proved a hollow reed. Although it banned racial discrimination in hotels and train stations, and on jury trials, it lacked teeth as federal troops and attorneys were being withdrawn from much of the South. The vision of Grant, and Lincoln, of a steady increase in black suffrage there disappeared.

CRISES IN CAROLINA

One of the final face-offs of Reconstruction happened in the cradle of the Civil War and, indeed, 1830s-era nullification: South Carolina. There Republicans had engaged in a fair amount of carpetbaggery, that is, the movement of Northern politicians and businessmen into the defeated South. There was also corruption and waste in the state government. Conflict simmered between whites and the majority-population blacks.

The Republican Governor in Charleston was Daniel Henry Chamberlain. He was a graduate of Yale and Harvard who had during the Civil War fought as a lieutenant in an African-American regiment. (He was unrelated to Gen. Joshua Chamberlain, famous for his defense of a strategic hill at Gettysburg.) Moving to South Carolina, Daniel Chamberlain became its attorney general, then was elected as its Republican Governor as in 1874. The Northern integrationist then faced off with a Southern war hero.

Wade Hampton III embodied resistance. The grandson of a ranking officer from the American Revolution and the War of 1812, he was the son of a military adjutant to Andy Jackson at the Battle of New Orleans. A famed bear hunter who killed with knife not gun, Hampton was wounded five times in the War Between the States. He led cavalry raids notable for succeeding without taking any casualties, while giving many. In antebellum times perhaps the state's largest slave owner, he lost all his servants due to the war, as well as his boyhood home, burned by Gen. Sherman.

Post bellum, Hampton quietly raised money for indicted Klan members. After he announced his bid for the South Carolina governorship in 1876, Red Shirt groups rode in his campaign tours. Violence erupted. In September 1876 in Aiken County, crowds of whites and paramilitary rifle clubs killed dozens of blacks. Some of those slain were in armed groups, others were lynched. Republican campaign rallies were broken up. In October, President Grant sent Gen. Sherman to South Carolina to keep the peace.

The Democrat's candidacy was helped by the fact that Gov. Chamberlain was an "interloper" from the North, who'd commanded black troops. Further, he was at odds with some of his fellow Republicans.

His G.O.P. predecessor, Franklin J. Moses, Jr., was a lawyer of Jewish descent and a Confederate colonel during the war. In 1861, he may have been the man who lowered the U.S. flag at Fort Sumter, the war's precipitating event. In Reconstruction, he was a prominent "scalawag", a local who switched sides over to the Radical Republicans. In his new role, he headed up the 14,000-strong, mostly black, state militia that battled the Klan. He helped integrate the University of South Carolina. As Governor, he astounded observers by having blacks as guests at his home.

But Moses also overspent, and worked with legislators and state officials, some of them uneducated blacks, who were underqualified for their roles.

Spending skyrocketed and corruption was common. Visiting reporters from Northern newspapers in Cincinnati and New York were shocked at what they saw.

In four years, the state's debts rose from $5 million to $18 million. On a salary of $3,500, Moses spent over ten times that on entertaining. Later in life, he was arrested for fraud at least four times.

After taking over from Moses, Gov. Chamberlain slashed taxes, corruption, and waste. One opposition legislator cried out in response: "Are you going to let Chamberlain frighten you off with his cry of reform and economy? Why, gentlemen, there are five years of good stealing in South Carolina yet!"

In the Governor's race of 1876, both Chamberlain and Hampton's sides engaged in voter fraud. Some districts backing Hampton reported voter turnout much in excess of 100 percent. The election ended in almost a dead heat, with both sides claiming victory. After six months of wrangling, the state's Supreme Court gave the win to Hampton. The following spring, Grant's successor, President Rutherford B. Hayes, pulled federal troops out of Charleston. The garrisoning of Louisiana and Florida ended as well.

Hampton went on years later to be an establishment Democrat who made political alliance with some blacks. In 1893 President Cleveland made him U.S. Railroad Commissioner. But in 1876, he rang Reconstruction's death knell.

A SPIRITED SCANDAL, AND PATENTLY FALSE OCCUPATIONS

In 1875, Grant was further wounded by revelations about major fraud involving whiskey and taxes. Starting in 1870, federal tax collectors, liquor distributors, distillers of spirits, and politicians in St. Louis, Milwaukee, Peoria, and other cities had engaged in a so-called Whiskey Ring. They defrauded the government of at least $3 million in tax revenues. Federal officers pocketed bribes in return for not taxing the distillers.

Treasury Secretary Bristow, without telling Grant, had his Department conduct secret, nation-wide raids against those suspected of being in the Ring. Authorities indicted 238 people, and convicted 110.

Secretary Bristow worked with then-Attorney General Edwards Pierrepont, who later helped take down Boss Tweed in New York. They gave the President evidence that his private secretary, Orville Babcock, was complicit in the fraud. Babcock was indicted. But at his trial, Grant testified for his friend. Further, he ended his close relationship, not with Babcock, but with Bristow, who resigned in 1876. The President also fired the special prosecutor heading up the federal trials of the accused, and pardoned some of those convicted. Usually unaware of misbehavior, this time Grant seemed almost complicit in it.

Also in 1875, yet another serious scandal hit several bureaus of the sprawling Interior Department. On the surface, Columbus Delano, a former Ohio congressman and the former federal Commissioner of Internal Revenue, seemed an unlikely man to head up a department riddled with corruption. He was a scion of the Delano family, who had helped craft the Mayflower Compact of the original Pilgrims settlers of the Massachusetts Bay colony. Among the descendants of this clan was future four-term President Franklin Delano Roosevelt. As Interior chief, Delano administered the first federally backed scientific exploration of Wyoming's Yellowstone.

But like President Grant, Delano was often blind to misbehavior around him. And as head of the revenue service he had missed the Whiskey Ring in which his agents were entangled.

His Department ran the Bureau of Indian Affairs. Many of its agents swindled Indian tribes. Their scam was to elicit payments from the Native Americans, by posing as high-powered Washington attorneys who would supposedly represent them in D.C.'s corridors of power.

The Interior Department also then ran the Patent Office, which was charged with administering and surveying federal lands as well as managing the copyright laws. During this time, its clerks handed out about 800 fake land grants. The Office hired surveyors who had no cartographical skills nor did any surveying work. Among those paid handsomely for doing nothing were the President's brother, Orvil Grant, and Delano's son, John Delano. Further, some managers made up the names of clerks, then pocketed the salaries of their ghost employees.

In October 1875, under attack from newspapers that exposed the scandals, Grant forced Delano to resign. He replaced him with the hard-driving Zachariah Chandler, formerly a mayor of Detroit and a businessman who'd helped slaves escape to Michigan via the Underground Railway. Grant, furious about the Patent Office clerks, told him: "Have those men dismissed by 3 o'clock or shut down the Bureau." Chandler cleaned up shop there, and dismissed the "Indian attorneys" as well.

The War Department wasn't immune to corruption. In 1876, Congress reprimanded Secretary of the Navy George Robeson, for apparently taking lavish gifts from a Philadelphia contractor, Alexander Cattell & Company. Secretary Robeson, the House of Representatives charged, had received horses, a New Jersey cottage, land in D.C., and a $10,000 loan. It was discovered Robeson, on an annual government salary of $8,000, had made bank deposits of over $300,000. In a play on the Cattell company's name, Civil War hero Admiral David Porter wrote in disgust of Robeson to Gen. Sherman: "Our *cuttle fish* may conceal his tracks for a while in the obscure atmosphere which surrounds him."

The Washington bureaucracies needed a shakeup, but Congress threw a roadblock. Eager for patronage, it rejected President Grant's proposals for setting up a non-partisan, professional Civil Service.

A DIPLOMATIC FOREIGN POLICY

In contrast to the domestic turmoil, foreign affairs under Grant was largely quiet, and foreign policy efficiently pursued. This was partly because the nation was recovering from the wounds of the Civil War, and had little taste for adventures beyond its own borders. Instead of using the huge military establishment that had been built up for conquest abroad, America dismantled most of its Army and almost all of its Navy.

And foreign threats were few. A French scheme which installed Emperor Maximilian in Mexico had collapsed in 1867, the year before Grant's election. Paris became preoccupied with the rising power of Prussia, which defeated it in the Franco-Prussian War of 1870-1871, leading to a potent, unified Germany.

The European nation with enough power to threaten America was Great Britain. And a major diplomatic dispute was underway with it. Britain had allowed the Confederacy to construct warships in its naval yards. These included the formidable *CSS Alabama*, which had destroyed 65 Union ships. (Its construction was arranged by Confederate agent James Bulloch, the uncle of future President Theodore Roosevelt.) The U.S. Congress demanded restitution. A "hawk" was Sen. Sumner, then as hostile toward the British crown as he was stern toward the defeated South. He demanded London make amends by handing over Canada, or by paying out a cool $2 billion in gold.

Grant's astute Secretary of State, Hamilton Fish, a former Governor of New York, persuaded the President to pursue diplomacy. London and

Washington turned the matter over to an international tribunal. The resulting 1871 Treaty of Washington sailed through the Senate. Britain evinced "regret" over the warships' construction, and paid $15.5 million in damages, while the U.S. handed over $5.5 million for a settlement over fishing rights. The two nations also brought in the German Emperor to broker a dispute over Puget Sound.

In 1873, however, a major blowup occurred with Spain over its troubled colony of Cuba, where rebellion brewed. A U.S.-flagged ship the *Virginius* was ferrying rebels and ammunition to the island, and a Spanish cruiser intercepted it. Before getting a directive from Madrid to spare the captives, Spanish authorities executed 53 U.S. and British citizens who'd been on board. The mass slayings triggered outcries for war with Spain.

Again, Fish urged a diplomatic course. He got the Spanish to release the 91 remaining prisoners, and to pay $80,000 ($1.5 million in 2015 dollars) in damages to the families of the slain. Grant and Navy Secretary Robeson then built a squadron of iron-hulled warships to deter further Spanish actions.

At the start of the Grant Administration, Fish also played a major role in a debate on whether to acquire Santo Domingo, the Caribbean nation adjoining Haiti. American businessmen sought profits there, and the Navy longed for a naval base. Grant sent Frederick Douglass to the mixed-race island to look into annexation. But Fish thought the impoverished, unstable nation a poor fit for the U.S. The Senate agreed, and blocked attempts at incorporation.

In Grant's final year, a famous military debacle took place on America's frontier. The disaster of Custer's Last Stand flowed out of Grant's policy of placing Indian tribes on reservations, and from the continuing encroachments of settlers on native lands. Grant had worked out an accord with the Sioux, or Lakota, Indians, whereby they agreed to reside on reservations in return for peace. However, after discovery of gold in the Black Hills of today's Wyoming and South Dakota, prospectors headed toward the Indian preserves. The U.S. Army moved in to protect the bushwhackers. Conflict loomed, as the Sioux shaman Sitting Bull had a vision of a calamitous Army defeat.

In June 1876, a band of Sioux, Arapaho, and Cheyenne warriors led by the Sioux chief Crazy Horse crushed the U.S. 7th Cavalry led by Gen. George Armstrong Custer, a cavalry hero of the Battle of Gettysburg. Of upwards of 600 soldiers at the Battle of Little Big Horn, over 260, including Custer and two of his brothers, were killed. In response, Congress and the Administration expanded the post-Civil War Army. They also forced the Sioux to give up the Black Hills and to reside permanently on reservations.

A happier development involved Gen. Oliver Otis Howard, a Civil War Medal of Honor winner and founder of D.C.'s African-American Howard University. In 1872 he forged a peace accord with the Apache nation of the Southwest, and its skilled guerrilla war leader Cochise.

A SCANDAL-TINGED ELECTION YEAR

So bad was the fallout from the Grant-era scandals that the President decided against running for his party's nomination for president, and for a third term, in 1876. In a reflection of the Administration's misdeeds, both the Republican and Democrat party nominations that year went to advocates of clean government.

The Republican was Rutherford B. Hayes, who as a Union Army general had received five combat wounds. As Ohio Governor, he was a champion of improved public schools. The Democrat was Samuel Jones Tilden, the New York Governor. Tilden had cleaned up a "Canal Ring", where crooked pols had overcharged the state for the upkeep of the Erie Canal. (In the 1870s, the term "Ring" was often employed, like "-gate" today, as in Watergate or Servergate, to indicate wrongdoing.)

The 1876 election and aftermath showed how Grant's efforts at Reconstruction had failed. That November Tilden, a conservative "Bourbon Democrat" who'd made a fortune as an attorney for the railroads, won the popular vote. Tilden edged out Hayes, 51 percent to 48 percent. Hayes took most of New England and the Midwest, and shut Tilden out of the West. But Tilden took most of the South, carried his home state of New York and adjoining New Jersey, and pulled in two other Northern states: Connecticut and Indiana.

However, Tilden's Electoral College tally, 184-166, fell just short of the number needed for victory. For the election came under dispute in the states of Louisiana, Florida, and South Carolina. These were the remaining Southern states under the control of Reconstruction Republicans. Their Army garrisons had yet to depart. All three, with their 19 electoral votes, ended up sending two groups of electors—one of them Republican of them and one Democratic—to the Electoral College! As Yogi Berra might have put it, it was 1800 all over again, with Hayes and Tilden standing in for Jefferson and Burr.

In January 1877, Grant and Congress decided on an electoral commission to sort things out. The 15-member panel had five Republicans and five Democrats from the House and the Senate, plus two of each party from the Supreme Court, and one independent, Supreme Court Justice David Davis of Illinois. The Democrats in the state then elected Davis to the U.S. Senate, in the hope of influencing his work on the commission. But Davis, citing the press of his new duties, resigned from the Court to serve in the Senate. Another Justice, a Republican, was picked to take his place.

The Democrats, feeling cheated, moved to filibuster the decision in the Senate. After much wrangling, the two parties cut a backroom deal two days before Inauguration Day. The commission voted on strict party lines, 8-7, to give all the electoral votes, and the election, to Hayes. In return, Hayes agreed to end the remnants of Reconstruction.

President Hayes would withdraw the last federal troops from Louisiana, Florida, and South Carolina, allowing Democrats to reassert control there. Ironically, the accord was struck at Washington's Wormley Hotel, run by entrepreneur James Wormley, an African-American friend of Radical Republican Sen. Sumner.

Denied the presidency, Tilden stated: "I shall receive from posterity the credit of having been elected to the highest position...without any of the cares and responsibilities of the office."

TROUBLE UNTIL THE END

Adversity lingered into Grant's post-presidential career. He and his family went on a well-received round-the-world tour, but he expended much of their savings on it. The ex-President did run for a third term in 1880, and initially garnered the most delegates at the Republican convention, then fell short.

He and his son Ulysses, Jr. opened a Wall St. investment house, which went belly up in 1884, with the Grants' partner sent to prison for fraud. Grant had to give away his Civil War mementos to settle his debts. Afflicted with throat cancer that year, possibly from his propensity for strong cigars, Grant spent his final months in object pain.

But heroically so, as the old soldier managed in his distress to write out his well-regarded *Personal Memoirs* which, with fellow Shiloh battle veteran Gen. Lew Wallace's *Ben Hur*, was among the 19th-century's bestselling books. Grant's literary agent was one Mark Twain, who'd been a Confederate soldier for a while, who secured him $450,000 in royalties. The proceeds saved

Grant's wife Julia from penury. Grant, though often swarmed by crooked colleagues, had never enriched himself from the public till.

Still, his tainted second term and final years were a sad counterpoint to the accomplishments of his first term and the triumphs of his military career. The famed warrior-politician could not evade the second-term presidential fall.

SECOND-TERM MISFORTUNE AFTER A FOUR-YEAR PAUSE GROVER CLEVELAND, 1893-1897

The second-term plague held up for the only president whose second term took place after a four-year hiatus, namely, Stephen Grover Cleveland of Buffalo, New York.

After first winning the presidency in 1884, and being generally well-liked as President, Cleveland narrowly lost his re-election bid in 1888. He bounced back to win again in 1892. However, due to the ill luck of an economic collapse, he would end his second term in 1897 as a man unpopular with the public and rejected by his own party.

ROCKET-LIKE RISE TO NOMINATION

Cleveland was a distant relation of Moses Cleaveland, the founder of Cleveland, Ohio. Grover grew up in Erie County, New York: his father was a Presbyterian minister and his mother was descended from Quakers. He never attended college, but went on to independently pass the bar exam. Among the young attorney's clients were Fenians. These were Irish-Americans—an important

Democratic constituency—who agitated for the independence of Ireland from Britain with armed raids into British Canada.

During the Civil War, Cleveland paid a man $300 to take his place in the war-time draft. It was a common practice of the time: Abraham Lincoln did it himself. Also like Honest Abe, he was plain-spoken and truth-telling. A biographer, Allan Nevins, wrote that Cleveland had "no endowments that thousands of men do not have. He possessed honesty, courage, firmness, independence, and common sense. But he possessed them to a degree other men do not".

In 1871, at age 33, he was elected Sheriff of Buffalo; in office he personally carried out several hangings. A bachelor, he and his friends would frequent saloons and, in a practice that would bring him grief later, have dalliances with the ladies. In 1881, he won Buffalo's mayoralty in a landslide, running against the corrupt machines of both parties, then slashing waste from rigged city contracting. Just one year later, he was elected Governor of New York, by 61 percent to 39 percent. It was the largest margin in state history up to that time.

In the state house, he vetoed spending bills. But he also vetoed a law, backed by Assemblyman Theodore Roosevelt, to cut the fares on New York City's elevated trains, owned by the unpopular Jay Gould, of the Grant-era Gold Ring scandal. Cleveland, though a reformer, deemed it unconstitutional for the government to set the prices of a private business. His veto was upheld, and Roosevelt changed his mind on the matter. By 1884, Cleveland was the golden boy of Democratic politics, and a favorite for the presidential nomination.

A KNOWN QUANTITY VERSUS AN UP-AND-COMER

The 1884 campaign, the 25th presidential contest, was raucous. Both major party candidates would be slammed by scandal. And the election turned out paper-thin close.

The incumbent President, Republican Chester A. Arthur of New York, had taken office after the 1881 assassination of President James Garfield, at D.C.'s old Sixth Street train station. The former Union general had been slain by a deranged man, Charles Julius Guiteau, who was convinced pro-Garfield campaign tracts he'd written were responsible for Garfield's election. When both the new President and his Secretary of State, James Gillepsie Blaine, both declined his bizarre demand to make him Ambassador to Austria-Hungary or to France, Guiteau reacted violently, and fatally.

As the deceased President had been, Arthur was well-liked, and he presided over growing foreign trade abroad and a vibrant economy at home. Unlike Grant, he succeeded in government reform, through a Pendleton Civil Service Report Act by which federal employees were hired by exam instead of by patronage. His shipbuilding plan helped reverse the sharp decline of the U.S. Navy after the Civil War. However, President Arthur's ill health precluded a serious bid for another term. In fact, he would die from the kidney disease nephritis in 1886.

Among the field of potential, well-regarded candidates to replace Arthur for the 1884 election was Gen. Sherman. But this was the campaign where the Civil War commander made his Shermanesque statement disavowing White House ambition: "If drafted, I will not run; if nominated, I will not accept; if elected, I will not serve." He left politics up to brother John Sherman, an Ohio Senator very influential on economic matters, and later a presidential candidate.

Another potential nominee with a famous name was Robert Todd Lincoln, the slain President's surviving son and then Secretary of War. But the younger Lincoln too had no desire for the presidency.

So that June, the G.O.P. convention in Chicago settled on a seemingly safe choice, James G. Blaine from Maine. He'd been Speaker of the House, U.S. Senator, and Garfield's Secretary of State, and had run for

President twice before. He represented a mildly reformist group known as the Half-Breeds, opposed to a pro-patronage faction dubbed the Stalwarts. Following its usual approach, the G.O.P. ticket paired a New Englander or Northeasterner with a man from the Midwest, in this case, Sen. John Logan of Illinois. Logan had been a Major General with Gen. Sherman, and a figure behind the creation of Memorial Day. Logan Circle in Washington, D.C. is named for him.

The Democrats in contrast anointed a fresh face—Cleveland. He faced a weak field of rivals. New York's Samuel Tilden, the winner of the 1876 popular vote and, perhaps, given widespread voter irregularities, the Electoral College as well, was the early favorite. But the man who would not be president stayed out due to allegations his aides in 1876 had themselves engaged in a major vote-buying scheme.

Massachusetts Gov. Benjamin Butler had become active in an issue of rising importance to the Democratic Party—curbing the power of large corporations. However, he was despised in the South for war-time profiteering as military governor of occupied New Orleans. On the other side of the spectrum, Sen. Thomas F. Bayard of Delaware, from the politically prominent Bayard family, had opposed using military force against the Confederacy, and so was anathema to many Northern delegates.

At the party convention in Chicago, Cleveland was chosen on the second ballot. In a slap at Tammany Hall, one of the nominating speakers said the delegates "love [Cleveland] most of all for the enemies he has made." The Tammany boss on hand, enraged, tried assaulting the speaker, but was held back. The vice-presidential pick was Thomas Hendricks of Indiana, a former Governor and Tilden's running mate from 1876.

Small, issue-oriented parties, whose concerns would become prominent over time, also held conventions. They included the American Prohibition Party, an amalgam of those opposed to liquor as well as to polygamy and masons. Further, a kind of Democratic Party spinoff was the Greenback Party, which opposed a hard dollar pegged to the value of gold. It picked Benjamin Butler as its man.

A NAIL BITER OF A FIRST ELECTION

After the convention, Cleveland was hit with very modern-sounding allegations, namely, that in 1874 he'd fathered an out-of-wedlock child. The boy was named Oscar Folsom Cleveland, named after Grover, and after his law partner and friend Oscar Folsom. Both Grover and Oscar had had a relationship with the mother, Maria Crofts Halpin. Although the paternity was unclear, Cleveland had supported the child financially, largely because he could afford it more than Oscar Folsom.

When the scandal emerged, Halpin poured oil on the fire, stating: "There is not, and never was, a doubt as to the paternity of our child, and the attempt of Grover Cleveland, or his friends, to couple the name of Oscar Folsom, or any one else, with that boy, for that purpose is simply infamous and false." Republicans cried: "Ma, ma, where's my Pa?!" (After the election the Democrats would cry: "Gone to the White House: Ha, ha, ha!") The Republican press, in that Victorian era of sexual propriety, presented the election as a choice between "the brothel and the family, between indecency and decency, between lust and the law."

The Maria Halpin imbroglio was enough to sink most politicians. But Cleveland countered with openness instead of a cover-up. He admitted to the affair, and to the child support, telling his aides: "Above all, tell the truth". A reform Republican backer of the Democrat dryly countered the charges: "We are told that Mr. Blaine has been delinquent in office but blameless in public life, while Mr. Cleveland has been a model of official integrity, but culpable in personal relations. We should therefore elect Mr. Cleveland to the public office for which he is so well qualified to fill, and remand Mr. Blaine to the private station which he is admirably fitted to adorn." Cleveland survived the scandal.

Another G.O.P. reformer supporting him was Rev. Henry Ward Beecher, formerly the ardent abolitionist, and brother of *Uncle Tom's Cabin* novelist Harriet Ward Beecher Stowe. Beecher was part of the "Mugwumps" faction of good-government types who backed the Democrat, despite Cleveland's hands-off approach to civil rights in the South. (The delightful term mugwump, meaning someone who won't stand with his own party, derives sarcastically from an Indian term for war chief.)

Blaine had his own flap, involving his and his party's long-time support of the politically connected railroads. Correspondence emerged from 1876 that he'd been behind laws boosting the railway firms, including the Crédit Mobilier-tainted Union Pacific. He'd owned bonds in it and an Arkansas concern. In one missive he'd scratched, "Burn this letter"—probably not as a cover-up, but out of a habit of confidentiality. But Democrats brandished the weapon handed them, crying: "Blaine, Blaine, James G. Blaine, the liar from the state of Maine—Burn this letter!"

In the end, Grover Cleveland eked out the narrowest presidential win until George Bush's win over Al Gore in 2000. Cleveland won the popular vote 48.85 percent to 48.28 percent, and the Electoral College 219-182. He took his home state, the deciding state of New York with its 36 electoral votes, by *1,049* ballots, of the 1,167,169 cast there.

The determining factor in the New York race was a memorable slur, made prior to the vote by a Presbyterian minister and ally of Blaine's. He branded the Democrats the party of "Rum, Romanism, and Rebellion". Meaning hard-drinking, Roman Catholic, and pro-Confederate. In angry response, Irish-Catholic voters turned out for Cleveland, not to mention Southerners.

The alliterative aspersion presaged Vice-President Spiro T. Agnew's memorable gibes in President Nixon's 1972 re-election campaign, per speechwriter and wit William Safire. That scribe wrote the Democrats stood for, "Acid, Abortion, and Amnesty". The acid meaning LSD, abortion meaning "pro-choice", and amnesty referring to a pass for evading Vietnam War-era conscription.

In the 1884 contest, highlighting the liquor issue helped the Prohibition Party in upstate New York, and thus inadvertently drew more votes away from the Republican Blaine. The Prohibition Party took 1.5 percent nation-wide. Hurting, but not decisive against, Cleveland, was the Greenback Party. It drew 1.3 percent of the vote nationally.

Cleveland swept the South, and proved just strong enough in and around his Northern home state of New York—taking it, New Jersey, and Connecticut by margins of under 2 percent. His running mate Hendricks carried his home state of Indiana, another usually Republican state, by 1.3 percent.

Blaine held New England, except Connecticut, the Midwest, except Indiana, and the entire West. He got blanked south of Mason-Dixon; indeed, he lost every border state too.

Reflecting the very narrow contest, the Republicans actually gained in both houses of Congress. By 23 seats in the House, cutting the Democrats' margin to 183-141. And by four seats in the Senate, to build their own majority to 42-34.

But for the first time in seven presidential elections, from before the Civil War, the Democrats had broken through to the White House.

FIRST-TERM ACHIEVEMENTS, AND A FIRST-TERM DEFEAT

In the Gilded Age, Cleveland would govern as a "Bourbon Democrat", a kind of modern-day conservative. (The term refers to a dynasty of French kings, not the liquor, and implies someone sympathetic to wealth and success.) He was pro-business at home, and wary of adventures overseas. Domestically, he backed the gold standard over a weaker-dollar silver. He feared the latter approach would encourage debt, by making it easier for debtors to pay off what they owed with cheap, inflated currency. Like his Republican predecessor Hayes, he tried to stop even the limited coinage of silver dollars.

He also vetoed agricultural spending and military pension bills; in fact, he issued more vetoes, 414, than any President except Franklin Roosevelt. Most vetoes involved pension claims, many of them fraudulent, by men claiming to be former Union Army soldiers. (Most of FDR's vetoes, during the Great Depression, would involve individuals petitioning for relief.)

Cleveland's most notable thumbs-down was of a drought relief act for Texas. He believed that "acts of God", such as natural disasters, were not the responsibility of Washington, D.C. He wrote: "I can find no warrant for such an appropriation in the Constitution, and I do not believe that the power and duty of the general government ought to be extended to the relief of individual suffering which is in no manner properly related to the public service or benefit.... Federal aid in such cases encourages the expectation of paternal care on the part of the government and weakens the sturdiness of our national character." (Cleveland would probably have opposed FEMA, the Federal Emergency Management Agency set up by President Jimmy Carter in 1979.) He practiced what he preached, declining use of the presidential yacht, and a presidential expense account.

He also tried to cut tariffs, and reformed the civil service. He opposed the Tenure of Office Act—the law that had caused so much conflict between President Johnson and the Radical Republicans—so that he could fire Republicans who held federal patronage jobs. Still, he kept on the payroll many Republicans he felt were competent, while reducing the number of political appointees.

With an eye on the Solid South, and retaining the prejudices of the time, he continued the 1876 bipartisan bargain of a hands-off approach to voting rights in that racially troubled region. This was the era when African-American educators such as Booker Taliaferro Washington, the head of Alabama's Tuskegee Institute, stressed black self-help, not political activism. (Behind the scenes, however, the wily Booker T. underwrote efforts to overturn discriminatory laws.) Black businessmen and professionals focused on the work of fraternal organizations, such as the ironically named International Organization of Odd Fellows.

HAYMAKERS AT HAY MARKET

For the country at large, the most troubling incident during the President's first term was the Haymarket Riot of May 1886 in Chicago. This was a vicious face-off between anarchists and police in the context of a labor movement that pitted union members against strike breakers.

Leading radicals in the town's labor movement were German immigrants working for the German-language newspaper *Arbeiter-Zeitung*, or Worker's Times. On May 1, union members in the Windy City, and throughout the country, went on strike or held protests to support an eight-hour work day. Two days later, a fracas broke out close to the McCormick Harvesting Machine factory, maker of the mechanized McCormick reapers that were revolutionizing agriculture. Strikers angrily faced off with strike busters, and hundreds of police guarding the latter fired into the throng, killing at least two.

Anarchists cried out for a demonstration in the city's Haymarket Square the following night. Speaking at the rally were socialists and anarchists that included *Arbeiter-Zeitung* editor August Spies. After the speeches, a large phalanx of police moved in on the crowd. A home-made bomb, thrown by an unknown hand, was tossed at the magistrates, killing or mortally wounding seven policemen, and injuring 60 others. The police then fired into the rally, killing four and wounding upwards of 70.

An enraged public was mostly sympathetic to the police. A series of raids followed, often without search warrants, on suspected anarchists. Eight men, radicals or workers for the newspaper, including editor Spies, were put on trial. None of the accused included any actual, suspected bomb thrower, and all faced an unsympathetic state judge.

All were convicted, and seven were sentenced to death. Four were hanged. Two had their sentences reduced to life by the Governor. One killed himself in jail by holding a blasting cap to his face. The radicals' association with violence had mostly alienated the man in the street. But the court's response was draconian, and the trial became a cause célèbre for civil libertarians, and for anarchists around the world. It spurred the movement to mark May 1 as a workers' holiday, or Labor Day.

LAISSEZ FAIRE, AND LOVE OF A FAIR LADY

No anarchist, Cleveland was a classical, 19th-century Liberal, with a capital L. In general, he believed private actions, not federal legislation, should address most societal matters.

An exception was his signing in 1887 of a bill that set up the Interstate Commerce Commission. It regulated the rates charged by the railroads and, later, truckers and telephone companies. (Regulation of truckers would ease in the 1980s, and the Commission itself would disappear in 1995 at the dawn of the cell phone revolution.) The Democrats had long distrusted the privileges granted the railroads, and the Cleveland Administration obliged this attitude by taking back 81 million acres of lands out West the federal government had granted the railroad operators.

On foreign policy, the President was practical and restrained. Cleveland worked to forge fishing and boundary-line agreements with Britain and Canada for Newfoundland and British Columbia. Regarding water resources, and ahead of his time, he banned the killing of seals in the Alaska Territory.

He did move Navy ships to the Pacific island of Samoa, when Germany tried taking over the island, but was opposed to the U.S. annexing the place.

On Cuba, Cleveland blocked the Senate's attempt to aid rebels there, and instead urged Spain to grant Havana independence in due course. He and the Senate rebuffed a prior accord with Nicaragua to jointly build a canal through that country, at a time when Frenchman Ferdinand de Lesepps failed to complete a similar project in Panama. And, while condemning violence against Chinese immigrants, Cleveland, believing the Asians assimilated too slowly into American society, restricted the number of Chinese entering the country.

Overall, Cleveland was viewed as a forthright, competent man of modest ambitions who steered clear of scandal and political favoritism.

On the personal front, the President's 1886 White House nuptials ignited a sensation among press and public. The 49-year-old Chief Executive wed 21-year-old Frances Folsom, daughter of Oscar Folsom, the friend of Cleveland who'd been the other man implicated in the Maria Halpin scandal! Frances would have five children with Grover; her charm and popularity as First Lady approached that of Dolley Madison's.

CONGRESSIONAL MIDTERMS AND A VETERANS' TEMPEST

For a party with an incumbent President, the Democrats did fairly well in the 1886 midterm elections. Usually the bloc in power loses seats, and this occurred in the House. The Republicans' push for a higher tariff to aid American industry resonated. At the time, Germany's steel and other industries were expanding behind a high, Hamiltonian wall of import taxes, and many U.S. industrialists wanted the federal government, and its rather Jeffersonian President, to respond in kind.

The G.O.P. gained 13 seats, to narrow the Democratic majority to 167-154. The Republicans rolled in the industrial Midwest: they took three seats in Indiana, four in Illinois, and five in Ohio, perhaps reflecting the labor unrest of Haymarket and other strikes, as well as the tariff issue. They also won five seats in Virginia, where a coalition, unusual for its time, of white and black voters sought funding for education and a rollback of voting restrictions.

However, the Democrats gained three seats in the Senate, narrowing the G.O.P. margin to 39-37. Congress was thus closely divided for the balance of Cleveland's first term.

In 1887 occurred a flap that rubbed wounds from the Civil War and hurt Cleveland's re-election hopes. Almost as an afterthought, the President assented to a notion of the Army's Adjutant General. Namely, to return to Southern governors some of the Confederate battle flags Union units had captured during the war.

The Grand Army of the Republic, a 400,000-member Union veterans' association, was apoplectic. The Grand Army's head, Gen. Lucius Fairchild, thundered of Cleveland: "May God palsy the brain that conceived it, and may God palsy the tongue that dictated it!" A West Virginian chapter on parade nearly rioted when marching near a picture of the President. Union Army Medal of Honor winner Oliver Wendell Holmes, the future Supreme Court Justice, noted "our hearts were touched with fire."

The President tried damage control. He backed out of an invitation to address the Grand Army's yearly meeting and encampment. And he withdrew his flag initiative, weakly claiming Congress, not the executive branch, had authority over such matters. In 1905, President Theodore Roosevelt, and both houses of Congress in a unanimous vote, would return the flags to their states. But for Cleveland, a year before another presidential campaign, the damage was done.

A RE-ELECTION LOSS BEFORE A RE-ELECTION TRIUMPH

The 1888 re-election campaign would be close, marked by some fraud on the G.O.P. side, and hinging on the Republicans' push for higher tariffs.

Cleveland ran without opposition within his own party; he was unanimously nominated at the Democratic convention in St. Louis, in the swing state of Missouri. The assembly's vice-presidential choice was the 74-year-old Allen Granberry Thurman of Ohio, by way of Lynchburg, Virginia. He was formerly the Democrats' leader in the Senate, and formerly a foe of emancipation and Reconstruction. He took the spot of Vice-President Hendricks, who'd died in office.

The Republicans turned to a man with a distinguished pedigree: Benjamin Harrison of Indiana. He was the grandson of Indian fighter and President William Henry Harrison, and great-grandson of Benjamin Harrison V, a signer of the Declaration of Independence whose forebears had settled Jamestown, Virginia. The younger Benjamin Harrison had been a brigadier general in the Civil War, and was a Senator from Indiana, a Northern state Cleveland had narrowly taken in 1880. He was for higher tariffs and higher spending on veterans, as well as educational aid for Southern blacks.

As Harrison hailed from the Midwest, the Republicans turned eastward for his running mate. This was Levi Parsons Morton, originally from New England, and in 1888 a congressman and financier from New York City, from the same, pivotal state as Cleveland.

The Prohibition Party and the Greenback Labor Party, with the latter calling for a soft dollar and stronger unions, also fielded candidates.

Far outspending Cleveland, the Republicans raised about $3 million from businessmen eager for taller tariff walls. The protectionist pitch also attracted skilled craftsmen thinking a tariff would defend their workplaces from foreign competition. Also, Union Army veterans wanted the White House back from a man supported by most Southerners, and willing to return them their rebel emblems.

During the well-financed campaign, the Republican treasurer of Indiana went too far, and was caught trying to set up a vote-buying scheme. A G.O.P. activist in California was cleverer: he wrote to Sir Lionel Sackville-West, the British Ambassador to the U.S., asking the envoy for voting advice. The Ambassador replied with an endorsement of Cleveland, and the activist, under the pseudonym Murchison, published the notorious "Murchison Letter" several weeks before Election Day. It pushed normally Democratic Irish-American voters, many of whom despised the British, to the Republican column, particularly in closely contested New York. The undiplomatic envoy was sacked.

Cleveland for his part ran a passive campaign. Sticking to tradition, he did not campaign personally. He uttered statements on the issues from the front porch of his home, leaving outreach to his elderly and listless running mate.

The outcome was unusual. The incumbent President, at a time of peace and a growing economy, and unblemished by scandal, lost his re-election try. Cleveland actually won the popular vote, narrowly, 48.6 percent to 47.8 percent, but failed in the Electoral College, 233-168. The Prohibition Party took 2 percent of the vote, and the Union Labor Party 1 percent. The former faction siphoned off more votes from the Republicans, but the Democrats still lost.

Cleveland took all the swing states and the Solid South, though he barely carried Virginia by 1,605 votes, and he again took the Northern states of New Jersey and Connecticut. But Harrison won all of the Northeastern states except those two, and all of New England and the Midwest. He carried the entire Farm Belt, excepting Missouri, and the entire West, including the mining state of Nevada, even though these were all places with some sympathy for Democrats. Cleveland's support for a gold dollar hurt him west and north of the Mississippi.

The extremely close election, with a voter turnout of 79 percent, again came down to pivotal Northern states. This time the Republicans took Indiana, by 2,348 votes, and Cleveland's home state of New York, by 49 percent to 48 percent. In the Empire State the President's long-term antagonism toward the corrupt, Democratic Tammany Hall machine cost him.

In the Senate, neither party lost a seat, as the Republicans maintained a narrow 39-37 majority. In the House, however, the Republicans made solid gains, and displaced the Democrats as the majority. Riding the tariff issue, they picked up 25 seats to gain control, by 179-152. From 1888 to 1890, they picked up every congressional district, seven in all, in each state newly admitted to the Union: North Dakota, South Dakota, Montana, Wyoming, Idaho, and Washington. It was a nightmare for aging ex-Confederates, as all the newer states from north and west of the old Mason-Dixon line went Republican.

Still, given his narrow defeat, and intact reputation, Cleveland's career wasn't over. In departing the White House, First Lady Frances Cleveland told the mansion staff: "I want you to take good care of all the furniture and ornaments, for I want to find everything just as it is now when we come back again four years from today."

INTERREGNUM

Like Cleveland, President Harrison attempted to reform the civil service. Like his predecessor, he ran an Administration generally free of patronage, and in so doing alienating his party's bosses. Unlike Cleveland, he was much more of an activist at home and abroad.

He pushed through in 1890 the McKinley Tariff, sponsored by Rep. William McKinley of Ohio, the future President. Part of the tariff deal included a subsidy for American sugar producers. The much higher tariff led to a large federal budget surplus, and debates over what to do with it: spend the money on infrastructure, or return it to the taxpayers. While raising import duties generally, Harrison also reached agreements with some countries to bilaterally cut tariffs.

Harrison used a show of force in 1889 to try to bolster American influence in the Pacific, on the distant, flashpoint island of Samoa, during the great scramble for overseas colonies of the late 19th century. However, he learned with dismay that a typhoon had wrecked U.S. Navy ships there, as well as German and British vessels, killing nearly 200 sailors.

President Harrison was more flexible than President Cleveland on the dollar—he advocated a silver-backed as well as a purely gold-backed currency. He signed in 1890 the Sherman Silver Purchase Act, a law sponsored by Gen. Sherman's brother, Sen. John Sherman. The Act increased the government's purchases of silver by 50 million ounces yearly, and thus boosted the amount of silver-backed dollars. Although a spur to the economy, it would help trigger a run on gold, and the dollar.

Harrison also in 1890 signed the Sherman Antitrust Act, sponsored by the same Sen. Sherman, to curb monopolies, not just of corporations, but of labor unions too. And, stealing an issue from the Democrats, he took grants of land originally intended for the railroads to set aside 22 million acres for the first national forests.

Remembering the role of the Grand Army of the Republic in his election, President Harrison much expanded pensions and disability payments for veterans. The benefits extended to injuries unrelated to the war, which much increased the budget of the Pension Bureau, the government's largest agency. He also pushed for protection of voting rights in the South, as well as federally funded education there. To these ends, Harrison worked with Rep. Cabot Lodge of Massachusetts, the future Senate Majority Leader, and scion of the Cabot family of Beacon Hill, Boston. But Congress blocked these attempts.

The growing federal programs, pushed by the flush of tariff revenues, meant higher government spending. In 1891, the federal budget would reach a billion dollars for the first time in peace time, angering many voters and offering a wedge issue for Democrats. That a goodly chunk of the expenditures went to Union Army veterans couldn't have pleased Southern Democrats.

THE VOTERS SEND A TARIFF TANTRUM

A notable sign of trouble for Harrison came with the autumn 1890 midterms. The Republicans suffered one of the worst defeats in U.S. electoral history, losing 93 seats, more than half of their Congressmen. Their modest 179-152 majority plunged to an almost 3-to-1 minority, 238-86.

The Democrats won big even in the Republican North and Midwest. They took nine seats in Ohio, eight in New York, seven in Illinois, and six each in Michigan and Wisconsin. All politics is local, it's said, and Republican support for "English only" and temperance laws in Ohio and Illinois badly hurt them with German- and Irish-Americans. The big, cross-cutting issues was the expense of the tariff and the size of the federal budget.

Loosely aligned with the Democrats was the new Populist Party, mainly hard-scrabble farmers in the South and the Great Plains opposed to big corporations and the gold standard. The Populists won eight House seats, five of them in Kansas, and gained two seats in the Senate. The Republicans lost four Senate seats overall, shrinking their majority to 47-39-2.

The election results weakened Harrison in his last two years. It was no coincidence that his major achievements—on the tariff, silver, and antitrust—took place before the drubbing.

AGGRESSIVENESS ON THE FRONTIER AND IN OVERSEAS MARKETS

A national tragedy occurred the month after the midterms. In Native-American affairs, Harrison had continued Grant's policy of keeping Indians on reservations, while somewhat contradictorily encouraging them to assimilate. He also permitted a policy of letting Native-American landholders sell their properties to American purchasers, which left many Indians landless.

In South Dakota in 1892, as at Little Big Horn in 1876, a charismatic Indian medicine man inspired Sioux tribesmen to rebel. U.S. Army cavalry responded. In mid-December Sitting Bull, the shaman active prior to Custer's Land Stand, was killed in a confrontation between Indians and troopers. Two weeks later, a brutal firefight took place during Christmas Week. Near Wounded Knee creek, the Army lost 31 soldiers while killing over 150 Indian women, children, and men.

Harrison, like any President, weakened politically or not, retained sway on foreign affairs. He lay the groundwork for constructing seven modern battleships, which would see service in the Spanish-American War of 1898. He was willing the use the Navy's growing might, seizing Canadian ships over fishing disputes near Alaska, and almost going to war in 1891 with Chile over the killing of two American sailors there.

That same year, Harrison secured exports of agricultural produce to Europe in exchange for a federal meat inspection law, to ensure the foodstuffs sent overseas were untainted. An appointee of his to the Civil Service Commission, Theodore Roosevelt, would much expand on this issue as President.

THREE CONVENTIONS AND NOMINEES

In the campaign year of 1892, the economy was slowing down, always a challenge for the incumbent and a boost for the challenger. Moreover, the higher excises from the McKinley Tariff meant inflated prices for many goods.

At the June convention in Minneapolis, Harrison was re-nominated, but only after a fight. The President's refusal to hand out patronage to party members alienated G.O.P. bosses, just as Cleveland's similar stance in 1888 had hurt his relations with Tammany Hall. Rebellious Republicans, including well-known party leaders, put together a Dump Harrison group, aptly termed the Grievance Committee.

A possible alternative candidate might have been Blaine, the 1884 nominee, and now Secretary of State. Harrison disliked his top diplomat, and his coyness on his presidential ambitions. In the end, Blaine's poor health precluded a serious White House run. Harrison won on the first ballot with 535 ballots; Blaine got 182 votes, the same number of a rising and future star, Gov. William McKinley of Ohio. Incumbent presidents usually fare poorly when facing internal opposition, so the auguries were ill for another inauguration.

The President tried shaking up his ticket. He replaced grandly mustachioed Vice-President Levi Morton, whose foot-dragging on civil rights legislation he disliked, with Whitelaw Reid of Ohio. Reid was the owner of Greeley's influential old pro-Republican publication, the *New York Tribune*. In future Administrations he'd serve as Ambassador to France as well as to Britain's Court of St. James.

At the Democratic convention in Chicago later that June, former President Cleveland, though the favorite, also faced rivals. A vulnerability was his firm backing of a gold dollar, while heading a party rooted in Southern and Western regions that clamored more and more for silver. Cleveland denounced the "reckless experiment of free, unlimited coinage of silver at our mints." Opposing the former President on the issue were the ex-Governor of New York, Sen. David Hill, the candidate of Tammany Hall, as well as Iowa Governor Horace Boies. In the end Cleveland, like Harrison, won a contested, first-ballot nomination.

To balance the ticket issue-wise, Cleveland chose as his vice-presidential nominee an advocate of silver greenbacks, the popular Rep. Adlai

Ewing Stevenson I of Illinois. His grandson, Adlai Stevenson II, would be the Democrats' presidential nominee in 1952 and 1956. When a two-term President, or a prospective one like Cleveland, has to give ground on a signature issue, in this case gold, it is usually a harbinger of trouble. It's a sign the issue landscape is shifting toward one's opponents.

The weak-dollar and pro-farmer People's Party, also called the Populist Party, was also in the mix in 1892. The favorite for nomination was the richly named Leonidas Lafayette Polk of North Carolina. He was a founder of the Grange movement of rural cooperatives, and a relative of the late, successful first-term President James Knox Polk. However, Leonidas Polk died that June. So in July his party turned to James B. Weaver, a congressman from Iowa who'd been a valorous Civil War general, and who was a member of the soft-money Greenback Party. Ahead of his time, Weaver pitched an eight-hour work day, as well as even more money for Union Army pensioners.

STEELING FOR A MANAGEMENT-LABOR BRAWL

Around the time of the summer conventions, the country faced one of the largest, and most violent, union and management actions in its history. In Homestead, Pennsylvania, on the Monongahela River near Pittsburgh, the Carnegie Steel Company had built a state-of-the-art, open-hearth steel mill. Back in 1882, the Amalgamated Association of Iron and Steel Workers union, the AA, had won hiring rights at the plant.

Owner and tycoon Andrew Carnegie, and plant supervisor Henry Clay Frick, chafed at these management restrictions, and sought to boost production. At the same time, prices for steel were dropping by half, making it hard for the plant to turn a profit. Determined to break AA, Frick arranged to bring in cheaper, non-union workers, many of East European immigrant stock, and fired the plant's 3,800 workers. He built "Fort Frick", a 12-foot-high, three-mile-long fence with rifle slits, strung around Homestead to keep out strikers. He and Carnegie brought in 300 Pinkerton security guards by river barge to protect the plant.

On July 6, enraged members of the AA attacked the Pinkerton men and burned their boats, even trying to set the river on fire with petroleum. In a 12-hour gun battle, three guards and at least seven workers were killed. The guards surrendered; some were badly beaten up. Worried about political fall-out, Harrison's running mate, Whitelaw Reid, futilely asked Frick to negotiate. Instead, Frick hired thousands of replacement workers, as the Pennsylvania governor brought in 8,500 troops from the state national guard to restore order.

By July 15, the factory was back on line; workers accepted lower wages and put in 12-hour shifts. Many of the new laborers were lower-wage blacks. A race riot with members of the AA, a segregated shop, would ensue. In August, Alexander Berkman, the lover of anarcho-socialist Emma Goldman, walked into Frick's office suite, and shot and wounded him.

The ongoing violence cost the workers public support, as authorities indicted and jailed many union leaders. The AA collapsed. The issue of management-labor relations, which threatened to dominate the campaign, faded for the time being.

ELECTIONEERING FOR A SECOND TIME AROUND

On the stump, Cleveland was more aggressive than in 1888, and the campaign's edge was sharpened with the addition of the articulate, 52-year-old Stevenson. A centerpiece of the campaign was a call to slash tariffs. Cleveland also appealed to German-Americans, who liked his reformist bent as well as his stance against a growing movement to prohibit alcohol.

The Democrats were stronger than ever in the South, as growing restrictions on black voters such as literacy tests and voter or poll taxes decreased the proportion of the Republican vote. Cleveland opposed the Force Bill, proposed by Rep. Henry Cabot Lodge and Sen. George Frisbie Hoar of Massachusetts, for federal supervision of voting in Dixie.

Two weeks before the election, First Lady Caroline Harrison died from tuberculosis. The death muted her widow's, as well as Cleveland's, final electioneering, just as a wife's passing had silenced Greeley in 1872.

In the end, Cleveland wound up with 46 percent of the vote, to Harrison's 43 percent. He handily won the Electoral College, 277-145. Still, he is one of five Presidents to win re-election with a smaller percentage of the popular vote than in his prior election. The others being Madison in 1812, Jackson in 1832, FDR twice, in 1940 and 1944, and Obama in 2012.

Weaver's Populist Party gained a surprising 8.5 percent, totaling over one million votes of the 11.5 million cast. In a sign, perhaps, the economy was approaching a fall, it carried four Western states: Kansas, Colorado, Nevada, and Idaho, as well as one Electoral College vote in both North Dakota and Oregon, for 22 electoral votes. The Democrats were not on the ballot in Colorado, Idaho, Kansas, and North Dakota; they backed the Populists there to deny those states to the G.O.P. The overlooked Weaver was the only third-party candidate to win electoral votes between 1860 and 1912, the latter being the year of Theodore Roosevelt's Progressive "Bull Moose" Party candidacy.

The Prohibition Party, which nominated pioneer and gold prospector John Bidwell of California, won 2 percent of the vote. For the first time since the early 1800s, some women voted, as Wyoming allowed female suffrage. That issue would snowball into the 1920s, when nation-wide female suffrage was won.

Cleveland had won the popular vote for the third time: in 1884, in 1888 when he lost the Electoral College, and 1892. He, Andrew Jackson (who also took the popular vote while losing the Electoral College in 1824), and

Franklin Roosevelt are the only Presidents to have gained the most votes for the presidency three times. Roosevelt of course would do it a fourth time.

Paralleling the close presidential race, Cleveland's party did well in the Senate, but poorly in the House. The Democrats gained five Senate seats, to become the majority party, 44-37. The Populist Party won two seats, and the Silver Party, a G.O.P. spin-off favoring a silver-backed dollar, picked up one. In the House, the Republicans gained 38 seats, after their drubbing in 1890. The Populist Party picked up three seats for a total of 11, while the Silver Party won its first seat. However, the Democrats retained a strong majority, 220-124-11-1.

TERRIBLE ECONOMIC TIMING

It was Grover Cleveland's awful luck that he reentered the White House in 1893, as one of the great financial depressions, the Panic of 1893, took hold. The Panic, which was world-wide in scope, was kicked off after the large Barings bank in London called in bad investments in Argentina.

As with the Panic of 1873 in the Grant Administration, the downturn was caused in part by overbuilding in the vast U.S. railroad industry. A bust in that sector hurt the related industries of steel and finance.

The value of the gold-and silver-backed dollar, meantime, was already under pressure due to the 1890 Sherman Silver Purchase Act. It directed the government to buy silver with gold-backed bonds. This both reduced the Treasury's gold stock while encouraging overinvestment in silver mines out West. A silver boom in the U.S. was followed by a bust in price, which put downward pressure on gold, the dollar, and stocks.

Just one month before the Panic had hit in May 1893, a decline in U.S. gold reserves convinced the hard-money Cleveland to defend the dollar. This limited his freedom of movement on the economy as the Depression took effect.

Indeed, Cleveland built his policy on the Panic around gold. Bankers, industrialists, and conservatives favored a U.S. dollar pegged to the value of gold, as it protected the value of investments and kept inflation low. There was also an overhang of fear from the Civil War, when the federal treasury had printed huge numbers of greenbacks to pay for the struggle against the Confederacy, whose own currency had collapsed from having neither the gold, nor cotton exports, to back it up.

Cleveland called for ending the redemption in gold of bonds backed by silver, and for boosting the nation's reserves of gold. Despite his Democratic base in the Western mining states and Southern farming states, he persuaded Congress to repeal the Sherman Silver Purchasing Act. In addition, the President had the U.S. Treasury offer sales of gold-backed bonds. He also tried to boost the economy by reducing tariffs, but the decrease was much watered down by exemptions Congress granted the powerful sugar industry, rake-offs that continue today.

As Wall Street stumbled, the most widely traded American stock, a maker of rope called the National Cordage Company, went bankrupt. So did major railroads such as the Northern Pacific and the Union Pacific, the latter the old progenitor of the Crédit Mobilier scandal. In 1893, almost 120 railroads failed. Over time, thousands of banks big and small, and many steel companies also went belly up. Several million workers lost their jobs as unemployment reached 15 percent, a level theretofore unprecedented in the U.S.

Soup lines formed in some cities. In Chicago, police patrolled train depots to keep vagrants out of the town. Some of the hardest-hit places were the financial nexus of New York City, industrial centers in Michigan, and farms in the West and South as prices plummeted for grain and cotton.

GDP fell a startling 6.7 percent in 1893, and 4.7 percent the next year. It roared back 9.9 percent in 1895, regaining most of what had been lost. But in Cleveland's final full year in office, 1896, it fell sharply again, by 3.8 percent.

Until the Herbert Hoover Administration in the initial years of the Great Depression, it was the worst economic performance of any presidential term.

Many factory or mine workers, seeing their wages cut, or colleagues laid off, went on strike. In 1894, three-quarter of a million laborers walked off their jobs, which further slowed the economy.

The Haymarket Riot of 1886 proved a presage. In 1894 the bituminous, or soft coal, union staged a violent walkout, met by violence from industry, after the union demanded restoration of wages to pre-Panic levels. Over 175,000 members of the United Mine Workers (UMW) struck, in mines from Pennsylvania to Colorado. In Illinois, UMW strikers injured 40 policemen. In Uniontown, Pennsylvania, 1,500 workers fought 15 guards armed with automatic weapons, and seven strikers died. Checked by the National Guard in other states, the union collapsed, for the time being, from a shortage of dues, as its jobless members ran out of savings. The walkout would stagger the economy in a calamitous midterm election year for the incumbent President.

A HEALTH CRISIS AT SECOND TERM'S START

The President's health seemed to echo the nation's commercial malaise. Three months after again taking the presidency, Cleveland faced a medical emergency. At a time when a diagnosis of cancer usually meant death, a doctor found a tumor in the President's mouth. "It's a bad-looking tenant and I would have it removed immediately," the physician stated.

Fearing the battered markets would plunge further with word of his illness, Cleveland determined on an operation carried out in secret, and at a highly unusual place. He dreaded a public spectacle like the one the late President Grant had been exposed to as a throat cancer sufferer.

It was summer in Washington, when politicians, then as now, often left the sweltering town for weeks. The President and his aides put out a story he would sail by yacht, with a long-time friend and fishing partner, from New York to a Cleveland-owned house in Cape Cod. When the ship was out of sight of land, six doctors strapped the 260-pound President to the mast, and on July 1 performed a 90-minute operation. They took out six teeth and much of his left jaw, masking the pain with the new anesthetics of ether and laughing gas. They then inserted an artificial jaw that remarkably conformed to Cleveland's face. It also allowed him to speak normally.

The White House told the public the President had had some bad teeth extracted. The physicians swore they wouldn't say a word. And when Vice President Stevenson got suspicious, Cleveland sent him on a weeks-long political trip to the West Coast. One journalist gleaned the truth from a loose-lipped doctor, and relayed the story, but the President's aides smeared the reporter's credibility.

Cleveland recovered. A few weeks after the surgery, he spoke in public, and voters were none the wiser. It wasn't until 1917 that one of the surgeons published the story of the President's furtive operation.

TROUBLE WITH A RAILWAY ICON

The Panic led to countless troubles for the President. In spring 1894, Jacob Coxey, a steel company owner in Ohio, grew distressed over layoffs he'd been forced to make. He led hundreds of workers in a march of "Coxey's Army" from the Midwest to Washington, D.C. Anticipating the Works Projects Administration of the Depression-era 1930s, he called for a large-scale program of road building, financed by soft-money currency. After gaining much publicity, however, his march fizzled. The normally tolerant Cleveland had Coxey and two top aides arrested on the Capitol Building's grounds, and forbade demonstrations there.

The most notorious incident of the Panic, and Cleveland's term, related to the railroad industry, and its legendary Pullman car. The Pullman Palace

Car Company was a large manufacturer of luxurious sleeping and dining cars for people traveling overnight on the rails of the nation's largest industry. Its visionary but hard-nosed founder was George Mortimer Pullman, originally from the Erie Canal region of New York. There the young Pullman had grown up observing packet ships carrying passengers on long-distance journeys; he decided to do the same for the rails.

To make his thousands of sleeper cars, he built a company town on 4,000 acres in Pullman, Illinois. There he supplied workers with lodging, shops, churches, and open spaces, though he forbade taverns, town hall meetings, and independent publications. He became the country's biggest-single hirer of African-Americans, many of them former servants on Southern plantations, employing them as sleeper car porters and waiters.

When the Panic struck, Pullman cut costs and retained profits by slashing the wages of the factory workers at his company town, while maintaining the rents they paid for lodging. Many of the hard-pressed men were members of the American Railway Union. It was headed by Indiana's Eugene Victor Debs, the son of a textile factory owner who later would be the presidential candidate of the Socialist Party. In June 1894, Debs urged the switchmen, critical to operating the rail lines, to refuse to handle trains with Pullman cars. They obeyed his directive, and other workers quickly followed—perhaps a quarter of a million strikers in over two dozen states.

The union chief urged non-violence but, at Blue Island, Illinois, strikers and their supporters set some buildings afire and pushed over a U.S. mail car. Elsewhere, unionists damaged federally owned property. Cleveland inveighed: "If it takes the entire Army and Navy of the United States to deliver a postcard in Chicago, that postcard will be delivered."

Some executives in business and government feared an all-out insurrection, as in Latin America or Europe, with anarchists in the mix. The labor movement was itself split. Samuel Gompers of New York's Lower

East Side, the head of the American Federation of Labor (AFL), opposed the strike.

Cleveland did not respond in the usual way, by letting a governor or mayor handle matters with the National Guard or the city police. Instead, he sent in federal troops, to Illinois and other states, 12,000 strong, along with thousands of federal marshals. His aim was to break the strike and to keep the railroads and the economy moving forward. He did this in Illinois even though the Democrat Governor there, John Peter Altgeld, was calling up nine companies of state militia to handle things himself.

The federal, and local and state forces, moved into Chicago, and its South Chicago Panhandle railway yards. Starting on July 4, 6,000 strikers and their supporters raged at this show of force, and wrecked hundreds of railroad cars. On July 7, a throng in Chicago attacked the National Guard, which fired back, killing some in the crowd. There were other face-offs around the country; upwards of 30 unionists were killed. Property damage from strikers and their backers grew to about $80 million, or about $2.2 billion in 2015 dollars. The railroads and the workers also lost huge amounts in profits and wages.

Due to the workers' destruction of property and the strike's paralyzing disruptions, the public soured on the railway union, after initial sympathy for the workers' plight during hard times, and disdain for Pullman. The President's Attorney General, Richard Olney of Massachusetts, the son of a textile manufacturer, obtained a circuit court injunction against Debs and four union lieutenants. The quintet, despite being defended by attorney Clarence Darrow, later of the Scopes "monkey trial" fame, wound up spending months in jail. For the federal government, the case set a precedent for ending major work stoppages.

At this time, as an olive leaf to laborers, the President and Congress created the Labor Day holiday. Further, a federal commission found Pullman, Illinois "un-American" for its restrictions on its resident-workers' liberties. In

1898 the Illinois Supreme Court ordered the firm to sell off the town, a year after its founder died of a coronary.

Cleveland, usually an apostle of federal restraint, was criticized for suppressing dissent, for using force, and for undermining states' rights. Politically, his action alienated the Democratic unions and their workers, giving an opening to populists in his own party, and to Republicans like McKinley who would advocate bargaining between management and labor.

A MIDTERM MALAISE

It was Cleveland's fate, as a limited-government Democrat, to regain office at a time when his party was becoming more activist, and increasingly so due to the economic depression. The leader of his party's opposition was Congressman William Jennings Bryan of Nebraska. A riveting orator, Bryan echoed back to his party's founding, capturing the heart of the Democratic Party with his denunciation of big banks and the influence of moneyed interests, with their attachment to the gold standard.

The public verdict on Cleveland and the Panic came quickly in the 1894 midterm elections. In the worst drubbing in the history of the House of Representatives, the Democrats lost 127 seats. The Republicans went from an almost 2-to-1 minority to an over 2-to-1 majority, from 124-220 to 254-93.

In their strongholds of the Midwest and Northeast, the Republicans had crushing, double-digit pickups: a 16-seat gain in Cleveland's home state of New York, and 11 each in Indiana and Illinois. The Republicans even gained with immigrant Catholics, and in Solid South states, including Alabama and North Carolina. In those states they formed a tactical alliance with local Populist Party factions against the long-entrenched Democrats. And at the state level, throughout the Midwest, Cleveland's supporters in the Democrats' conservative wing were displaced by advocates of silver.

A BITTER PILL TO SWALLOW

For the embattled President, as bad as dealing with cancer or the nation-wide strikes was the continuing run on gold, and the threat of national bankruptcy. In early 1895, near the trough of the Depression, worried investors sold off dollars for the safe haven of the precious metal. The Treasury Department's gold reserves, normally set at $100 million, fell well below that mark. By February 1895, they were down to $45 million, then suddenly slid to about $15 million. The Treasury was literally at risk of running out of money, and bankrupting the U.S. government.

Enter John Piermont "J.P." Morgan, the era's most powerful financier, and as such the bane of the President, leading a party that traditionally was Wall Street's foe. Originally from Connecticut, and having cut his teeth in his father's London-based investment bank, Morgan had made his early fortunes by buying companies and commodities on the cheap during recessions. After the Civil War he consolidated much of the railroad industry into a trust. In 1892 he'd formed what became the General Electric, and in 1901 he'd create U.S. Steel. In the 1893 Panic, he saw an opportunity for profit as well as public service.

The industry titan rushed from Manhattan to Washington, took up residence at a Lafayette Square hotel near the White House, and demanded to see the President. Cleveland at first put him off. Morgan stubbornly told a presidential confidant: "I have come down to see the President. And I am going to stay here until I see him." With the Treasury Building across the way from the Executive Mansion almost out of cash, Cleveland buckled.

At their meeting in the President's office, Morgan coolly played his cards, noting the Treasury's reserves were down to about $10 million, with an investor about to call in his $10 million worth of federal securities. "If that $10 million draft is presented," the mogul told the President, "you can't meet it. It will be all over before three o'clock."

Cleveland threw in his cards: "What suggestion have you to make, Mr. Morgan?" Morgan recommended that his syndicate, which included the wealthy Rothschild banking family of Britain, sell gold to the Treasury in exchange for federal bonds. Cleveland doubted this was within the law. Morgan pointed out President Lincoln had done the same during the crisis of the Civil War. Attorney General Olney, pouring through a tome of federal statutes, confirmed this.

Cleveland asked how much gold Morgan had in mind. "100 million," came the response. The President thought such a large round sum would play very badly to the public, as if the House of Morgan had purchased the country. So he and the powerful financier settled on about $60 million. In return, the financier's group would collect a cool $7 million in interest off the bonds.

The Treasury was saved from bankruptcy, and Wall Street rallied. The following year, the Depression began to ease. In all, Cleveland held four auctions of federal bonds to defend the dollar.

But the deal with Morgan, along with the end of silver purchases, played into the hands of Rep. Bryan. While Cleveland staunchly defended the dollar and gold, Bryan made the free coinage of silver, as well as cheaper money and greater lending for farmers, a rallying cry. He would become the Democratic nominee for President three times. And, though failing short of the White House, he'd bury Cleveland's Bourbon Democrats for control of the party.

AN EXILE AT HIS OWN CONVENTION

With his popularity damaged by the Depression, and with the G.O.P. and insurgents in his own party in the ascendancy, Cleveland found his clout reduced. In 1893 and 1894 he nominated two reformers to the Supreme Court, but machine politicians in New York whom Cleveland had alienated blocked his picks.

Even in foreign affairs, usually the President's prerogative, he was checked. One defeat was on the issue of Hawaii, which the Harrison Administration had moved to annex. Cleveland withdrew the treaty of annexation with the new republic there. It was run by American businessmen and plantation owners, headed by Sanford Dole, a cousin to the founder of the Dole food enterprise. The President, normally wary of foreign expansion in any event, believed the magnates had overthrown Hawaii's queen against the will of the native population. The Democratic Congress, however, ignored its President, and forged diplomatic ties with Hawaii's government. The U.S. would annex the islands under Cleveland's Republican successor in 1898.

In 1895, the President bristled at Britain's effort to take over part of Venezuela's Orinoco River basin. With this violation of the Monroe Doctrine, the usually pacific President threatened war, and London acceded to peaceful arbitration.

Cleveland spent his last year as a lame duck. One positive act was to speak out against the mass killings of Armenian Christians by the Muslim Ottoman Turks.

At their July 1896 convention in Chicago, the Democrats turned away from the incumbent Cleveland, and nominated the silverite Bryan. The fiery Nebraskan had galvanized his party with a speech stating, "You shall not crucify mankind on a cross of gold!" Bryan's running mater was a long-time Missouri congressman, Richard "Silver Dick" Bland, who'd been a silver prospector. Gold had been thoroughly gelded.

Some at their convention followed Cleveland's lead in backing 79-year-old Illinois Sen. John Palmer, a Liberal devotee of gold, and a former Union general. He wound up as the nominee of a splinter faction, the National Democratic Party, or Gold Democrats. His running mate was the 73-year-old Simon Bolivar Buckner of Kentucky, a former Governor and an ex-Confederate general. Union and Confederate generals on the same ticket!

Underlining the notion that the President's ideas were out of date with his own party were the combined 152 years of the two candidates. The Republicans, hoping Palmer and Buckner would steal votes from Bryan, secretly funneled campaign funds their way. But the pair would draw just 1 percent in the election, and no electoral votes.

In November, Bryan lost by a modest amount to Republican William McKinley, a firm backer of hard money. McKinley took 51 percent of the popular vote to 47 percent for Bryan, and won the Electoral College, 271-176.

Cleveland lived until 1908, when a heart attack felled him. His last remark was, "I have tried so hard to do right."

President Cleveland was admired by many as an honest and well-meaning executive. But he helped lead the way to the other party's chokehold on the presidency. After McKinley's win, the Republicans would not relinquish the White House until Woodrow Wilson's victory in 1912. And they'd continue to dominate national politics until the Great Depression began in 1929.

Cleveland's entire second term was colored by the ill fortune of a commercial collapse. He had major trouble with unions and with farmers, the bedrocks of his party. His party got walloped in his second term's midterms. Further, the Democrats nominated a successor with economic views the antithesis of his own. And then lost the election anyway, then many more to come.

Grover Cleveland was clearly caught in the second-term jinx.

SECOND-TERM PROSPECTS
FOILED BY AN ASSASSIN
WILLIAM MCKINLEY, 1897-1901

President William McKinley, a former Union Army major and Governor of Ohio, had a very successful first presidential term, following his election in 1896 over the skilled orator William Jennings Bryan of Nebraska. After a solid re-election triumph in 1900, McKinley had a brief and tragic second term of office that cheated him of a real chance of being one of the most accomplished of Presidents.

PERSONAL CONNECTIONS IN A PIVOTAL STATE

Politically, McKinley was born at the right time at the right place, in 1843, in Niles, Ohio, near his state's burgeoning industrial centers of Akron and Youngstown, during the surge of America's industrialization. The manufacturing centers of the North were to defeat the agrarian South in the Civil War, and the Northern industrial hub of Ohio was to supply a number of Presidents from the 1870s to the 1920s. McKinley himself hailed from a family that worked in iron manufacturing. His mother was a devout Methodist who adamantly supported free-wage, as opposed to slave, labor.

William McKinley was the last president to fight in the War Between the States, and the contacts he made during that conflict much influenced his career. A long-time friend and fellow Ohioan who he met during military service was future President Garfield. His commander in the Union Army was Col. Rutherford B. Hayes, another fellow Ohioan and future President, who McKinley would later campaign for and befriend.

Yet another soldier under whom McKinley served was a hero of Gettysburg, Gen. Winfield Scott Hancock. In the 1880 presidential election, McKinley, as a rising Ohio politician, would campaign for the Republican Garfield against Hancock, the Democrat nominee.

At the Civil War's end, Hancock, impressed by McKinley's efficiency and valor, urged him to remain in the peace-time Army. Instead, McKinley set up a lucrative law practice. Then, after turning to politics, he was elected to Congress and later to the Ohio governorship.

His work as attorney and Governor were marked, during a time of bitter strife between workers and business owners, by compromise. In 1876, a coal miner strike in Canton, Ohio led to a violent clash between laborers and the state militia, under then-Gov. Rutherford B. Hayes. As a result, 23 of the workers faced court action. McKinley represented the miners, and got all but one of them off. Oddly enough, this impressed an operator of one of the mines, wealthy Ohio businessman Mark Hanna. Hanna would become manager of McKinley's national campaigns.

A BROAD APPEAL ON MONEY MATTERS

While many corporate chiefs refused to treat with employee organizations, McKinley backed arbitration between unions and management. He appointed labor officials to his state government, and had amicable meetings with a seminal figure in the U.S. labor movement, AFL chief Gompers.

When McKinley agreed, after the Panic of 1893, to pay back a huge $100,000 loan he'd guaranteed for a bankrupt friend, his stock among the man on the street rose further. He also gained sympathy for his affection for his long-suffering wife Ida, who had epilepsy, and for their family tragedies. Before she had lapsed into the illness, the McKinleys' two daughters had died, at ages four and ten. Later, when President McKinley presided over White House dinners, the First Lady would sometimes be gripped by a seizure. McKinley would quietly place a napkin or handkerchief over her head to hide her distorted facial features, then remove it after the fit had passed, his calm action itself helping Ida regain her composure.

While McKinley had the great political knack of appealing to the other side of the aisle, he was ever careful to maintain his political base. He was an advocate of American business, and was especially supportive of tariff barriers to protect U.S. manufacturers. Such taxes on imports, while raising the price of imported goods, tended to increase the profits of manufacturers, and the wages of factory workers, in Ohio and other industrial states. McKinley would show some flexibility on such imposts, but it would be a signature issue throughout his career.

McKinley was cagey on another major economic issue of the time, the gold standard. He backed two laws, the 1878 Bland-Allison Act and the 1890 Sherman Silver Purchase Act, which directed the U.S. Treasury to buy and make silver-backed money, while still making gold-backed money as well. Later, when economic and political conditions warranted, McKinley shifted to a firm stance for a dollar backed by gold alone.

TAKING ON A PRAIRIE POPULIST

In the 1896 campaign, McKinley benefitted from a relatively weak field of Republicans, and from a vastly superior political organization. Former

President Benjamin Harrison, the favorite, decided not to run. In the race for delegates, McKinley's team outhustled candidates like Republican Speaker of the House Thomas Reed of Maine and Levi P. Morton, then the Governor of New York and formerly President Harrison's Vice President. Aide Mark Hanna buttonholed convention delegates, in particular the often-ignored but delegate-rich G.O.P. state conventions from the solidly Democratic South.

The Ohioan secured the nomination on the first ballot, 661 votes to 84 for Reed, his nearest rival.

McKinley then faced a dynamic candidate on the Democratic side who appealed to the masses of people hurt by the Panic and depression of 1893. At the party convention William Jennings Bryan, all of 36 years old, a former congressman from the Midwestern farm country, seized the nomination at the convention. Bryan swept up the delegates with a "Cross of Gold" speech—a class warfare appeal that decried the purported effects of a gold-backed currency on laborers and farmers.

"Upon which side," cried Bryan, "will the Democratic Party fight; upon the side of 'the idle holders of idle capital', or upon the side of 'the struggling masses'?...The miners who go down a thousand feet into the earth and bring forth from their hiding places the precious metals to be poured into the channels of trade are as much business men as the few financial magnates who, in a back room, corner the money of the world!...Burn down your cities and leave our farms, and your cities will spring up again as if by magic; but destroy our farms, and the grass will grow in the streets of every city in the country!"

Posing with arms outstretched like Jesus during the Crucifixion, Bryan concluded: "Having behind us the producing masses of this nation, supported by the commercial interests, the laboring interests, and the toilers everywhere, we will answer their demand for a gold standard by saying: "You shall not press down upon the brow of labor this crown of thorns; you shall not crucify mankind upon a cross of gold!" The enraptured listeners responded by carrying Bryan around the convention hall on their shoulders for 20 minutes. The next day they nominated him.

To lessen unease on Wall Street about his alleged radicalism, Bryan picked as his running mate Maine's Arthur Sewall, who'd run a bank, railroad, and a major shipyard. Bryan was also selected the nominee of the Populist Party, and as such picked up its running mate too, Rep. Thomas E. Watson of Georgia, known for establishing the Postal Service's rural free delivery.

In response to the formidable Bryan, McKinley plotted strategy with an old friend and advisor, Hanna, the highly skilled political operative.

Even more than McKinley, and rather like Lincoln, Mark Hanna represented the Northern industrial infrastructure that dominated the nation's politics from the 1860s until the 1930s. A Union Army veteran, Hanna went on to shrewdly make a fortune in the iron and coal trade. One of his middle school classmates was none other than John D. Rockefeller, the mogul of the new oil industry. Like Lincoln in his early days as a corporate lawyer, Hanna advised and managed companies charged with the nitty-gritty of industry, those building or managing ships, canals, bridges, and railroads, particularly for the up-and-coming city of Cleveland. President Grover Cleveland, that distant relation of that city's founder, had placed him on the board of the Union Pacific railroad.

In 1880, Hanna had been by some accounts the key operative in electing Garfield as President. Thereafter, he ran the presidential campaigns for another formidable, if unsuccessful, candidate, Ohio Sen. John Sherman. The author of the Silver Act, and the Sherman Antitrust Act that presaged Teddy Roosevelt's trust busting, Sherman would become a Secretary of the Treasury and a Secretary of State.

McKinley and Hanna split the key aspects of running a White House bid, and in so doing invented the modern campaign. McKinley tackled the big picture: crafting the overall strategy, formulating stands on the issues, giving speeches, and meeting with reporters to get the message out.

As the theatrics of his Cross of Gold talk attested, Bryan was a superb orator, and he had a young man's energy to mount an 18,000-mile whistle-stop campaign tour of the Midwest. McKinley choose the opposite tact, one which played to his own quiet strength. When Hanna advised him to mimic Bryan's electrifying style, he replied archly: "I might just as well set up a trapeze on my front lawn and compete with some professional athlete as go out speaking against Bryan. I have to think when I speak."

Thus, in a classic "front porch" campaign, McKinley made his public pronouncements, over 300 speeches worth, from his home in Canton, Ohio. Yet it wasn't a static scene. Some three-quarter-million of his supporters traveled to his house to meet and treat with him. The campaign was a study in modern "spin". At the local train depot, aides carefully schooled the throngs of arriving officials on what they were to say on meeting McKinley. And McKinley's own comments were carefully scripted. A surprise came when Bryan himself showed up on McKinley's porch. The two chatted amicably.

Hanna handled the guts of the political contest: he organized state offices, and mastered what today would be called outreach. He sent out 1,400 speakers to stump the nation, and printed and distributed 200,000 pamphlets—the eagerly read attack ads and infomercials of the day.

Above all, Hanna fundraised. Wall Street's investors were leery at the idea of Bryan, a tax-raising, farm-country populist, as President, and Hanna took advantage. He set up one of two campaign headquarters in the nation's financial center, New York City, to solicit campaign cash. Spectacularly so, raking in $3.5 million (about $95 million in 2015 dollars) at the federal level alone, not counting donations in kind. The Republicans outspent Bryan 5-to-1.

Running the Midwest headquarters in Chicago was an unusually talented young businessman, Charles Gates Dawes. Dawes was later Vice-President for President Coolidge, and winner of a Nobel Peace Prize for crafting a lenient debt repayment plan for a post-First World War Europe.

THE MCKINLEY-BRYAN BRAWL

A main issue of the campaign, given Bryan's advocacy for silver currency, was the gold standard. In fact, a major supporter of Bryan was publisher William Randolph Hearst, whose family had made its wealth by founding the Comstock Lode silver mines near Virginia City, Nevada.

McKinley had previously backed letting the Treasury purchase and use silver for some U.S. money. Now, sensing a defining issue to distinguish him from his rival, he came out strongly for gold. He declared it "better to anchor the U.S. economy to American gold than to the silver of English bonds". The stratagem worked, after voters tired somewhat of Bryan's incessant focus on the matter. As Hanna put it: "[Bryan's] talking Silver all the time, and that's where we've got him."

Bryan and McKinley also differed on the income tax: the populist Democrat was for it, the pro-business Republican against it. Unlike Bryan, McKinley also was for a steep tariff. He was able, given his past support for workers right to strike, and for worker-management arbitration, to credibly pitch this as a boon to American workers, their wages and jobs sheltered by a protectionist wall. Both candidates agreed—partly to protect domestic wages, partly due to the era's biases—on limiting the immigration of cheap labor from China.

The election turned out to be fairly close, surprisingly so given McKinley's huge fundraising edge. The narrow margin was probably due to the lingering effects of the Panic on workers and farmers. The Ohioan took the popular vote, 51 percent to 47 percent. His Electoral College margin was wider, 271-176, and revealed a sharp regional split. McKinley dominated the North and Midwest. Bryan took the entire South, except the border state of Kentucky, and all the Mountain and Great Plains states, except North Dakota.

The new President and his advisor Hanna had adroitly put together a winning coalition of businessmen, skilled workers, and city dwellers. German-Americans also went for McKinley. Although often voting Democratic, they tended to be fiscally conservative, and were thus suspicious of Bryan's silverite inflation, as well as his fundamentalist-style rhetoric. Most historians see 1896 as a watershed year where the Republicans set up a nation-wide dominance that lasted until FDR's Depression-era Democratic landslide of 1932.

This seems a bit understated—as only Republicans, or the conservative/ reform Bourbon Democrats Samuel Tilden and Grover Cleveland—won the popular vote for the White House starting in 1860, and clear through 1928. (Tilden lost out in the 1876 Electoral College tally, and Cleveland lost it in 1888, while winning like Tilden the popular vote.) After the collapse of Southern Democrats nationally in 1860, the G.O.P.'s dominance was longer and stronger than is generally thought.

The Democrats seemed to fare better in the 1896 congressional elections, but these results may have been misleading. In the House, the party made major gains, winning 31 seats, while the Democratic-leaning Populist Party gained 13 seats. The Republicans lost 44 seats, yet kept a solid majority of 210-124, with 22 seats for the Populists. Some historians think the results reflected not dissatisfaction with the Republicans nationally, given McKinley's win, but a return to the fold of many normally Democratic voters. After all, in the 1894 midterms, after the Panic of 1893, many had voted Republican because of economic fears.

This view is backed up by the Senate results. There the Republicans lost just one seat, while the Democrats lost seven, mostly to the moderate Silver Republican party, consisting of Republicans who favored, like most Democrats, and McKinley previously, a currency based on silver as well as gold. The Republicans retained a majority of 43-33, with five seats for the Silver Republicans.

HAPPY DAYS ARE HERE AGAIN

In the first term of the McKinley Administration, the country strongly recovered from the severe 1893 recession. Economic historians can debate the causes. Business did rebound after the Administration raised tariffs to very high levels.

This was an era in which newly rising economic powers such as Germany, with its *Zollverein*, or toll or tariff union, and established powers such as the British and French Empires, with their huge overseas territories, followed mercantilist means to defend their homeland or colonial businesses. The United States, under a triumphant Republican party that had from its start adhered to the tariff policies of its Whig Party and Federalist forebears, followed suit.

The campaign over, President McKinley showed flexibility on gold, and offered to mint some silver money if foreign powers did likewise. Negotiations ensued with Britain's Lord Salisbury, who failed to dissuade imperial interests in India to embrace the mining and production of silver. The U.S. stayed with the hard-money policy of a gold standard. Meantime Charles Dawes, promoted from campaign organizer to Comptroller of the Currency, collected debts from banks owed the Treasury since the Panic.

Although the strong-dollar policy raised the cost of American exports, and tariffs the price of imported raw materials, the nation generally prospered. The McKinley Administration benefitted from a stroke, or strike, of luck— the discovery of vast gold deposits in the Klondike region of the Canadian Yukon as well as around Nome, Alaska. From 1896 to 1899, as a hundred thousand prospectors rushed north, supplies of gold flooded the market, producing the same inflationary effect as a silver-backed currency.

Also lifting the economy was the innovations of industrialization. Coming onto the market from 1895 to 1901 were the gasoline-powered auto, Thomas Edison's rechargeable battery, Nikola Tesla's electronic remote control, and mundane aids to commerce like the mechanical key punch and the business filing cabinet. And fueling demands for the new goods and devices was a growing population. Boosted by massive influxes of immigrants from southern and eastern Europe, the number of Americans soared between 1890 and 1900 by 13 percent, from 63 million to 76 million.

A BUILDUP AT SEA

McKinley's term in office occurred at a time of intense rivalries world-wide. The newly unified nations of Germany and Italy, and the newly modern one of Japan, longed for empire along the lines of the British, French, and Spanish. So did many in the United States, whose ambitions were aided by an expanding Navy.

In military as in economic matters, the McKinley Administration went along with the times. Under the 25th President, a newly powerful U.S. military would crushingly win its first foreign war since the Mexican-American conflict of 1848.

Throughout America's military history, the strength of its Navy has risen and fallen markedly during times of war, peace, and perceived threat. At the end of the Civil War in 1865, a vast U.S. Navy had over 50,000 seamen serving on about 700 ships. Yet 15 years later, the peace-time service had only 6,000 sailors, and fewer than 50 ships.

In 1881, however, under the Garfield Administration's Navy Secretary William H. Hunt, and continuing under President Arthur, the U.S. constructed a fleet of powerful battleships and cruisers. After Grover Cleveland cancelled the construction of some vessels to cut waste and expenditures, the Navy built additional capital ships under President Benjamin Harrison and under McKinley. By 1898, the American Navy had the third largest war fleet in the world.

It's interesting to note the buildup occurred under Republican Administrations and slowed some under Democrat Cleveland's two terms—continuing the schism over the proper size of the military going back to Hamilton's Federalists and Jefferson's anti-Federalists. The debate continues today, after over 225 years, with those parties' distant successors, the Republicans and the Democrats.

The naval renaissance was cheered by influential scholars who urged the U.S. to take up a Great Power mantle. In 1890, West Point-born Alfred Mahan, a former president of the Naval War College, authored his highly influential book, *The Influence of Sea Power upon History*. The ex-U.S. Navy captain argued that powerful battle fleets had throughout history been essential for a nation's military and commercial success. Mahan's world-wide bestseller spurred all the major powers, and would-be powers, to build up their navies.

In 1893, University of Wisconsin historian Frederick Jackson Turner published a persuasive essay, "The Significance of the Frontier in American History". Turner posited that expansion into the western wilderness shaped a uniquely American character. From his idea some statesmen deduced that the nation, with its western territories settled, would best thrive with further expansion beyond its North American limits.

TOWARD A CUBA LIBRE

As America grew more powerful in terms of commercial and military clout, and its ideology more aggressive, a crisis erupted on its southern doorstep.

The people of Cuba, ruled by Spain since soon after Columbus, rose up in 1895 to start a three-year war of independence. Seventy years after Simón Bolívar had liberated much of the rest of Latin America, it seemed inevitable that Havana, one of imperial Spain's final, tottering outposts, would fall. But Madrid replied harshly, sending tens of thousands of troops to the island. It also set up *reconcentrado*, or concentration, camps—massive holding pens for civilians outside Spain's fortified towns. During this struggle, about 100,000 native Cubans, out of a population of roughly two million, died from disease or battle.

The oppression angered the democratic sense of the American people on the nearby mainland. Also roused were the fears of American businesses with vast commercial interests in Cuba. For decades, the U.S. had been purchasing over three-quarters of the island's exports. Cuba was already an economic outpost of America.

At the same time, the sensationalistic "yellow press", Hearst's *New York Journal* and Joseph Pulitzer's *New York World*, among others, sold out their penny papers by playing up Spanish tyranny. The Cuban issue saw a peculiarly American mix, which endures for its foreign policy today: human rights wrapped up with economic interest and patriotism, plus a rush of screaming headlines.

At first, McKinley steered a middling course. He opposed sending troops into Cuba, but as a sign of strength ordered the warship the *USS Maine* to Havana harbor. He also offered Madrid a financial way out. The U.S. had long gazed with longing past Spanish-founded Florida to Spanish Cuba. "I candidly confess," former President Jefferson had written to President Monroe in 1823, "that I have ever looked on Cuba as the most interesting addition which could ever be made to our system of States." Back in 1854, the U.S. had tried buying Cuba from Spain, and McKinley did so again in 1897, for $300 million, or about $9 billion in 2015 dollars. Further, President McKinley urged the Spanish to grant Cuba autonomy and to shut down their prison camps.

Spain did close the *reconcentrados*, an act which irked Cuba's Spanish nationalists, who clashed further with members of its liberation movement. In the States, hawks filled with the philosophy of Turner and Mahan and the war-like spirits of Clay and Calhoun demanded a fight, and dreamt of the Caribbean as an American lake.

The path toward war was steady, and became inevitable on February 18, 1898, when the *Maine* blew up, with the death of 266 U.S. sailors. Americans cried, "Remember the Maine!", adding, "To Hell with Spain!"

From 1898 to 1999, four investigations of the *Maine*'s demise took place. The first two, by the Navy, concluded the ship's hull was blown inward by an outside explosion, consistent with the explosion of a mine. The third, a private inquiry led by Admiral Hyman G. Rickover, the father of the nuclear-powered submarine, was held in 1976. It surmised the explosion came from within, likely from a coal fire, a common peril for the ships of the time. (The bulwarks of the *RMS Titanic* were weakened by such a blaze.) The fourth, in 1999 by the National Geographic society, noted the *Maine*'s crew carefully checked for coal fires, and deemed an external detonation most likely. The matter remains unresolved, bearing out Theodore Roosevelt's statement, the day after the explosion, that "we shall never find out" the cause for certain.

In any event, the fate of the *Maine* shoved McKinley toward war. On April 20, he signed a congressional resolution demanding Cuban independence. The next day, he ordered a naval blockade of the island. Two days later, Spain declared war, and two days after that Congress followed suit. Wary of seeming too imperialistic, Capitol Hill had already approved the Teller Amendment assuring Cuban independence, not U.S. annexation, after the island's liberation.

OVERWHELMING NAVAL VICTORIES

The War Department went on handily defeat the poorly equipped and badly funded navy and army of the Spanish imperium, now a shadow of its glory under the *conquistadores*. In swift order, the U.S. would gain control over Cuba, Puerto Rico, and the waters of the Philippines.

The latter, a vast archipelago, had been a Spanish possession since the mid-1500s. Magellan, a Portuguese working for Spain, came across it during the first circumnavigation of the world. Since 1896, anti-Spanish rebels had been fighting, like their brethren in Cuba, for Filipino independence. As war with Madrid loomed, Washington debated whether to take the whole island chain, or settle for something less, such as a Navy base.

The naval buildup, and thorough preparations in the region, led to an overwhelming American victory at sea. In January 1898, the Navy ordered the American commander of its Asia station, Commodore George Dewey, originally from Vermont, to concentrate his fleet near Hong Kong, within striking distance of the archipelago. Dewey held onto sailors whose enlistments had expired, and purchased private steamships to serve as a coal tender and ammunition vessel. A young Assistant Secretary of the Navy, Theodore Roosevelt, had plied Congress for more arms and more seamen, helping prep the sea service. The War Department telegraphed Dewey the U.S. declaration of war, and he steamed out the next day, appearing at Manila Bay four days later.

The Spanish fleet of 10 ships was woefully obsolete, lacking torpedoes and even armor, even though metal-plated ships had become standard since the 1862 Civil War battle of the *Monitor* and the *Merrimack*. After a five-hour fight, Dewey's fleet sunk or seized all the Spanish ships, with the loss of exactly one American. U.S. Army troops occupied the capital of Manila.

The Spanish Navy's defeat was so quick and overwhelming that McKinley, following the enthused public reaction to the win, decided to seize the entire Philippines.

In Cuba, the U.S. ground forces took on a "motley crew" aspect not seen since Andy Jackson's army at the 1815 Battle of New Orleans. Roosevelt, after resigning from the Navy and enlisting as an Army Lt. Colonel, cobbled together a Rough Riders volunteer cavalry regiment of gold prospectors, cowboys, Ivy League scholars, and American Indians. Helping lead the American expeditionary force were former Confederate generals: including Robert E. Lee's nephew, former Virginia Gov. Fitzhugh Lee, and the commander of Roosevelt's division, Maj. Gen. Joseph Wheeler. Joining in with the old rebel yells were African-American formations, as McKinley gave a green light for all-black regiments to fight. (It is said Wheeler, after glimpsing his Buffalo Soldiers attacking, shouted, "Give them Yankees hell!")

The peace-time Army had had just 28,000 soldiers, but almost ten times that number poured in from volunteers and National Guard units. The effort was somewhat amateurish and ad hoc, and ultimately successful.

Still, a major problem was supply. After 33 years of peace, the War Department's logistics for a major land conflict were pitiful. Canned meat hastily procured from Chicago's meatpacking plants arrived at the front spoiled, dubbed "embalmed beef".

In all the war-time theaters, 332 Americans died in battle, yet almost over 2,500, many in Cuba, perished from yellow fever and malaria. A silver lining: a U.S. Army officer stationed in Cuba, Virginia's Dr. Walter Reed, would draw on his experience to make the landmark discovery of yellow fever as a mosquito-borne disease.

On July 1, 1898, the Army mounted bloody frontal assaults to win the battles of El Caney, San Juan Hill, and Kettle Hill. In the meantime, the Marines seized Guantánamo Bay, bottling up the rest of the Spanish Army in the port city of Santiago, and securing a prison camp for a war in another century against another foe.

On July 3, the Spanish fleet of six ships attempted to escape its harbor. Although these crafts were modern, they were short of ammunition, with many shells filled with sawdust for target practice. One warship hadn't had its guns installed. Commodore Winfield Scott Schely, standing in for Rear Admiral William Sampson, who was at a planning session with Army officers onshore, won a victory as clear-cut as Manila Bay. His seven vessels sank, ran aground, or forced the scuttling of all the Spanish ships. Over 300 Spaniards were killed, over 1,600 surrendered. The Americans lost one seaman.

Meanwhile U.S. forces easily occupied Puerto Rico. In August, Madrid called a halt to the one-sided struggle, and to its 400-year-old New World empire.

Under the Paris Peace Treaty in December, the U.S. acquired the Philippines and the Pacific island of Guam, and annexed Puerto Rico. Cuba became a U.S. protectorate in 1902, and would gain an often-troubled independence starting in 1934. Washington paid Madrid $20 million for Manila.

"It was a splendid little war," wrote Secretary of State John Milton Hay, formerly an aide to Lincoln during a far bloodier time. After speaking softly of compromise, McKinley had wound up wielding a big stick.

ACROSS THE PACIFIC

Thrilled by these smashing successes, the man on the street clamored to annex Hawaii, as intellectuals spoke of "manifest destiny" carrying clear across the Pacific. Military thinkers feared the Japanese Navy would move into Pearl Harbor if a U.S. fleet didn't.

On these old "Sandwich Islands", Western missionaries had banished many of the native chieftains' beliefs, and sometimes vicious practices. U.S. planters controlled the islands' economy. In 1893, American interests had overthrown the monarchy and set up a republic of sorts. Despite the Cleveland Administration's opposition, Congress had pursued negotiations for annexation. McKinley continued these discussions, despite the opposition of the native Hawaiian majority.

The Senate was wary, so McKinley in July 1898 acquired the islands through a joint resolution of Congress, not through a formal Senate-approved treaty, as the Constitution might have called for. The votes were about 2-to-1 in favor: 42 to 21 in the Senate, and 209 to 91 in the House.

Hawaii would prove a jewel of the mid-Pacific, and Cuba's economic value to the U.S. would grow even greater. In the long run, Hawaii would be a center of the U.S. military action in the Pacific theater of the Second World War, after the 1941 Japanese attack on Pearl Harbor. Cuba in 1959 would be taken over by Communists led by Fidel Castro, and would become the fulcrum of the perilous 1962 nuclear missile crisis with the Soviet Union.

In the short term, the war was popular, and entailed few battle deaths. The sprawling conquests were impressive and adroitly executed by the American military and its volunteers. They were also part of the times, a time of empires of all the established and rising powers. With its victories, the U.S. took its turn as a great power, soon the greatest power.

THE CRY OF DOVES

However, there was significant opposition to the Spanish-American War, a conflict which led immediately to another war with many casualties.

Opponents spanned the spectrum. Left-wing anarchists saw it as imperialism. Some, especially among the progressive movement of the day, feared bringing non-white peoples under American rule. Former President Cleveland opposed it. A reluctant Mark Hanna commented, "Remember that my folks were Quakers. War is just a damn nuisance."

The Senate resisted the terms of the Treaty of Paris which ended the war and ratified the conquests. Statements from a trio of senators illustrated the divergent range of opinion. Henry Cabot Lodge of Massachusetts said rejecting the treaty would brand Americans "a people incapable of taking rank as one of the greatest world powers". But from the same state, Sen. George Frisbie Hoar opined, "This Treaty will make us a vulgar, commonplace empire, controlling subject races and vassal states." Minnesota Sen. Knute Nelson countered, "Providence has given the United States the duty of extending Christian civilization. We come as ministering angels, not despots."

The Treaty narrowly gained the requisite, two-thirds Senate margin, in about the same 2-to-1 proportion as the resolution on Hawaii. 57 Senators voted Yes, and 27 voted No.

Along with the treaty, Congress passed the Platt Amendment. To allay critics of imperialism, it forbade annexation of Cuba. To appease expansionists, it permitted U.S. military intervention there to fend off foreign powers.

The acquisition of the Philippines and Hawaii was particularly problematic. Unlike Cuba and Puerto Rico, neither was in the U.S. "sphere of influence", and the defense of them necessitated long supply lines trailing thousands of miles from the American mainland.

AN EARLY ASIAN WAR

In the Philippines, McKinley's decision to acquire the entire island chain led to a major war right away. A bloody conflict erupted between U.S. troops and the Philippine fighters who'd been seeking independence from Spain.

The U.S. Army there was led by Gen. Arthur MacArthur, Jr., a Medal of Honor winner in the Civil War, and father of the Second World War's conqueror of the Philippines, Gen. Douglas MacArthur. The armed Filipino opposition to the U.S. occupation was led by Gen. Emilio Aguinaldo, who had led the resistance to Spanish rule.

Aguinaldo was no saint: he established a regime that ruled by decree; in the Second World War, he would vocally take the side of the occupying Japanese. Indeed, an idealistic motive behind the American occupation was to prevent a native authoritarian regime, while eventually bringing about local democratic rule.

American soldiers would capture Aguinaldo in early 1901. Guerrilla war then replaced large-scale conventional fighting the following year, then sputtered on past 1906. Casualties, especially compared to the sea battles of Manila and Santiago, were huge. Upwards of 6,000 American soldiers, and perhaps 15,000 Filipinos, were to die in battle or succumb to disease.

It would be the first of seven long American land wars in Asia (Philippine-American War, Pacific theater of the Second World War, Korean War, Vietnam War, Afghanistan, the Second Persian Gulf War, and the war against the Islamic State, or ISIS). At the time, Mark Twain stated of the Philippines broil: "We have got into a quagmire from which each fresh step renders the difficulty of extrication immensely greater."

Like many successful presidents, McKinley possessed the trait of exercising restraint, and of knowing when to say no. With the Philippines, however, after initially following his usual caution, he probably overreacted to public sentiment, in deciding to occupy the entire island chain. In retrospective, it would have been much less costly in blood and treasure to settle for a military base. Rather as the U.S. would lease the naval installation at Subic Bay after Filipino independence, and indeed Guantánamo Bay from Cuba.

McKinley was savvy enough to adjust his policy, however. He brought in the skilled jurist, William Howard Taft, to craft an effective plan of administration. The Americans enacted widespread legal and social changes, such as separation of the state from the formerly official Catholic Church, and making English the official language. Under Taft, the U.S. put the islands on a gradual path to independence. The Philippines would become a commonwealth in 1935, a stalwart ally in the Second World War, and a fully independent, and friendly, nation in 1946.

TO THE MIDDLE KINGDOM

In China, Secretary of State Hay was responsible for a landmark "Open Door" policy, by which the U.S. urged all nations to practice free and open trade with that vast and troubled land. As part of this policy, the U.S. there eschewed the acquisition of "spheres of influence" desired by many European powers and by Japan. With its missionary work and the establishment of schools, the American approach to China would continue to be characterized by such idealism, along with economic self-interest.

Ideals ran into realities from 1899 to 1901, when the Boxer Rebellion of Chinese nationalists erupted against foreign encroachments. Europeans gave the rebels, called "righteous militia" in Chinese, their pugilistic nickname. With the help of the Chinese imperial government, they burned churches, killed Christians and foreigners, and besieged Beijing's embassy district.

Along with the militaries of six European nations and Japan, McKinley dispatched 3,300 U.S. troops to put down the rebellion. Reprisals and looting among the militaries were severe, and Beijing was forced to pay large reparations. The U.S steered much of its share to missionary efforts in China.

From the U.S. perspective, the intervention was successful, as the Rebellion collapsed, and many threatened Americans were saved. Moreover, the U.S. had again acted successively on a world stage. It was an extraordinary and unprecedented deployment of a large American military force on a "peacekeeping mission" on a distant shore.

However, some of the foreign powers, including Japan, Germany, and Russia, went on to seize territories and special privileges in the Middle Kingdom. As for the U.S., McKinley had sent in the American military without congressional authorization, laying down a precedent for military actions on the Asian continent without formal declarations of war.

Today's American relationship with a powerful China—marked by widespread trade and investment, mixed with marked military and technological competition—much reflects the markers originally laid down by McKinley and Hay.

Reflecting the popularity and success of the Spanish-American War, the congressional elections of autumn 1898 produced mixed results, instead of the normal falloff for the incumbent President's party. The Democrats did gain an impressive 37 seats, many at the expense of the sister party to their left, the Populists, who lost 16 seats. In the Senate, however, the Republicans added eight seats, to build their formerly modest majority to a more than 2-to-1 edge, 51-24. Reflecting the continuing adherence to the gold standard of McKinley and Roosevelt, the Silver Republican Party lost three seats.

A DELEGATOR YET A DECIDER

As modernity arrived, McKinley invented the modern presidency. He was the first Chief Executive to meet regularly with reporters, to go on frequent nation-wide speaking tours or, if confined to the White House, to regularly use the telephone. He also much increased the size of the White House staff.

Like most successful executives, he usually made good personnel selections, and he knew how to delegate. As during his campaigns, he maintained a "big picture" of the important issues, and made the big decisions himself.

When McKinley did pick the wrong man for the job, he got rid of him. An illustration was the key job of Secretary of State. Partly due to Hanna's desire to take over John Sherman's slot as Senator from Ohio, McKinley appointed Sherman to head up Foggy Bottom, even though the then-74-year-old legislator was probably senile. At the same time, Sherman's Assistant Secretary of State was very taciturn—and his senior staffer was deaf! This led to a lament: "The head of the department knows nothing; the first assistant says nothing; the second assistant hears nothing."

In 1898, with the Spanish-American War approaching, McKinley replaced Sherman with the able attorney William Day. Later, after he appointed Day to the Supreme Court, he picked Hay as Secretary of State. John Hay defined the phrase "long and distinguished career." In the Civil War, he'd been President Lincoln's private secretary. Soon he would be behind a number of historic achievements for McKinley and for President Theodore Roosevelt.

After the war with Spain broke out, McKinley chafed at the administration of the invasion of Cuba by his Secretary of War, Russell Alger, a self-made timber baron and distant relation of the symbol of self-help, Horatio Alger.

The President went behind his Secretary's back for military advice, and later replaced him with the able, high-powered New York lawyer Elihu Root, whose clients ranged from Jay Gould to former President Chester A. Arthur. Root eventually overhauled the military, and established the Army War College and a General Staff that was perform adeptly during the two world wars. One of the most influential diplomats of the early 20th century, Root would be Theodore Roosevelt's Secretary of State.

For his Vice President in the 1900 campaign, McKinley acceded to Hanna's recommendation of New Jersey's Garret Augustus Hobart. A skilled Republican state legislator in a Democratic state, Hobart had become Speaker of the New Jersey Assembly by age 30, and then President of the State Senate. As an attorney, he'd made a fortune as a reorganizer of bankrupt railroads. In 1895, Hobart had run the first successful gubernatorial campaign of a New Jersey Republican in three decades. Although he didn't attend McKinley's regular Cabinet meetings, he served as a close presidential adviser, and one willing to do the "dirty work", such as telling Alger to pack his bags.

When Hobart died in office in 1899, of heart disease at age 55, McKinley needed a successor. One option was the youthful star of the Republican party, New York Governor Theodore Roosevelt, admired for his thoroughgoing reforms as New York City Police Commissioner, and for his dash during the Spanish-American War. But McKinley was wary, telling a Roosevelt acquaintance: "I want peace, and I am told that your friend Theodore is always getting into rows with everybody."

Hanna was firmly opposed to the bellicose New Yorker. During the run-up to the Spanish-American War that Hanna disliked, Roosevelt, at D.C.'s yearly Gridiron Dinner of press and politicians, had had a run-in with the President's aide de camp. Shaking his fist at Hanna, Roosevelt exclaimed: "We will have this war for the freedom of Cuba!"

Still, at the 1900 convention, the President went for Roosevelt after pressure from New York's Republican political chiefs, such as Sen. Thomas C.

Platt, who disliked Roosevelt's reform and interventionist inclinations. They calculated they could get rid of a pest by exiling him to the powerless office of the vice presidency.

Hanna, when he heard of the VP decision, thundered at McKinley: "Do whatever you damn please! I'm through! I won't take charge of the campaign! Why, everybody's gone crazy! Don't any of you realize that there's only one life between that madman and the Presidency?" After he calmed down, Hanna wrote to President: "The ticket is all right. Your duty to the country is to live for four years."

In the end, despite Hanna's anguish, McKinley's decision seemed sound. After Roosevelt took over for the slain McKinley, he proved a vigorous and accomplished two-term president.

Hanna himself, after becoming Senator from Ohio in 1897, remained a close counsel of McKinley's. Access is influence in Washington, and he took up residence across from the White House in a Lafayette Square manse, where he and his wife often entertained the President and First Lady.

McKinley's inclination was more toward mainstream and moderate Republicans, men like William Howard Taft, than the restless Roosevelt. After his time as McKinley's Governor General of the Philippines, Taft was to serve as Secretary of War, President of the United States, and Chief Justice of the Supreme Court.

Another example of McKinley's judge of talent was his appointment of Cleveland's chief clerk, New York barrister George Cortelyou, as his private secretary. Cortelyou would try mightily if futilely to strengthen the security around McKinley prior to his assassination. When Theodore Roosevelt was sworn in, the new President retained Cortelyou, as his press liaison, and later picked him for various Cabinet posts. After leaving government, the talented man headed up what became Consolidated Edison.

McKinley's performance on personnel matters was poorer on the matter of civil service reform. Where Presidents Cleveland, Arthur, and Hayes believed the civil service could rein in corruption, McKinley preferred to make appointments himself, to reward loyalists.

Another weakness of McKinley's, indeed for almost all presidents from Hayes up until Truman, was civil rights. Although he allowed African-Americans to fight during the Spanish-American War, he made fewer appointments of blacks than had his predecessors.

He was largely silent on a national disgrace, the era's record number of lynchings of blacks, which during each of three years of his presidency exceeded 100.

A CLEAR RE-ELECTION WIN

President McKinley headed into his second White House campaign with several advantages.

The nation had won an overwhelming and very popular military victory, thus acquiring new territories from a defeated European nation. Prosperity had returned, partly due to the discovery of gold in the far North. The Republicans campaign slogan was, "Four More Years of the Full Dinner Pail".

The President had positioned himself in the center or center-right on other economic issues. Although not an active "trust buster", he took a stand against absolute monopolies. Though a friend of big business, he approved of labor's right to strike and believed management had a duty to bargain with worker unions.

He again faced Bryan as the Democratic nominee. But Bryan's signature issue of silver money had faded with prosperity and the gold boom. Further, McKinley had added to his ticket a youthful, appealing Vice President,

Roosevelt. As a New York reformer, the choice of Roosevelt countered Bryan's own pick of a progressive, Adlai E. Stevenson I, Cleveland's former Vice President.

The President also had the skilled Hanna as a campaign manager, and they repeated their successful strategy of 1896. McKinley conducted another "front porch" campaign, making his pronouncements from his Canton home. As a stand-in on the campaign trail, they sent out the aggressive Roosevelt, who exceeded even the huge amount of miles that Bryan covered by railroad, 21,000 to 18,000. Bryan tried making his big issue the Spanish-American War and the Philippines insurgency, but the public had liked the war, and early in the re-election year McKinley appointed Taft to oversee what proved a viable exit strategy from Manila.

McKinley and Hanna finessed a potentially disruptive strike in September by Midwest coal miners, led by their powerful union, a revived UMW, the United Mine Workers. During the McKinley Administration years, the union had garnered greater pay for its enrollees while increasing its membership by tenfold. With the election but six weeks away, Hanna worked with the moderate National Civil Federation and with financier J.P. Morgan to convince management the strike could hurt McKinley enough to elect Bryan, a skeptic of big business. As a result, the mine owners conceded to higher pay and a process for handling grievances to the workers, without formally recognizing the union.

President McKinley gained a respectable re-election win. He had a modest popular vote margin, 52 percent to 46 percent. His Electoral College edge was more impressive, and larger than four years prior: 292-155. He carried all of the North, the West Coast, and all of the Midwest except Missouri. He even carried Bryan's home state of Nebraska. Bryan held the agrarian Solid South and took some of the Rocky Mountain states.

The congressional results were mixed. In the House, the Republicans picked up 12 seats to hike their majority to 201-151. In the Senate, the

Democrats gained five seats, at the expense of the Populists, who dropped from seven seats to two. The G.O.P. majority fell from 54-23 to 53-28.

EARLY SECOND-TERM SUCCESS

In the four months after his re-election, and for the first six months of his second term, success continued for McKinley. At home, a vast oil deposit, the first of many to come, was discovered in January 1901 at Beaumont, Texas. It promised to lift his second term as the lucky strikes of gold had boosted his first. Petroleum would be the black gold of the new century, and America its dominant producer for much of it.

Abroad, more foreign policy successes reflected the continuing growth of American power.

The Spanish-American War had greatly heightened the ongoing U.S. desire to build a canal in Central America to link the Atlantic to the Pacific. During the war, it had taken a Navy ship over two months to steam from San Francisco to the Cuban war zone by way of Cape Horn, at the southern tip of South America.

Hay, the adroit Secretary of State, negotiated an agreement with Britain where London acceded to the eventual construction by the U.S. of the Panama Canal. Construction of the giant ditch would begin under Roosevelt, after his Administration helped instigate Panama's independence from Columbia. Thus McKinley set up this famous feather in Roosevelt's cap.

And spectacularly, on March 23, just 19 days after McKinley's second inauguration, the U.S. Army captured Aguinaldo, the leader of the bloody Filipino insurrection. The erstwhile rebel was persuaded to call for an end to the revolt.

On the economic front, McKinley represented the nation's manufacturers, who had long prospered through protectionism. Yet the President pledged that month to slash tariffs if other nations did the same. The U.S., now the world's largest economy, exceeding Great Britain and Germany, seemed strong enough to allow overseas competitors vie for its vast domestic market. America also seemed powerful enough to begin laying down some of the rules of the world economy. Moreover, the President was acting as the enlightened statesman: a strong defender of the national interest, but willing to engage in mutually beneficial compromise with other nations.

At age 58, McKinley was popular and admired. At the national level his political party was on a roll, preeminent in the presidency all the way from the Civil War to the Great Depression. And McKinley was President right in the middle of the streak.

STALKED BY A KILLER

But his fortune-strewn time in office came to the most unfortunate end in September 1901, just six months into his second term.

McKinley's presence at the time and place of his demise was due to circumstance. The President was making a nation-wide speaking tour in support of "reciprocation", his scheme for lowering tariffs if other trading nations did likewise. The President had made plans to travel in June to Buffalo, New York, for the Pan-American Exposition, which itself highlighted America's deepening commercial involvement with Latin America. However, his sickly wife Ida fell very ill, and to spend time with her McKinley delayed his appearance. The visit was rescheduled, with much publicity, for September.

Meanwhile a villain had begun stalking him. 28-year-old Leon Czolgosz was the son of Polish immigrants in Michigan. For much of his adult life an unemployed drifter, he lost his Cleveland factory job over a strike during the Panic of 1893. In industrial and mining regions, the years that followed were often a time of bullets and bombs between striking workers and police, as in the time of the Pullman strike of 1884.

Leon Czolgosz became fascinated by the growing anarchist movement, a kind of extreme socialist movement. Anarchists despised wealthy corporate chiefs and the ruling governments of Europe and America. Some had staged assassinations of prominent Europeans.

Czolgosz himself was so wild-eyed he spooked his fellow anarchists, notably the movement's leader Emma Goldman, originally from Lithuania, Russia, whose lover Alexander Berkman had tried to assassinate steel magnate Henry Clay Frick in 1892. Czolgosz asked so many questions of Goldman's group that it was certain he was a corporate or government plant.

Five days before the McKinley assassination, its newspaper issued a remarkable warning about him: "ATTENTION! The attention of the comrades is called to another spy... he disappeared when the comrades had confirmed themselves of his identity [and] were on the point of exposing him. His demeanor is of the usual sort, pretending to be greatly interested in the cause, asking for names or soliciting aid for acts of contemplated violence."

Czolgosz was no plant, but a fanatic. He later recalled: "People seemed bowing to the great ruler. I made up my mind to kill." He proceeded to the President's stop-off in Buffalo.

Ill omens greeted McKinley's arrival at the city's train depot. Local officials fired off a cannon in greeting, and its boom shattered his train's windows, leading onlookers to think anarchists had thrown a bomb.

As the President disembarked, Czolgosz was waiting. His revolver loaded, he got close—but too many guards surrounded McKinley to get off a clear shot.

The following day, the President delivered a speech at the Exposition's esplanade. With lowering of tariffs and foreign incursions into China in mind, he declared that "commercial wars are unprofitable." Czolgosz was in the front of the audience but, jostled by the crowd, felt he couldn't get off an accurate shot. Besides, he knew McKinley was scheduled to speak again the next day at the fair's Temple of Music.

A TRAGIC END

During this time the President's conscientious private secretary, Cortelyou, was deeply worried about his boss' safety. He pleaded with McKinley to cancel the Temple speech, to be held at a large auditorium with thousands of spectators. He actually deleted the appearance from the President's schedule. Twice. The President put it right back on his agenda, twice. McKinley noted: "No one would wish to hurt me."

So Cortelyou took other steps. He increased the Secret Service guards from one to three, and persuaded a group of Buffalo police detectives to attend as well. In addition, he placed 12 artillery soldiers, on hand for ceremonial reasons, around the President. However, the troops weren't trained for their role, and they obstructed the view of the guards.

Presidential security was then a different world. As Lincoln had been, McKinley was frustratingly lax about his own safety. He would often walk to church or take a carriage ride with his wife without a body guard. On the morning of his Temple speech, he had slipped out of his guest house for a stroll without his guards noticing him leaving.

McKinley's ill luck that day extended to the smallest detail. At the Temple, the President stood at the head of a reception line. At such events, his chief security guard, George Foster, normally stood at his side. However, that day, because the Exposition's marshal wanted to be right next to the President, Foster stood across the aisle from McKinley, where he couldn't stop a determined assailant.

The Chief Executive began shaking hands with the hundreds of well-wishers who were lined up. Presidential protocol called for greeters to approach the Chief Executive with open, uncovered hands, but that September 6, perhaps due to the day's warmth, greeters were allowed to carry handkerchiefs. Czolgosz approached, his .32-caliber revolver wrapped in one.

McKinley saw the man's right hand wrapped in the kerchief and, thinking he was injured, reached out to shake his left hand. As their fingers touched, Czolgosz fired off two rounds.

One bullet didn't penetrate the target's body. The other entered deep within the abdomen. The President staggered, and the men around him lowered him into a chair. As stunned onlookers began to beat the assassin, who muttered, "I done my duty," the gallant President and war veteran cried out that they not take revenge. He asked Cortelyou to gently break the news of the shooting to his wife.

McKinley was taken to the Exposition's hospital, and met more ill fortune. The clinic had no operating room, and at first no doctor was on hand. The region's finest surgeon, Dr. Roswell Park, was then indisposed, performing a dissection in Niagara Falls, 20 miles away. Less than a month later, he would save a patient with a wound similar to McKinley's.

Two other doctors arrived, and determined to operate. But they performed the procedure without surgical retractors, and with poor lighting—to help the surgeon see more clearly aides reflected the setting sun onto the bullet wound.

In the era before the widespread, effective use of the X-ray, the President's physicians were unable to find the bullet lodged in his abdomen. A similar lapse had contributed in 1881 to the death of President Garfield, despite the efforts of inventor Alexander Graham Bell to detect the lead lodged in his body with a prototype X-ray. Days after McKinley's shooting, with the President still alive, an X-ray device from inventor Thomas Edison arrived at the patient's hospital. However, the machine was missing a vital component, and wasn't used.

During the operation the attending physician, Dr. Matthew Mann, a gynecologist, did not accurately trace the course of the bullet. Some forensic historians believe he did not clean the wound properly. Mann concluded: "A bullet once it ceases to move does little harm."

During an age where stomach wounds were almost always fatal due to infection, the optimism of McKinley's doctors was strange. They were fooled perhaps by the President's demeanor. After the surgery, McKinley was upbeat and talkative. His medical team publicly professed confidence he was steadily improving. The Cabinet believed this. Vice President Roosevelt felt secure enough about McKinley's health to go on a hiking trip deep in the Adirondack Mountains. A doubter was State Department chief Hay, formerly the secretary of the slain President Lincoln and formerly an associate of the slain President Garfield as well. He told the Exposition's marshal that McKinley was doomed.

On September 12, the doctors pronounced McKinley well enough to take toast and broth. On September 13, he collapsed into critical condition.

His final words were, "We are all going…God's will be done, not ours." He died early the next morning, eight days after the shooting.

His death was from gangrene poisoning, probably a result of pancreatic infection, which even today is very hard to treat. An autopsy discovered the bullet had pierced his stomach, colon, and kidney, and damaged the pancreas and adrenal glands as well. The projectile was never found, likely lodged deep in his back muscles.

Vice-President Theodore Roosevelt, at age 42, returned from his trek to take the oath of office. The Secret Service, until then an unofficial means of protection, was soon formally given the role of guarding the President.

Czolgosz was tried by a New York state court, and electrocuted on October 29. His last words were, "I killed the President because he was the enemy of... the good working people."

One can speculate on what might have happened if McKinley had survived the assassination, or avoided it altogether. McKinley's death probably robbed him of his own successful second term. Historian Eric Rauchway noted: "It looked as if the McKinley Administration would continue peaceably unbroken for another four years." The years from 1901 to 1905 were ones of peace, prosperity, and technical innovation, a fortunate era that McKinley's successful first term had in some measure set up.

However, due to an assassin's hand, McKinley's happy prospects were cut short. Among the second-term presidents, only Abraham Lincoln too suffered such an abrupt and fatal turn of fate.

TWO-TERM SUCCESS PRECEDING
A LATE-CAREER FALL
THEODORE ROOSEVELT, 1905-1909

This book considers both McKinley and Theodore Roosevelt to be "two-term" Presidents. McKinley with a very brief second term, with Roosevelt's first term serving out the balance of it, before his own second term.

Roosevelt is an exception to the general rule—a successful two-term president, well-thought-of in his time, and popular today among most historians and among the public. He did have his blemishes, however, in his first term and his second.

PRESIDENTIAL PEDIGREE

In taking over the White House, the restless Roosevelt had previously served as Vice-President of the United States and as Governor of New York, and had primed the nation for war with Spain as Assistant Secretary of the Navy. As head of New York City's Police Commissioners, he'd substituted merit for politics in recruitment, and walked a beat through the town's tenement slums with muckraker Jacob Riis, author of *How the Other Half Lives*. Roosevelt had even served as a Wild West sheriff, who ran down boat thieves from his North Dakota ranch. He'd been ambitious since his student days at Harvard Law. He recalled: "I intended to be one of the governing class."

Two Presidents from different parties, the Republican Hayes and the Democrat Cleveland, thought him effective and honest enough to appoint, and reappoint, to the U.S. Civil Service Commission. He'd already been a conservationist out West, and had written a classic naval study of the War of 1812. He considered his Spanish-American War charge near San Juan Hill "the great day of my life".

Yet he was only in his early forties when he had accomplished all that, when he took office as the youngest president ever.

Roosevelt's character stemmed from a stern yet loving father, as he himself would be, and an irrepressible mother.

His father, Theodore "Thee" Roosevelt, Sr., was the nephew of a congress-man, and the son of a merchant importer: Cornelius Van Shaack Roosevelt. Of Dutch and British ancestry, Cornelius Roosevelt co-founded what became Chase Manhattan Bank. And he was the grandfather of Eleanor Roosevelt, the spouse, and fifth cousin once removed, of four-term President Franklin Roosevelt.

Thee Roosevelt, intensely philanthropic, helped established New York's Children's Aid Society and its world-class Museum of Natural History, as well as the war-time Union League Club. During the Civil War, and with support from President Lincoln, he set up a paycheck plan that sent the wives of fighting men a portion of their husband's wages. His six-year-old son Teddy watched Lincoln's funeral procession, which had wended its way from Washington, D.C. to New York City, from the window of Thee's Manhattan mansion.

In words that could have described himself, the younger Roosevelt later recalled of Thee: "I never knew any one who got greater joy out of living than did my father, or any one who more whole-heartedly performed every duty." It was Thee who rode with the young Teddy in a swift, open carriage, trying to force air into his son's asthmatic lungs. And encouraged him to take up manly sports like boxing, to transform his weak body into a powerful physique.

Thee, the ardent Unionist, married a Southern belle, a denizen of Georgia's historic Bulloch Hall. Martha "Mittie" Stewart Bulloch was the great-granddaughter of her state's first governor. Author Margaret Mitchell, of *Gone with the Wind*, probably used Mittie, a willful beauty, as a template for Scarlett O'Hara.

Mittie was from a plantation family that owned 33 slaves; three of Mittie's brothers or half-brothers fought for the Confederacy. Teddy Roosevelt said of his mother's regional loyalties: "She was entirely 'unreconstructed' to the day of her death." He further remembered: "From hearing of the feats of my southern forefathers and from knowing my father, I felt a great admiration for men who were fearless and who could hold their own in the world."

Roosevelt, Jr. married Alice Hathaway Lee, an alluring banker's daughter from Boston's elite Cabot family. In 1884, she died from kidney failure during childbirth, at age 22, on the same day that Mittie died. Stricken, barely able to utter Alice's name again, Roosevelt journeyed to the Dakota badlands to forget. Then in 1886 he remarried, to his childhood friend, Edith Kermit Carow, daughter of a Union Army general. They would reside in Sagamore Hill on Long Island, New York, and have five children.

Their progeny would include Theodore Roosevelt, Jr., who would die during the 1944 invasion of Normandy, where he won the Medal of Honor; and Kermit Roosevelt, Jr., would lead a CIA coup in 1953 that installed a strongman in Iran called the Shah. TR's other child, with his first wife Alice, was Alice Lee Roosevelt. She blossomed into a headstrong Washington socialite, marrying House Speaker Nicholas Longworth, before having an affair with Idaho Sen. William Borah. Few dynasties have pursued their aims with greater passion.

RISE AND CONTINUITY

Teddy Roosevelt got to a stepping stone of the White House, the vice-presidency, in unusual fashion. As New York's head of police and as its Governor, his efforts at reforming the state's civil service had irked the state's Republican bosses. Businesses resented his advocacy of taxes and regulations on insurance firms and state-granted franchises. The Democrat bosses at Tammany Hall disliked his zeal for blue laws cracking down on vice.

So, when President William McKinley's Vice-President Garret Hobart died in November 1899, G.O.P. chieftains persuaded McKinley to make Roosevelt his number two. As noted, the President, though concerned about Roosevelt's forward personality, had few other big-name alternatives, and figured correctly the New Yorker would make an attractive asset in his 1900 re-election bid. Also as noted, the bosses figured they'd dropped the busybody reformer into permanent exile at a do-nothing post in faraway D.C. Few political calculations have turned out more wrong.

In the 1900 campaign, Roosevelt played a role typical of a vice-presidential candidate: attack dog. TR vigorously traveled the country to accuse the Democratic nominee William Jennings Bryan of radicalism. This would prove ironic, as in later years some of Roosevelt's fellow Republicans would accuse him of "Bryanite socialism".

The McKinley-Roosevelt ticket won handily. But just six months after their inauguration, the anarchist Leon Czolgosz shot and mortally wounded President McKinley. On September 14, 1901, Roosevelt was sworn in as President.

After taking office, the new Chief Executive announced he would continue McKinley's policies. This would be true on many issues, such as maintaining the gold standard, high tariffs, and low internal taxes. On other, domestic matters, Roosevelt would over time prove considerably more "progressive", or activist, especially so on federal regulation of lands and industry. After leaving the presidency he moved much further in that direction.

On foreign affairs, he largely followed McKinley's initiatives: intervention in the Caribbean and Central America to maintain order and American interests, as well as decisive action to bring about McKinley's and his own vision of a Panama Canal.

TR retained McKinley's Cabinet, which was generally of high quality. It included Secretary of State John Hay, who would help Roosevelt win a Noble Peace Prize and build the Panama Canal, and reformist Secretary of War Elihu Root, himself later to win a Nobel. Roosevelt's Attorney General was Philander C. Knox, a friend of Pennsylvania industrialists such as Henry Clay Frick, and later Taft's Secretary of State. Knox proved adaptable: although he'd been a partner in Pennsylvania of business barons Andrew Mellon and Frick, he'd prosecute many of TR's anti-trust lawsuits. The Attorney General slot was later filled by the able Charles J. Bonaparte, a grand-nephew of Napoleon.

For the first Secretary of Commerce and Labor, TR picked the first Jewish Cabinet member, Oscar Straus, former ambassador to the Ottoman Empire, and brother of the co-owner of Macy's. To the Supreme Court, Roosevelt made three appointments, including the very influential judge Oliver Wendell Holmes, Jr. of Massachusetts, a decorated officer of the Civil War. He also made McKinley's dedicated secretary, Cortelyou, his press secretary, and together they created the contemporary White House press office.

ETHNICITY, LABOR, CAPITAL

Roosevelt's first flap as president came in October 1901, one month after taking office, when he dined at the White House with Booker T. Washington, the black educator, author of *Up from Slavery*, and advocate of personal uplift. Southern race baiters fiercely criticized the President over the high-profile, biracial sit-down. The presidential war hero responded lamely he had only had sandwiches with Washington, not dinner, and refrained from publicized meetings with black leaders for the rest of his presidency. In time an icon of presidential strength, TR was like so many Chief Executives in the era of official segregation, weak or absent on such matters.

President Roosevelt was stronger in his first year on immigration. The nation was then in the midst of the largest mass migration in human history, until the movement in the late-20th century of rural Chinese to Middle Kingdom megalopolises. In the decade before TR took office, about 10 million newcomers had come to America, and about 13 million more would arrive over the succeeding 20 years.

Most entered through the processing center at New York City's Ellis Island, itself a successor to the federal facility of Castle Island at The Battery on the tip of Manhattan. In 1901, the new President picked a new Ellis Island immigration commissioner, who rooted out corruption among some officials who'd taken bribes in exchange for favorable treatment of arrivals.

On immigration, TR balanced between a welcoming stance, a stern nationalism, and the ethnic biases of the day. On the one hand, he declared as President a lack of prejudice toward the religion, ethnicity, or place of origin of the immigrant: "We can not afford to consider whether he is Catholic or Protestant, Jew or Gentile; whether he is Englishman or Irishman, Frenchman or German, Japanese, Italian, or Scandinavian or Magyar. What we should desire to find out is the individual quality of the individual man." His declaration was notably enlightened, for referring to Catholics and Jews at a time of wide unease over masses of non-Protestants entering America, and for mentioning the Japanese after decades of restrictions on Asian immigration. Yet he also signed, in 1902, a congressional bill to continue to exclude Chinese coolies from migrating to the U.S.

Later, in his 1907 "Gentlemen's Agreement" with Japan, he would persuade California public schools to admit Japanese-American students, in return for Japan ending most immigration to the U.S. (Some Japanese and Americans got around the restriction with "picture brides", whereby Americans married, and made citizens of, Japanese women who publicized their beauty and availability through photographs.)

TR's vision was one of an unabashed 'melting pot', of a single flag and language, not the multicultural mosaic often advocated today. "We must Americanize in every way," Roosevelt said before coming President, "in speech, in political ideas and principles, and in their way of looking at relations between church and state. We welcome the German and the Irishman who becomes an American. We have no use for the German or Irishman who remains such." And the immigrant "must revere only our flag."

Further, leaders like Roosevelt fashioned the immigration laws in an effort to strengthen the nation by keeping out what they deemed undesired categories of people. By Roosevelt's second term, the 1907 Immigration Act barred from America the following: criminals, the insane, the contagious, political radicals, and migrants deemed likely to wind up on the public dole. Roosevelt stated that, "we cannot have too much immigration of the right sort, and we should have none whatever of the wrong sort."

At that time, many immigrants from Eastern Europe worked the mines in Pennsylvania's anthracite coal region, the scene of TR's first test on the economy. A crisis erupted there in May 1902, with a strike by 140,000 miners, who dug up what was then main fuel for heating homes.

Roosevelt looked for a solution through arbitration between employees and management. A month before the midterm elections, with winter coal heating shortages lurking, he worked out an agreement that echoed the one which McKinley and Hanna had forged in 1900 with the Midwestern coal miners.

President Roosevelt brought representatives of both sides to the White House, threatened to send federal troops into the mines, and hammered out a deal. A commission was set up that persuaded the owners of the mines to increase worker pay, while at the same time allowed higher prices for their coal. Management did not have to officially recognize the miner's union. But the union in effect had won out on some of its key issues.

Roosevelt pointed to the accord as emblematic of his "Square Deal" for every man, by which "labor" and "capital", as he put it, would both benefit. This was a continuation, and extension, of the McKinley-Hanna approach, with its expectation of give-and-take between these two sides of the industrial equation.

Reflecting this trend administratively was TR's creation, in 1903, of the federal Department of Commerce and Labor, later split into two separate Departments. At the time it reflected the Progressive Era notion of the government managing different sectors of society more effectively. Over time, however, critics would charge, the Department of Commerce and the Department of Labor turned into expensive bureaucracies supporting politically connected interests, such as highly profitable corporations granted federal subsidies, or unions hindering the ability of companies and agencies to respond nimbly to changing economic and technological conditions.

WHO DO YOU TRUST?

Much related to the trend toward a great federal role over corporate management, President Roosevelt became famous for his "trust busting", or the breaking up of interconnected firms which controlled much of an industry.

As a leader in New York's State Assembly in the 1880s, Roosevelt had sparred with corrupt financier Jay Gould, and he harbored distrust for the aggressively rich, as well as some wariness toward them as a rival to federal power. Laws like the Sherman Antitrust Act of 1890 had been used to break up perceived union labor monopolies. TR's Justice Department filed and won over three dozen anti-trust suits against corporate trusts, including some mammoth conglomerations.

In 1902 it sued the Northern Securities Company, a railroad trust run by the grand tycoons of the time: John D. Rockefeller, J.P. Morgan, New York's Edward H. Harriman, and Canadian-American magnate James J. Hill, the trust's president. It controlled the Union Pacific, the Northern Pacific, the Burlington, and other major rail lines. It aimed to end price wars and to strengthen profits among the different companies. In 1904, following the Justice Department's suit, the Supreme Court ruled 5-4 to break Northern Securities into its component firms. (66 years later, the same firms would merge to form the Burlington Northern Railroad.)

Such anti-trust cases set up the landmark suit against Standard Oil, Rockefeller's petroleum conglomerate, under Roosevelt's successor, President Taft. In 1911 Standard Oil would be broken up into many other, state-based companies. Some economic historians argue the suit was unnecessary, as Standard Oil had started to lose its market share and monopoly to rival firms. The same argument would be made 90 years later in the federal suit against Microsoft, that competition from Internet-based rivals would overthrow its long-term control of the industry. In any event, the companies resulting from the petroleum breakup were the direct ancestors of most of today's biggest U.S. oil companies, such as ExxonMobil.

Throughout the 20th century and beyond, a similar dynamic would play out for industries such as trucking, telephones, and airlines.

Alexander Graham Bell's old American Telephone and Telegraph Company, or AT&T, operated as a monopoly under federal regulation until 1982. In that year, "Ma Bell" was broken up into component companies such as Bell Atlantic and a portion of Bell Labs. Ever since, the telecommunications industry has undergone an explosion of innovations and lower costs, accelerated by the new cell phone and Internet sectors to which it helped give birth.

The airline sector was increasingly regulated until 1978, when setting of fares and routes was ended, although the Federal Aviation Administration retained a major role in air traffic control. In recent decades, supervision of the airlines has led to greater safety, if less innovation. Fierce debates over the proper amount of regulation over the preeminent firms in an industry continue today.

DAMS AND A DITCH

Later famous for land conservation, Roosevelt in his first term also put together legislation that had wide-reaching economic effects in the West and over time deleterious impacts on its environment. This was the National Reclamation Act, or Newland Act, of June 1902. "Newland" was a play on words of its sponsor, Nevada Rep. Francis Newlands.

For years, farmers in Western states had demanded federal support for irrigation projects, akin to the government financing of infrastructure such as canals and harbors in the East. The result under the Act was a Reclamation Service, later the Bureau of Reclamation within the Interior Department. It administered a Reclamation Fund of money from sales of federal lands.

Over time, the Bureau of Reclamation would be a force behind the building of thousands of dams, both small and gigantic. These included the world's largest concrete edifices at the time of their construction—the Hoover Dam (1936), in Nevada/Arizona; Washington State's Grand Coulee Dam (1942), and California's Shasta Dam (completed 1945).

Practically every naturally wild river in the West, with the Yellowstone an exception, was tamed. The water projects turned millions of acres of desert to bloom, were much responsible for making California the world's leading grower of fruits and vegetables, and created countless recreational parks for fishing, boating, and swimming.

However, the projects were also expensive, costing on average over four times as much per acre as the prior, smaller-scale local projects which officials had tried to have pay for themselves. In theory self-sustaining financially, by the 1920s the Reclamation Fund would have to dip into the federal government's general treasury. Farmers were supposed to pay for project costs with user fees, but in 1939 the Bureau essentially ended payback requirements. And by the 1960s, growing awareness of the dams' destructive impact on natural fish, insect, and animal habitats threw a less-positive light on one of the greatest construction binges in world history.

On a major foreign policy matter, the construction of a canal across Central America, Roosevelt took a series of forceful, even Machiavellian, acts during his first term. First, in November 1901, he and Secretary of State Hay got the British to agree to an American-sponsored "big ditch". In summer 1902, he further set the table, by signing a Canal Act that called for the financing and construction of a waterway across the narrow isthmus of Panama.

At the time, Panama was a strife-torn province of Columbia. So Roosevelt winked in November of the following year when the Panama Canal Company instigated a revolution against Columbia. Within three days of the insurrection, the U.S. recognized the new Republic of Panama. Hay quickly signed the Hay-Buneau-Varilla Treaty.

For a 10-mile-wide Panama Canal Zone, the U.S. gave Panama $10 million in gold in return for an annual $250,000 lease. TR soon set up a commission to start the digging. By his second term, tens of thousands of Caribbean laborers aided by 160 locomotives were digging and hauling out millions of metric tons of soil and rock from a vast construction zone. The construction cost of the Canal would be about $9 billion in 2015 dollars; it was opened to ships in 1914. The former number two at the Navy got his fast path between the seas, which would remain property of the USA until 1999.

A THUMPING RE-ELECTION

In the 1902 midterm elections, the opposition party, as is the norm, gained. The Democrats picked up five Senate seats, including two former Populist Party seats, though the Republicans retained a large 55-33 majority. In the House, with the reapportionment that followed the census of 1900, both parties gained seats, reflected the swelling U.S. population.

But the Democratic Party gained more seats: 25, to just nine for the G.O.P, while absorbing the former House seats of the Populists. The Republicans retained a modest majority, 210-176. Much of the population growth came from immigrants from eastern and southern Europe, who were often lesser skilled laborers who voted heavily Democratic.

Over the next two years, the nation was at peace, with the insurgency in the Philippines having faded. Major union strikes were absent. Roosevelt, with his anti-trust actions, co-opted a major Democratic theme, concern over the power of large businesses. Along those lines he signed the 1903 Elkins Act, which permitted the federal Interstate Commerce Commission, or ICC, to fine railroads giving rebates to shippers. The rebates were in fact at times kickbacks. Supporters of anti-trust argued they were among the means the railroads used to retain customers and restrict competition.

As with many two-term presidents, Roosevelt was aided in his re-election by weakness in the rival party. William Jennings Bryan announced a bid but, as a two-time loser, his moment had passed. The former two-term President, Grover Cleveland, was considered for the nomination but, at age 67, he decided to stay out. Bryan's major backer from his prior runs, publisher Hearst—by then a pro-labor congressman as well as a newspaper baron—threw his hat in the ring. But New York's Democratic Tammany

Hall machine, stung by Hearst's editorial broadsides, impeded his reformist campaign.

Facing a popular incumbent, the Democratic Party turned to Alton B. Parker, the chief justice of New York's Court of Appeals. Parker was generally well-regarded by both parties in his populous state. Another benefit of his nomination was he had few known views on the issues, making him hard to attack. But Parker's thin life story was far less compelling than Roosevelt's. As author Irving Stone noted in the 1940s, Parker was the only major party nominee to have no major biography written of him. (In the 21st century, he still has no bio, apart from an entry in the Encyclopedia Britannica.)

Yet Judge Parker wasn't a complete cipher. Like Cleveland, he was a conservative Bourbon Democrat. For instance, from the bench he'd labeled unconstitutional the eight-hour workday, believing that was something a business owner should decide. At the convention, he enraged Bryan's free silver supporters, and the party's easy-money grassroots, by stating: "I regard the gold standard as firmly and irrevocably established." The party platform tried to unite the factions by opposing high tariffs and overseas imperialism. Parker took the nomination, beating Hearst, 679 ballots to 181.

As his running mate, the New York judge selected a former U.S. Senator from West Virginia, Henry Gassaway Davis, the millionaire founder of a large coal company. Once again the Democrats faced a well-financed Republican machine, and as in 1896 they hoped an affluent vice-presidential nominee would help bankroll the campaign. Also as in 1896, they countered charges of being anti-business radicals by placing an entrepreneur on their ticket. At 80 years of age (he would live to 92), Davis was, and remains, the oldest person ever chosen as a nominee to either of the nation's two highest political offices.

At the G.O.P. convention, there were rumblings against TR's progressivism among some conservative Republicans. The Republican Speaker of the House, Joseph Gurney Cannon of Indiana, would later say of the President, "he's got no more use for the Constitution than a tomcat has for a marriage license." But the one powerful party member considering a bid against the incumbent, Mark Hanna, had died at the start of the campaign year.

For his own Vice President, Roosevelt wanted Robert Hitt of Ohio, an ex-ambassador to France and, long before that, Abraham Lincoln's aide during the Lincoln-Douglas debates. But he was persuaded to pick Charles Fairbanks, of Indiana. A moderate Midwesterner, it was thought Fairbanks might lend regional, policy, and even personal balance to the young New Yorker impatient for change. (The Alaskan town of Fairbanks is named for him.) Roosevelt consoled the "Old Guard" with this choice. In a first-ballot nomination, the President got every vote.

In the campaign, the conservative Parker attacked Roosevelt's "individual caprice" and placement of more authority in the executive branch. And TR's former Commerce and Labor Secretary, Cortelyou, then the Republican National Committee chairman, flirted with scandal. He used his connections with business to solicit campaign donations, as exposed by newspaper publisher Joseph Pulitzer. But Roosevelt was little hurt. And Cortelyou, in the role of party chairman, waged a far more effective outreach to swing voters, such as German-Americans, than Parker did with heavily Democratic groups, such as Americans of Irish descent.

In autumn 1904, given a weak challenger, landmark executive actions, and a dynamic personality in the White House, a big TR victory was written in the stars. He and Vice-President Fairbanks won the popular vote, 56 percent to 38 percent.

The Electoral College edge was also big, 336-140. Missouri, which had leaned to the South since the Compromise of 1820, went for the G.O.P. for the first time in 36 years. Parker took only the South, and won the border state of Maryland by a bare 51 votes. Vice-presidential nominee Davis failed to carry his home state of West Virginia. (In at least five Southern state counties, Roosevelt—as often happened to Republicans in that region during that era—got no votes.)

In the election, the Socialist Party, under Eugene V. Debs of Indiana, emerged on the national stage. It took 3 percent of the vote. Debs drew on the support of many Scandinavian and German immigrants in the Midwest who had a European, Social Democratic outlook. The Prohibition Party also attracted some support. Its ironically named candidate, Silas Swallow, of Pennsylvania, received 2 percent.

Riding on the President's coattails, the Republican Party made significant congressional gains. The G.O.P. picked up 41 House seats, to build its majority under Speaker Cannon to a strong 251-135. It added two Senate seats, for a big 58-32 edge.

FOLLOWING THE REGULATIONS

In his second term, Roosevelt continued the wide-reaching initiatives of his first. As a follow-up to breaking up business monopolies, in 1906 he pushed through the Pure Food and Drug Act, and the Meat Inspection Act, which aimed to ban harmful or mislabeled products. The latter was inspired by the muckraking book *The Jungle*, by reporter Upton Sinclair, later a Socialist politician. The twin Acts laid the groundwork for pervasive federal regulation of the food and pharmaceutical industries.

They helped continue the growth of the vast, healthful, and profitable food industry of modern America. Yet, over the long run, they also helped lead, under the federal Food and Drug Administration, to today's often slow and very expensive regulatory process for new medical drugs and devices. Approval for some pharmaceuticals, for instance, can take a decade in time and $1 billion in development costs, slowing therapies for the ill.

Also in 1906, President Roosevelt signed the Hepburn Act, a follow-up to his first-term Elkins Act regulating the railroads. (Iowa Rep. William Hepburn, the sponsor, was the great-grandson of Rep. Matthew Lyon, jailed by President John Adams under the Alien and Sedition Acts, which helped elect President Jefferson.) Passed by Congress with just three Nay votes, it authorized the ICC to set "just and reasonable" railroad rates. It let the Commission examine the financial books of the rail companies, and effectively ended their rebates.

In the Progressive Era, Roosevelt firmly believed he and administrative experts should decide on such things as the proper size and practices of an industry. However, although popular, the Hepburn and Elkins Acts would show the difficulty of regulating a complex sector like the railways.

After their passage, shipping costs for farmers and middlemen barely decreased. Forbidden from granting rebates, the railroads then turned to other means of attracting customers. With rates restricted, their profits dropped, which contributed to a financial crisis the year after the Hepburn Act became law. And over the long run, the rail companies were constrained in competing for carrying freight against new technologies, such as the trucking and automotive industries that began to take off at this time. By the mid-20th century, they lost even more business, such as carrying the nation's mail, to the new industry of the airlines, which were often able to flexibly enact new routes with less regulatory oversight.

TR's extensive regulation of business may have contributed to slow economic growth during his presidency. Increases in GDP for his eight years in office averaged only between 1-2 percent a year, well below the norm of about 4 percent a year since 1790.

LAND MANAGERS

Theodore Roosevelt was a lover of, and hunter in, the natural world, and it showed in his penchant for a growing federal role on public lands. In his second term he kept on establishing new national parks, and 18 national monuments, including the Grand Canyon as well as Devil's Tower. In 1905 he created the Forest Service, which quadrupled the land in national forests to 172 million acres. 16 million acres fell under a "Midnight Forests" order, a play on President John Adams' "Midnight Judges" executive action, whereby

Roosevelt shifted the lands to a federal reserve just before a congressional law forbade their transfer.

Roosevelt's point man on land issues was Gifford Pinchot, a future governor of Pennsylvania, and the affluent son of a Connecticut family wealthy from its speculation in timber and real estate. President McKinley had tasked Pinchot, the chief of his Division of Forestry, with creating a plan for managing federal lands. Roosevelt made him in 1905 the first head of the Division's successor, the U.S. Forest Service.

In the spirit of Progressivism, Pinchot tried to apply professional techniques of land management, imported from European experts and practiced at new forestry schools like one at Yale University he helped found. In contrast to naturalist and photographer John Muir, Pinchot did not push for establishing wilderness areas, but urged mixed use of public lands where lumbering and mining were allowed under regulatory supervision and with payment of user fees. He also advocated more lands under federal administration, in contrast to advocates of regional or private control.

In 1910, President Taft would fire Pinchot after he publicly attacked Taft and his Interior Secretary, Richard Achilles Ballinger, formerly the pro-development Mayor of Seattle, after Ballinger transferred millions of acres back to private uses, and supported private mining of Alaskan coal fields. The dismissal of Pinchot enraged TR, and helped spark his 1912 run against Taft as a pro-conservation Progressive.

Roosevelt and Pinchot's (and Muir's) approach had the benefit of reserving many scenic lands for the enjoyment of the citizenry. In the long run, as the federal government acquired or retained vast amounts of property other than the well-trod centers of the national parks, this tact came under dispute. By 2015, the federal government possessed over 50 percent of the acreage in many states, including Utah and Alaska. This contributed to "brush fire rebellions" by the businesses and ranchers of such states on the one hand, and Washington, D.C. and conservationists on the other, over land and resource use.

GOOD COP, BAD COP

For his second term's foreign policy, Roosevelt both spoke diplomatically and brandished his big stick.

With Secretary of State Hay, in September 1905 he brokered an end to the Russo-Japanese War. The bloody conflict had raged between Moscow and Tokyo in Manchuria and its adjoining seas since early 1904. Japan had won crushing victories, gaining preeminent influence over Manchuria and Korea. Roosevelt gained the 1906 Noble Peace Prize for his mediation, although by the time of the negotiations Russia had in effect already lost the war.

The treaty had an impact bigger than ending a conflict. At the talks hosted by the U.S. in Portsmouth, New Hampshire, Roosevelt tilted toward Russia. He blocked Japan's demand for indemnities and for occupying all of Sakhalin Island off of Siberia. He thus tried to maintain a balance a power in the region, by restricting Japan somewhat and by continuing the Open Door policy with China that Hay and President McKinley had established. His view somewhat anticipated that of his distant relative Franklin Roosevelt 35 years later, when FDR took the side of an embattled China against Japan in the run-up to the 1941 Pearl Harbor attack.

In 1907 Roosevelt, although usually a firm nationalist, tried to help set up a 'world court' for the settlement of some international disputes, in the Dutch city of The Hague. Such a body, the Permanent Court of International Justice, would be established there at the end of the Second World War.

TR continued, and heightened, McKinley's policy of intervention in the Caribbean and Central America. In December 1904, he'd issued his "Roosevelt Corollary" to the Monroe Doctrine, by which the U.S. could intervene in Latin America in the event of abusive governance or chaos, as an "international police power". This was a step, in some historians' analysis, in America taking on the role of a 'world cop'.

In 1905, the U.S. took over part of the Dominican Republic's finances in order to pay its debts back to European creditors, in lieu of the European powers themselves taking military action. In 1906, TR dispatched troops to Cuba, per the Congress' Platt Amendment, after a political uprising there. Under his Secretary of War Taft, the U.S. put into effect a second Cuban occupation, which lasted until February 1909, through an American Civil Governor. In 1907, the President sent Marines to Honduras after turmoil there threatened American commercial properties.

And in December 1907 he sent the Navy's powerful, and brightly painted, "Great White Fleet" on a 14-month tour of the world, arriving back home the month before he left office. (U.S. Navy ships were then slabbed white during peace time, and a stealthy gray during war.) TR had presided over another major increase in U.S. naval strength, and his armada contained 16 new battleships, and 50 coaling ships to keep them steaming. Perhaps something of a "wag the dog" ploy, the voyage took minds off the effects of an ongoing financial recession. It also affirmed the reach of a new world power.

By the middle of his second term, unusual for a two-term president, Roosevelt retained his broad personal popularity. The 1906 midterm elections, meanwhile, yielded mixed results. A two-term President's party almost always loses ground in the House elections, and the Republicans lost 26 seats, lowering their margin to 224-167. In the Senate, however, the G.O.P. picked up three Senate seats, for a large edge of 61-31.

To his discredit, before the election the President shabbily handled the Brownsville, Texas riots of that July and August. A soldier from the black 25th Division of infantry stationed near the town murdered a white man at a brothel, leading to a riot where two whites and a black soldier were killed. Two weeks later, after a white bartender in town was killed, townspeople falsely accused members of a battalion of the 25th, all of whom had been in their barracks at the time, of the man's death. After an Army inquiry, Roosevelt waited until after the midterms—so as not to dampen the normally pro-Republican black vote—and ordered dishonorable discharges to all 167 men of the battalion. The Army would reinstate 11 of the soldiers in 1910, during the Taft Administration. In 1972 President Nixon posthumously gave pardons and honorable discharges to all of those dismissed.

A PLUTOCRAT BAILS OUT A TRUST BUSTER

A serious threat to second-term success arrived the following October, with the Panic of 1907. This entailed a collapse of some New York City banks, and a sharp recession that endured into 1908, TR's final full year in office.

Probably contributing to the bust was the unintended consequences of limiting the rates charged by the railroads, via Roosevelt's Hepburn Act of the previous year. Major holdings in the stock market included railroad giants like Union Pacific, whose value fell sharply. In the eight months after passage of the law, stocks overall dropped 17 percent, and by a full third in the year following the Act. The immense property losses from the 1906 San Francisco earthquake, and the need of banks and insurance firms to cover their losses from it, were another factor. The Panic's immediate cause was an attempt to corner the market in copper, which led to a run on a number of New York banks and trust companies.

Alarmed by the financial implosion, Roosevelt rushed back to Washington from a hunting trip, but the real action took place in the financial center of New York. Ironically, the trust-busting President was to be bailed out of a jam by the barons of wealth with whom he often jousted.

Racing back to Manhattan from a church assemblage in Richmond, Virginia was none other than J.P. Morgan, the man who'd saved President Cleveland's Treasury. As New York's most powerful banker, Morgan reacted to the panic by pledging tens of millions of his own monies to the city's cash-strapped banks. Wheeling and dealing from the library of his brownstone on Madison Avenue, now the Morgan Library, he got solvent bankers and industrialist friends like John D. Rockefeller, the country's richest man, to pledge millions more. He met with the ubiquitous Cortelyou, now TR's

Treasury Secretary, who deposited $25 million into Gotham's financial firms, or about $650 million in 2015 dollars. Morgan arranged for U.S. Steel, despite having a near monopoly of the metal, take over a Tennessee firm on whose survival a vital New York bank depended.

The potential stumbling block was Roosevelt, who opposed acquisitions by dominant trusts like U.S. Steel. The latter's head, Henry Clay Frick, the former plant manager from the Carnegie Steel violence of 1892, hurried down to Washington on a Sunday night. Frick met with Roosevelt, Secretary of State Root, and Secretary of the Interior James Rudolph Garfield, President Garfield's son. The men feared a stock market crash on its opening Monday morning. Trading principle for practicality, the President agreed on the takeover. "It was necessary for me to decide on the instant," he recalled, "for the situation in New York was such that any hour might be vital."

Still, the Panic touched off a severe recession that endured until the following summer. Joblessness rose to 8 percent from near full employment, as industrial production plummeted by over 10 percent. Fortunately for Roosevelt's party, the economy began to recover before the 1908 election.

The major consequence of the Panic of 1907 may have occurred in 1911, at Jekyll Island off of Georgia. Meeting at a secretive conference there were many of the New York bankers who'd fought off the collapse, including a number of Morgan's associates, and Rhode Island Sen. Nelson Aldridge, father-in-law to Rockefeller's son. These powerful men agreed on a plan that led to the formation in 1913 of the Federal Reserve. Its main founding goal was to provide liquidity to stave off a future banking collapse. Later it would morph into other roles.

Thus was resurrected Hamilton's vision of a powerful federal bank, the bane of the Jeffersonians and Jacksonians who had interred the Second Bank of the United States back in 1836.

GROOMING A SUCCESSOR, AND A FUTURE RIVAL

With the Panic dissipating, TR was popular enough to go for a third term. At the Republican convention in June 1908, party chairman and friend Henry Cabot Lodge spoke warmly of him. This ignited a massive demonstration in the President's favor. But TR had pledged after his 1904 re-election not to run again. He had decided, for the time being at least, to stick to George Washington's longstanding precedent of a two-term limit.

In fact, TR had groomed Taft, whom he much admired for his administrative skill and for being a "genuine Progressive", to succeed him. On taking office from McKinley, he'd retained Taft as Governor-General of the Philippines, then appointed him in his second term to the key position of Secretary of War. Taft further served as Acting Secretary of State and managed construction of the President's pet project, the Panama Canal.

At times TR also wanted Taft on the Supreme Court, but the Ohioan turned him down three times. Roosevelt told Taft: "If only there were three of you; I could appoint one of you to the Court, one to the War Department, and one to the Philippines." The President's views of his favorite were to dramatically change.

With Roosevelt's backing, Taft took the G.O.P. presidential nomination against no strong rival. Continuing the Republican practice of choosing a ticket of men from the Midwest and the East, Taft picked as his running mate the genial Rep. James "Sunny Jim" Sherman of New York. Sherman was a descendent both of Civil War Gen. William Tecumseh Sherman, whose brother John Sherman had run twice for the G.O.P. nomination, and of Founding Father Roger Sherman of Connecticut. Along with genealogy and geniality, "Sunny Jim" offered ideological balance. A gold-standard conservative, he was strongly for the tariff, unlike the more progressive Taft, who like McKinley desired to lower imposts on imports.

In fact, Taft's progressive campaign platform sounded like a post-Cleveland Democrat. He called for labor safety and public health laws, and for preventing "at once the accumulation of dishonest wealth, thereby carefully distributing the national wealth more fairly."

Having lost badly to the progressive Roosevelt in 1904 with the conservative Parker, the Democrats turned for the third time to the populist Bryan. The Republicans countered with the slogan, "Vote for Taft Now, You Can Vote for Bryan Anytime." The Nebraskan orator tried to make hay of the lingering effects of the Panic, and Republican ties to the moguls of Wall Street. Instead of reaching to the Northeast for a running mate, the party chose John W. Kern, an Indiana lawyer, and later U.S. Senate Majority Leader.

Taft and Sherman won a solid victory, if not the Roosevelt landslide win of 1904. They took every Northeast and Midwestern state, and swept the West Coast too. Bryan and Kern won the Solid South, and the border states of Maryland and Kentucky, the silver state of Nevada, the mining state of Colorado, and Bryan's home state of Nebraska. Taft's popular vote margin was 52 percent to 43 percent. His Electoral College edge was two to one: 321 to 162. The congressional elections came out fairly even, as the G.O.P. lost one Senate seat, to keep a commanding 60-32 margin, and lost five House seats, to retain a 219-172 edge.

THE COATTAILS OF TWO TERMERS

It's interesting to note that would-be successors to two-term presidents from the same political party usually win the White House. It held with the Republican Taft succeeding the Republican Roosevelt. It holds true in 10 out of 17 cases, as outlined below. However, the incidence is sharply decreasing in recent times. (Lincoln-Andrew Johnson, McKinley-Theodore Roosevelt, and Harding-Coolidge are all combined and counted as 'two-term' presidencies):

* Washington/John Adams (Federalists)
* Jefferson/Madison (Democrat-Republicans)
* Madison/Monroe (Democrat-Republicans)
* Jackson/Van Buren (Democrats)
* Lincoln-Johnson/Grant (Republicans and pro-Union Democrats). (Although the Democrat Johnson opposed the Republican Grant as his successor. A special case, as the Republicans impeached Johnson.)
* Grant/Hayes (Republicans) (Although Hayes' backers likely stole the 1876 election from the Democrat Tilden.)
* McKinley-Theodore Roosevelt/Taft (Republicans)
* Harding-Coolidge/Hoover (Republicans)
* Franklin Roosevelt/Truman (Democrats)
* Reagan/Bush I (Republicans)

In fewer cases, the would-be successor to the two termer failed win the presidency:

* Cleveland/Bryan (Democrats) (Cleveland actually opposed Bryan as his successor, after the second of his interrupted two terms.)
* Truman/Adlai Stevenson II (Democrats) (Truman was a "two termer" in the sense he had been in the White House for over three years, after FDR's death, before his own victory in the 1948 presidential election.)
* Eisenhower/Nixon (Republicans) (Although Nixon may have actually won the 1960 election, with Kennedy's backers stealing the pivotal state of Illinois.)
* Kennedy-Johnson/Humphrey (Democrats)
* Nixon/Ford (Republicans)
* Clinton/Gore(Democrats)
* Bush II/McCain (Republicans)

All of this implies that, although there is a second-term liability, there is also an after-the-fact benefit to a second term. A popular President's "coattails" are powerful, and apparently outlast even his term of office, even if his second term is troubled.

Yet it should be pointed out that six of the seven failures have taken place from 1952 to 2008. The "post-presidential coattail effect" has generally declined. (As of mid-2016, Obama was supporting Hillary Clinton as his successor.)

BACK FOR AN ENCORE

After his two terms in the White House, TR was just 50 years old, and faced the unique problem of what a very accomplished and still relatively young man was to do with the rest of his life. And this during an era when, as F. Scott Fitzgerald would put it, "There are no second acts in American lives."

But TR began his second act with aplomb. Partly to dispel accusations he would control Taft's new presidency from behind the scenes, the ex-President embarked on a 12-month safari to east Africa. There, his outsized appetite for life was undiminished, as he and his fellow hunters trapped or shot over 11,000 animals, then handed the hides over to the Smithsonian.

After his return, TR found the Republican party brawling between conservatives, who rallied around President Taft, and progressives, led increasingly by Robert LaFollette, Sr. of Wisconsin, a founder of the National Progressive Republican League.

Taft, so able as a lieutenant, lacked a deft touch as leader. He alienated conservationists, and Roosevelt, by firing Roosevelt's friend Pinchot. And he alienated almost everyone by first coming out for low tariffs, then keeping most tariffs high after making deals with various industries. He did file some 90 antitrust suits, but liberals distrusted his oratory and his other pro-business actions. Meantime Roosevelt was shifting further and faster toward the Progressives.

The ex-President was irked that Taft had not consulted him on appointments and policy. Out of principle and ambition, he moved steadily toward the incumbent President's political foes. In summer 1910, he openly broke with his successor in a major speech, the "New Nationalism", where he adopted many of the Progressives' stands. Roosevelt declared that workers' welfare trumped property rights. He called for sweeping changes that future Chief Executives would enact. These included a federal income tax, a steep inheritance tax, a form of social security, workman's compensation, and farm relief. He also demanded direct election of U.S. Senators, instead of election by state legislatures, and limits on campaign contributions.

His oration, delivered in Osawatomie, Kansas to honor the abolitionist John Brown, who'd fought battles against pro-slavery forces there—urged speakers to "destroy this invisible Government, to dissolve the unholy alliance between corrupt business and corrupt politics." It was a stark break with the traditional business base of the Republican Party. Later Roosevelt demanded popular votes to overturn unpopular judicial decisions, a stance that sounded demagogic to the judicially minded Taft, who dismissed backers of such measures as "extremists". The ex-President was influenced by New York City journalist Herbert Croly. His 1909 book *The Promise of National Life* favored a strong central government that promoted major industrial corporations, large unions, and wealth equity, while deemphasizing individuals and constitutional rights.

TR seemed to have his finger on the country's pulse. In the 1910 midterms, the Democrats made huge gains, mostly in the North and Midwest, outside their traditional base. They picked up 12 Senate seats, to narrow the Republicans' once overwhelming margin to 48-44. Their victory in the House elections was even greater, gaining 58 seats to seize clear control of the House, 230-163. They surged on the state level too, taking the governorships of G.O.P. bastions such as Taft's Ohio. In New Jersey, the former head of Princeton University, Democrat and future two-term President Woodrow Wilson, was elected Governor.

Amid the progressive tide, President Taft looked very weak for re-election. Prominent Ohioans, like James Rudolph Garfield, the son of President Garfield, and Dan Hanna, the son of McKinley's confidant, abandoned their own native son. Roosevelt publicly said of Taft: "I am sure he means well, but he means well feebly, and he does not know how!"

A THIRD PARTY FOR AN ATTEMPTED THIRD TERM

In 1912, Roosevelt saw which way the tide was flowing, and wished to stay with the current, while saving the G.O.P. Yet Taft, although sometimes politically obtuse, was a highly intelligent and usually able man. And he was no quitter. Working in his favor is that, historically, it is very difficult for an insurgent to win his party's nomination against an incumbent president.

In recent times, the last such major challenges were former California Gov. Ronald Reagan against President Ford in 1976, and Minnesota Sen. Eugene McCarthy and New York Sen. Robert F. Kennedy against President Lyndon Johnson in 1968. None of the three won their party's nomination. Further, while 1976 was a time of inflation and recession, and 1968 a time of foreign war and domestic dissent, TR attempted his bid during a time of peace, whatever his personal and policy differences with Taft. This makes his performance in the G.O.P. race all the more remarkable.

The Republicans held 12 state primaries in 1912, and Roosevelt won most of them, including Ohio. However, the President controlled the party machinery and delegate selection in most of the other 36 states. At the convention, Taft was nominated fairly narrowly. The President actually trailed after the first ballot: 367 delegates to 411 for Roosevelt. But then the party steered many delegates to the incumbent, nominating Taft. A small block of delegates went to the progressively minded LaFollette.

The willful Roosevelt, believing with some reason he'd been cheated, bolted the party. Sounding rather like Bryan, he thundered, "With unflinching hearts and undimmed eyes, we stand at Armageddon, and we battle for the Lord!" He ran as an independent, a "Bull Moose" Progressive. Inevitably, he and Taft split up those opposing the Democrats' nominee, Wilson, and they trailed him throughout the fall.

The campaign was otherwise notable for TR's astonishingly calm reaction to being shot during an assassination attempt at a campaign trip in Milwaukee. After taking a bullet in the chest, from the deranged German immigrant John Flammang Schrank, the veteran soldier and amateur taxidermist judged the wound was not life-threatening. "It takes more than that to kill a bull moose," he announced. Roosevelt went on to deliver a 90-minute speech before heading to a hospital.

Yet his political and personal decline began with this third-party bid. Health-wise, as the bullet lodged in his abdomen would plague him to the end of his life. Politically, as he ensured the election of Democrat Woodrow Wilson, whose two terms were a major pause in the Republicans' post-Civil War presidential dominance.

Wilson won the Electoral College crushingly, with 435 delegates to 88 for Roosevelt, and just 8 for Taft. Yet Wilson's percentage of the vote (42 percent), combined with that of Socialist Eugene Debs (6 percent), was just 49 percent. This total was less than that of Roosevelt (27 percent), and Taft (23 percent), at 50 percent. In theory, if Roosevelt had stayed out, and Taft had held on to TR's votes, he might have won.

However, 1912 was definitely a progressive's year, as the combined Democratic, Progressive, and Socialist vote of Wilson, Roosevelt, and Debs was an overwhelming 75 percent.

If, however, Roosevelt had held off until 1916 to make a third White House run, he might very well have won that year. Given his political skills and his charisma, he likely would have united progressive Republicans with more conservative Republicans, who would have turned to him as the viable alternative to President Wilson. Moreover, with the First World War raging, the paramount issue of preparedness would have played to TR's strength as a war hero and to his nationalist bent. With Cleveland, he might have become the only President to leave and then return to the White House, and the only President to do so after two terms.

A BULL MOOSE IN WINTER

In his later years, Roosevelt grew increasingly bellicose and sickly. During a harrowing 1913-14 expedition of discovery on Brazil's River of Doubt, he nearly died of a leg infection. The great outdoorsman had to quit exercise, and grew fat.

Yet when the First World War erupted in August 1914, he lusted for military service. He savaged President Wilson's policy of neutrality, and called for U.S. intervention in support of the British and the invaded Belgians. As during the Spanish-American War, he saw the conflict as a test of America's values, and whether it could match the mettle of the other Great Powers.

Probably with an eye to another White House term, and given the collapse of the Progressive Party without him, he rehabilitated himself within the Republican party. In 1916, thumping for war-time preparations, he campaigned hard for party nominee Charles Evans Hughes, the former and future Supreme Court Justice and, like Roosevelt, a former New York Governor. The incumbent President Wilson, meantime, ran on his slogan of, "He kept us out of war."

With Roosevelt's Progressives mostly voting Republican again, the G.O.P. much reduced their margin of defeat from 1912. Hughes lost to

Wilson by just 277-254 in the Electoral College, and by 49 percent to 46 percent in the popular vote. Perhaps reflecting the wounds that Roosevelt had inflicted on Taft, however, the Democrat President easily carried Taft's rib-rocked Republican state of Ohio. Its 24 electoral votes were enough to determine the contest.

In March 1917, as U.S. intervention in the war loomed, Congress approved TR's ambitious plans to raise and help lead for combat in Europe some four divisions of volunteer troops, an expanded version of the Rough Riders. President Wilson was in no mood to help his political foe, however, and quashed the notion. It became a moot point as Germany re-launched its unrestricted submarine attacks on American shipping. Congress declared war on Germany in April, and the U.S. began readying a vast Expeditionary Force of regular Army and Marine units for France.

Wilson then bitterly disappointed Roosevelt by blocking him from volunteering to fight. In response, he published a fierce critique of the President, *The Foes of Our Own Household*. Near the war's end, in July 1918, Roosevelt was devastated by the death in aerial combat over France of his 20-year-old son, Lt. Quentin Roosevelt.

When the First World War ended in November 1918, TR was still regarded the favorite for the 1920 Republican nomination. But his activism was out of tune with his party, and the nation, which was to yearn for a "return to normalcy" after the Great War's interventionism and Wilson's, and Roosevelt's, own domestic activism.

For the presidency, he backed Gen. Leonard Wood, his commander in the 1898 Cuban expedition. But a candidate that Taft supported, Sen. Warren Gamaliel Harding of Ohio, got the nod, and went on to win the presidency. He and his successor, Calvin Coolidge, put together two terms of a *laissez faire* approach that was a counter to TR's progressivism.

A Roosevelt candidacy in 1920 had become impossible in any event, as Roosevelt's health fell apart. He suffered from malaria, and from his River of Doubt leg injury, and from the lingering effects of the 1912 assassination attempt. He died in January 1919, at age 62.

Wilson's Vice President, Thomas Riley Marshall, eulogized: "Death had to take Roosevelt sleeping, for if he had been awake, there would have been a fight."

LOOKING BACK AT TR

Despite Roosevelt's mostly exalted status today, there are historians with revisionist views. Some critics, generally from the Left, take him to task for his war-like attitude and Anglophile views on race and immigration. He was for the sterilization of criminals, and said of Native Americans: "I don't go so far as to think that the only good Indians are dead Indians, but I believe nine out of ten are, and I shouldn't like to inquire too closely into the case of the tenth."

Others, generally of a conservative or libertarian lilt, chide him for his statist, interventionist approach. At the time, House Speaker Cannon was a harsh, reoccurring critic: "That fellow at the other end of the avenue wants everything from the birth of Christ to the death of the devil." A modern biographer stated it more mildly: "Even his friends occasionally wondered whether there wasn't any custom or practice too minor for him to try to regulate, update or otherwise improve." One ridiculed overreach of Roosevelt's was an effort to simplify and standardize English spelling. Another of his reforms, with happier results, were rules that greatly reduced the number of college athletes who died in the smash-mouth football games of the early 1900s.

Some dislike him for paving the ground for Wilson's sharp move toward progressivism. President Wilson would establish, as TR wanted, a permanent income tax, as opposed to, say, Lincoln's temporary, war-time excise. He would also set up the Federal Reserve, a huge increase in Washington's power over the banking system and the economy. Like Wilson, TR sought popular elections of U.S. senators, not their selection by state legislatures, an attempt at greater democracy which would have the effect of eroding the power of the states. And Wilson's call for a "war to end all wars", like Roosevelt's and McKinley's interventions in the Caribbean and Asia, lowered the bar for America's future entry into overseas broils, in contravention of President Washington's admonition against "entangling alliances".

Yet President Roosevelt was perhaps more of a centrist, and a continuer of President McKinley's policies, than is generally acknowledged. He intervened abroad, in the Caribbean and Central America, but more to maintain the conquests and spheres of influence McKinley had obtained, and not to expand them. In 1903 he maintained the Monroe Doctrine by getting German and Britain to eschew force, and agree to arbitration, over a financial dispute with Venezuela. The Panama Canal itself was an intensified continuation of McKinley's policy.

Like other successful two termers, Teddy Roosevelt benefitted from luck. He hailed from an accomplished family. He held office between the Spanish-American War and before the First World War, at a time of peace, one brief recession, and technical progress. This was the dynamic, innovative America of the Wright Brothers and Ford's Model T.

But he also made his luck. At home he was the opposite of stand-pat, at a time when the Democratic Party and many Republicans were becoming more activist and interventionist.

As with his predecessor, Roosevelt strove to reconcile labor and management to avoid crippling strikes. He was much more of a trust buster than McKinley. Yet he followed the recommendations of the big bankers and Morgan to allay the Panic of 1907. Further, his accomplishments in land management exceed those of any President or Congress—for the good, as with the national parks, and the not-so-good, as with land reclamation. He tended to overreach with federal regulation, although some of the consequences of this did not come clear until much later. His passion for regulation was likely a factor in the sluggish economic performance during his terms.

Yet Theodore Roosevelt dominated the politics of his two terms, and even the failed bid for a third. A very popular man, he won his second term in a landslide, and avoided a sharp, second-term slide in clout. Further, he set up his chosen successor Taft for his own White House term. He was also largely responsible for Taft's defeat, but that was after he had left the White House. His final years were ones of woe, but again, that was after he had departed the Oval Office that he had constructed in the White House's West Wing.

Based on his presidential record and personal accomplishments, Roosevelt was a natural choice, in 1927, to join Washington, Jefferson, and Lincoln among the esteemed personalities on the newly sculpted Mt. Rushmore.

And he was the only one of those four two termers to handily beat the jinx.

SELECT BIBLIOGRAPHY

Adams, Charles Francis, ed. *Memoirs of John Quincy Adams: Comprising Portions of His Diary from 1795 to 1848.* Philadelphia: J.B. Lippincott & Co., 1874.

Adamczyk, Joseph. "Homestead Strike". *Encyclopædia Britannica Online.* 2016.

Ambrose, Stephen. *Undaunted Courage: Meriwether Lewis, Thomas Jefferson, and the Opening of the American West.* New York: Simon & Schuster, 1997.

Ammon, Harry. *James Monroe: The Quest for National Identity.* New York: McGraw-Hill Book Company, 1990.

Andrew Jackson's Hermitage. "Slavery: Understanding the Other Families at the Hermitage". http://www.thehermitage.com/mansion-grounds/farm/slavery

Andrews, Evan. *History.com.* History in the Headlines. "The 'Black Friday' Gold Scandal, 145 Years Ago". September 24, 2014. http://www.history.com/news/the-black-friday-gold-scandal-145-years-ago

Armstrong, William H. *Major McKinley: William McKinley and the Civil War.* Kent, Ohio: The Kent State University Press, 2000.

Beede, Benjamin R., ed. *The War of 1898, and U.S. Interventions, 1898-1934: An Encyclopedia.* New York: Garland Publishing, 1994.

Berry, Trey, Pam Beasley, and Jeanne Clements, eds. *The Forgotten Expedition: The Louisiana Purchase Journals of Dunbar and Hunter, 1804–1805.* Baton Rouge: Louisiana State University Press, 2006.

Blow, Michael. *A Ship to Remember: The Maine and the Spanish-American War.* New York: Morrow, 1992.

Brands, Henry William (H.R.). *Historynet.com.* "Upside-Down Bailout", June 3, 2010. http://www.historynet.com/upside-down-bailout.htm

Brands, H.W. *TR: The Last Romantic*, New York: Basic Books, 1997.

Brown, Dee Alexander. *Bury My Heart at Wounded Knee: An Indian History of the American West.* New York: Holt, Rinehart and Winston, 1971.

Bryant, Keith L., Jr., ed. *Encyclopedia of American Business History and Biography, Railroads in the Twentieth Century.* New York: Facts on File, 1990.

Buel, Richard Jr. *America on the Brink: How the Political Struggle over the War of 1812 Almost Destroyed the Young Republic.* New York: Palgrave Macmillan, 2005.

Chernow, Ron. *Washington: A Life.* London: Penguin Books, 2010.

"Cleveland's Veto of the Texas Seed Bill". *The Writings and Speeches of Grover Cleveland.* New York: Cassell Publishing Co. 1892.

Coffey, Walter. *The Reconstruction Years: The Tragic Aftermath of the War Between the States.* Bloomington: AuthorHouse, 2014.

Cox, Isaac Joslin. "The American Intervention in West Florida". *The American Historical Review. (Oxford University Press on behalf of American Historical Association).* January 1912.

Cox, Isaac Joslin. "The Freeman Red River Expedition". *Proceedings of the American Philosophical Society.* Vol. 92, No. 2, May 1948. (Studies of Historical Documents in the Library of the American Philosophical Society).

Croly. Herbert. *The Promise of National Life*. London: MacMillan, 1911 edition.

Dalton, Kathleen. *Theodore Roosevelt: A Strenuous Life*. New York: Knopf Doubleday Publishing Group, 2002.

Dangerfield, George. *The Awakening of American Nationalism: 1815-1828*. New York: Harper & Row, 1965.

Davis, Gene. *High Crimes and Misdemeanors: The impeachment and trial of Andrew Johnson*. New York: Morrow, 1977.

DeRose, Chris. *Founding Rivals: Madison vs. Monroe, The Bill of Rights, and The Election that Saved a Nation*. Washington, D.C.: Regnery, 2011.

Dickinson State University. Theodore Roosevelt Center. Digital Library. http://www.theodorerooseveltcenter.org/Research/Digital-Library.aspx

Dodd, William Edward. *American Statesmen: James G. Blaine*. Boston: Houghton Mifflin, 1905.

Douglass, Frederick. *The Narrative of the Life of Frederick Douglass*. Project Gutenberg EBook. (Originally published in 1845). https://www.gutenberg.org/files/23/23-h/23-h.htm

Ellis, Joseph J. *Founding Brothers: The Revolutionary Generation*. New York: Alfred A. Knopf, 2000.

Encyclopaedia Britannica. "Pullman Strike". 2016. http://www.britannica.com/event/Pullman-Strike

Encyclopedia.com. "Embargo Act of 1807". 2003. http://www.encyclopedia.com/topic/Embargo_Act_of_1807.aspx

Encyclopedia.com. "Panic of 1893". 1997.
http://www.encyclopedia.com/topic/Panic_of_1893.aspx

Federal Judicial Center. *History of the Federal Judiciary.* "The Aaron Burr Treason Trial — Historical Background and Documents".
http://www.fjc.gov/history/home.nsf/page/tu_burr_doc_1.html

Fischer, David Hackett. *Albion's Seed: Four British Folkways in America (America: A Cultural History).* Oxford: Oxford University Press, 1989.

Flexner, James Thomas. *Washington: The Indispensable Man.* New York: Back Bay Books, *1994.*

Flores, Dan L., ed. *Southern Counterpart to Lewis and Clark: The Freeman and Custis Expedition of 1806.* Norman: University of Oklahoma Press, 1984.

Foner, Eric. *Reconstruction: America's Unfinished Revolution, 1863-1877.* Gloucester, MA: Peter Smith Publisher Inc., 2001.

"Gigantic Miners' Strike Ordered.; Over 200,000 Men in Eleven States May Quit Work", *New York Times,* April 12, 1894.

Gordon-Reed, Annette. *Andrew Johnson.* The American Presidents Series. New York: Henry Holt and Company, 2011.

Gould, Lewis L. *The Presidency of Theodore Roosevelt.* Lawrence, Kansas: University Press of Kansas, 1991.

Gould, Lewis L. *The Presidency of William McKinley.* Lawrence, Kansas: University Press of Kansas, 1980.

Hamand, Lavern M. "Lincoln's Particular Friend". *Essays in Illinois History.* University of Illinois. 1968.

Hamilton, Alexander, and James Madison. *The Federalist Papers*. New York: Signet, 2003.

HBO. *John Adams*. Television miniseries. 2008. Based on the David McCullough book *John Adams*.

Herbert, Paul N., "Profiteers Rifle North", *The Washington Times*, May 26, 2008.

Humphrey, Jim, and Rich Wallace. Shelby County Historical Society. Traveling Through Time. *"Randolph Slaves"*, February 1997.

Hutton, Anne Hawkes. *Portrait of Patriotism: Washington Crossing the Delaware*. Radnor, PA: Chilton Book Company, 1975.

Jaffa, Harry V. *A New Birth of Freedom: Abraham Lincoln and the Coming of the Civil War*. Lanham, Maryland: Rowman & Littlefield Publishers, 2000.

James Madison's Montpelier. Research and Collections. https://www.montpelier.org/research-and-collections

Jefferson, Thomas. Peterson, Merrill D., ed. *Thomas Jefferson : Writings : Autobiography / Notes on the State of Virginia / Public and Private Papers / Addresses / Letters.* : Library of America. 1984.

Jessup, Phillip C. *Elihu Root*. 2 vols. New York: Dodd, Mead and Company, 1938.

Johnson, Paul. *A History of the American People*. New York: Harper, 1998.

Koster, John. "The Belknap Scandal Fulcrum to Disaster". *Wild West,* pp. 58–64, June 2010.

Kranish, Michael. *Flight from Monticello: Thomas Jefferson at War*. Oxford: Oxford University Press, 2010.

Krause, Paul. *The Battle for Homestead, 1890-1892: Politics, Culture, and Steel*. Pittsburgh, PA: University of Pittsburgh Press, 1992.

Lawrence, William J. *A concise life of Admiral George Dewey*. Boston: J.F. Murphy, 1899.

Leech, Margaret. *In the Days of McKinley*. New York: Harper & Brothers, 1959.

Library of Congress. A Century of Lawmaking for a New Nation. "Habeas Corpus Suspension Act", 12 Stat. 755. March 3, 1863.

Lincoln, Abraham, Basler, Roy, ed. *The Collected Works of Abraham Lincoln*. 9 Vols. Springfield, Illinois: Abraham Lincoln Association, 1953.

Linklater, Andro. *An Artist in Treason: The Extraordinary Double Life of General James Wilkinson*. New York: Walker Publishing Company, 2009.

Loring, Kyle A. "National Reclamation Act of 1902". *Encyclopedia.com*. 2004.

Madison, James. *Notes of Debates in the Federal Convention of 1787*. Columbus: Ohio University Press, 1985. 2nd Edition.

Magie, David. *Life of Garret Augustus Hobart*. New York: G. P. Putnam and Sons, 1910.

Mahan, Alfred Thayer. *The Influence of Sea Power Upon History, 1660–1783*. Boston: Little, Brown and Company, 1890.

McCullough, David. *John Adams*. New York: Simon and Schuster, 2001.

McDougall, Walter A. *Freedom Just Around the Corner: A New American History 1585-1828*. New York: Harper, 2004.

McFeely, William S. *Grant: A Biography*. New York: Norton, 1981.

McPherson, James M. *Battle Cry of Freedom: The Civil War Era*. Oxford: Oxford University Press, 1988.

Meacham, Jon. *Thomas Jefferson: The Art of Power*. Westminster, Maryland: Random House, 2012.

Melton, Buckner F. *Aaron Burr: Conspiracy to Treason*. John Wiley & Sons, New York, 2002.

Miller Center of Public Affairs, University of Virginia. "George Washington". https://millercenter.org/president/washington

Miller Center of Public Affairs, University of Virginia. "James Madison". https://millercenter.org/president/madison

Miller Center of Public Affairs, University of Virginia. "James Monroe". https://millercenter.org/president/monroe

Miller, Hunter, ed. *Treaties and Other International Acts of the United States of America. Volume 2. Documents 1-40. 1776-1818*. "Treaty of Ghent; 1814". Washington, D.C.: Government Printing Office, 1931.

Miller, Nathan. *The U.S. Navy: A History*. 3rd ed. Annapolis: Naval Institute Press, 1997.

Mintz, S., & S. McNeil. *Digital History*. "The Growth of Political Factionalism and Sectionalism". 2016. http://www.digitalhistory.uh.edu/disp_textbook.cfm?smtID=2&psid=3531.

Mitchell, Stewart. *Horatio Seymour of New York*. Cambridge: Harvard University Press, 1938.

Monroe, James. Hamilton, Stanislaus Murray, ed. *Writings of James Monroe*. 7 vols. New York: G.P. Putnam's Sons, 1898-1903.

Monroe, James. Letter. February 19, 1820. To Thomas Jefferson. (Missouri Compromise). http://founders.archives.gov/documents/Jefferson/98-01-02-1093.

Moore, Bob. Zebulonpike.org. "Zebulon Pike: Hard-Luck Explorer". http://zebulonpike.org/pike-hardluck-explorer.htm

Morison, Samuel Eliot. "Our Most Unpopular War," *Massachusetts Historical Society Proceedings*. 1968 80: 38-54.

Morison, Samuel Eliot. *The Oxford History of the American People*. New York: Oxford University Press, 1965.

Morgan, H. Wayne. *William McKinley and His America*. Revised ed. Kent, Ohio: The Kent State University Press, 2003.

Morris, Edmund. *The Rise of Theodore Roosevelt, 1. To 1901* (1979); *vol. 2: Theodore Rex 1901–1909* (2001); *vol. 3: Colonel Roosevelt* (2010). New York: Random House.

Morris, Roy, Jr. *Sheridan: The Life and Wars of General Phil Sheridan*. New York: Crown Publishing, 1992.

Moser, Edward P. *A to Z of America*. Nashville: Turner Publishing, 2011.

Moser, Edward P. "Lafayette Square Tour of Scandal, Assassination, and Intrigue". Tours and research on George Washington, Thomas Jefferson, James Madison, James Monroe, Andrew Jackson, War of 1812, Capitol

Building grounds, Civil War, Abraham Lincoln, Andrew Johnson, Grover Cleveland, Theodore Roosevelt, et al. https://www.facebook.com/LafayetteSquareTourOfScandalAssassinationIntrigue

National Archives and Records Administration. "Electoral College Box Scores 1789–1996". July 30, 2005.

National Archives and Records Administration. "The Emancipation Proclamation, A Transcription". January 1, 1863.

Nau, Henry. *Conservative Internationalism: Armed Diplomacy under Jefferson, Polk, Truman, and Reagan.* Princeton: Princeton University Press, 2013.

Nevins, Allan. *Grover Cleveland: A study in courage.* New York: Dodd, Mead & Company, 1962.

PBS. *American Experience.* "The Burr Conspiracy".
http://www.pbs.org/wgbh/amex/duel/sfeature/burrconspiracy.html

PBS. *American Experience.* "The Homestead Strike".
http://www.pbs.org/wgbh/amex/carnegie/peopleevents/pande04.html

PBS. *Crucible of Empire: The Spanish-American War.* "January 1899: Senate Debate over Ratification of the Treaty of Paris". 1999. http://www.pbs.org/crucible/tl17.html

PBS. *American Experience.* "Thomas Clark Durant (1820-1885)".
http://www.pbs.org/wgbh/americanexperience/features/biography/tcrr-durant/

Putnam, Samuel. *The tour of James Monroe: president of the United States, through the northern and eastern states, in 1817; his tour in the year 1818.* Facsimile Publisher, 2015. Reprint.

Rauchway, Eric. *Murdering McKinley: The Making of Theodore Roosevelt's America*. New York: Hill and Wang, 2004.

Regan, Geoffrey. *Naval Blunders*. London: Andre Deutch, 2001.

Remini, Robert V. *Andrew Jackson*. New York: Harper Perennial, 1999. First edition, 1969.

Remini, Robert V. *Henry Clay: Statesman for the Union*. New York: W. W. Norton & Co, 1993.

Rezneck, Samuel. *Business Depressions and Financial Panics*. New York: Greenwood Press, 1968.

Rines, George Edwin, ed. "Crédit Mobilier of America". *Encyclopedia Americana*. 1920.

Risjord, Norman K. *Chesapeake Politics, 1781–1800*. New York: Columbia University Press, 1978.

Robertson, Jr., James I. *Stonewall Jackson: The Man, the Soldier, the Legend*. New York: Macmillan, 2001.

Roosevelt, Theodore. *An Autobiography*. 1913. Great Books Online. http://www.bartleby.com

Rothbard, Murray. *The Panic of 1819: Reactions and Policies*. New York: Columbia University Press, 1962.

Schlesinger, Jr., Arthur Meier, and Gil Troy, and Fred L. Israel. *History of American Presidential Elections, 1789-2008*. Fourth Edition, 3-Volume Set. New York: Facts on File, 2011. Library of American History.

Serratore, Angela. *Smithsonian Magazine*. "Alexander Hamilton's Adultery and Apology". July 23, 2013.

Sidbury, James. *Ploughshares into swords: race, rebellion, and identity in Gabriel's Virginia, 1730–1810*. New York: Cambridge University Press, 1997.

Smith, Jean Edward. *Grant*. New York: Simon & Schuster, 2001.

Suarez, Ray. *PBS Newshour*. "'The President Is a Sick Man' Details Secret Surgery of President Cleveland". July 29, 2011. http://www.pbs.org/newshour/bb/white_house-july-dec11-groverclevelan_07-29/

Swanson, James L. *Manhunt: The 12-Day Chase for Lincoln's Killer*. New York: HarperCollinsPublishers, 2006.

Taylor, John M. *Old Farmer's Almanac*. "Grover Cleveland and the Confederate Flags". 1987. http://wesclark.com/jw/g_cleve.html

TeachingAmericanHistory.org. "Annapolis Convention Resolution, 1786". Ashland, Ohio: Ashbrook Center at Ashland University, 2016.

The Economist. "The people's road", Oct 27, 2005. (Henry Clay and Andrew Jackson).

Thomas Jefferson Monticello. Research and Collections. "Embargo of 1807". https://www.monticello.org/site/research-and-collections/embargo-1807

Thomas Jefferson Monticello. Research & Collections. "Northern Tour of 1791". https://www.monticello.org/site/research-and-collections/northern-tour-1791

Toll, Ian W. *Six Frigates: The Epic History of the Founding of the U.S. Navy*. New York: W. W. Norton. 2006.

Trefousse, Hans L. *Andrew Johnson: A Biography*. New York: W.W. Norton & Company, 1989.

Tucker, Spencer C. *The Encyclopedia of the Wars of the Early American Republic, 1783–1812*. Santa Barbara: ABC-CLIO, 2014.

Tumbler. *Dead Presidents*. "Presidential Rankings (#4): James Monroe". http://deadpresidents.tumblr.com/post/26764124156/presidential-rankings-4-james-monroe

Turner, Frederick Jackson. "The Significance of the Frontier in American History". 1893. University of Virginia. American Studies. http://xroads.virginia.edu/~hyper/turner/chapter1.html

Unger, Harlow G. *The Last Founding Father*. (James Monroe). Cambridge, MA: Da Capo Press, 2009.

University of Missouri-Kansas City, School of Law. "Proceedings of the Senate Sitting for the Trial of Andrew Johnson". http://law2.umkc.edu/faculty/projects/ftrials/impeach/articles.html

Urofsky, Melvin I. "Judiciary Act of 1801". *Encyclopaedia Britannica*. http://www.britannica.com/topic/Judiciary-Act-of-1801

U.S. Congress. U.S. Senate. Senate History. "Daniel D. Tompkins, 6th Vice President (1817-1825)"

U.S. Congress. U.S. Senate. Senate History. "The Impeachment of Andrew Johnson (1868): President of the United States".

U.S. Congress. U.S. Senate. Summary of Bills Vetoed, 1789-present. http://www.senate.gov/reference/Legislation/Vetoes/vetoCounts.htm

Washington, Booker T. *Up from Slavery*. New York: Avon Books, 1965. (Originally published in 1901).

Washington Post. "Montgomery Blair: A Prominent Figure in Political History Passes Away". July 28, 1883.

Webb, Steven B. "Tariffs, Cartels, Technology, and Growth in the German Steel Industry, 1879 to 1914," *Journal of Economic History*. Vol. 40, No. 2, June 1980.

Wikipedia. "James Madison". https://en.wikipedia.org/wiki/James_Madison

Wikipedia. "United States presidential elections", "United States House of Representative elections", "United States Senate elections". (Election results).

Woodward, C. Vann. *The Strange Career of Jim Crow*, 3d ed. New York: Oxford University Press, 1974.

Zeender, Jim. The National Archives. "Thomas Jefferson: Governor of Virginia, Part II." May 16, 2013. http://blogs.archives.gov/prologue/?p=12175

INDEX

33859203R00216

Made in the USA
Middletown, DE
30 July 2016